D1011133

For All Those Pupils Whose Lives Touched Mine

A · W A R D L A W · B O O K

For All Those Pupils
Whose Lives Touched Mine

By Stella Gipson Polk

Texas A&M University Press
College Station

Copyright © 1989 by Stella Gipson Polk
Manufactured in the United States of America
All rights reserved
First Edition

Original pen and ink sketches by Charles Shaw

The paper used in this book meets the minimum requirements of the American National Standard for Permanence of Paper for Printed Library Materials, Z39.48-1984. Binding materials have been chosen for durability.

LIBRARY OF CONGRESS CATALOGING-IN-PUBLICATION DATA
Polk, Stella Gipson.
    For all those pupils whose lives touched mine / by Stella Gipson
Polk. – 1st ed.
        p. cm. – (A Wardlaw book)
    ISBN 0-89096-405-X (alk. paper) :
    1. Polk, Stella Gipson.   2. Teachers – Texas – Biography.   3. Rural
schools – Texas.   I. Title.   II. Series.
LA2317.P65A3   1989
371.1′0092′2 – dc19
[B]   88-29359
                                                                            CIP

Contents

For All Those Pupils Whose Lives Touched Mine

Prologue: The Voices

Yesterday, down a weed-grown lane, I drove by a dilapidated one-room schoolhouse. Its yard still was bare, for, as was said of Attila's mighty army, no grass could grow where so many feet had trod. But the rotted rope swing, the broken-down seesaw, and the two outhouses leaning backward against a barbed-wire fence told their story of change and progress.

They were so very much alike, those little one-room schools I had known, each looking as if it had been carelessly dropped in a cup of hills enclosing a Texas-sized pasture.

I stopped the car. Voices were calling to me, calling from across the years . . .

"Teacher, can I go out?"

"Connally, please ask 'May I be excused?' Tiptoe to the door."

Travis, giving thanks at Thanksgiving: "I was thankful that, when my aunt started to spank me, I had a pair of pliers in each back pocket."

Fourth-grade Lena Jane writing her first descriptive paragraph: "I like my teacher very much. She has dark hair turning grey and a very loud voice."

I started the car. As I drove across the cattle guard,

I looked back, and some lines from Whittier's "School Days" came to me:

> Still sits the schoolhouse by the road.
> A ragged beggar sleeping. . . .

1. Hilda

I was sixteen in November and graduated from high school the following May. After a summer in San Marcos at the normal school for prospective teachers, I came home with visions of entering a four-year college or university that fall.

Truly Shakespeare was wise when he talked about the divinity that shapes our lives. To me that summer of 1918, World War I seemed far away. It was the noon mail delivered on the college campus and the sober faces of those who hurriedly scanned the pages of black-ink names, praying their loved ones' names were not among them.

Then my brother-in-law Lee Loeffler was called into service. He and my oldest sister, Jennie, were teaching in the little two-room school in the Hilda community, where they lived. What was the community to do? With all able-bodied men in the service, with a few women teachers, and with little country schools dotting the land like so many daisies, where could they get a teacher to replace Lee?

Then the State Board of Education at Austin came to their rescue: It decreed that anyone sixteen years old who passed the state examinations could teach. I wasn't too interested. However, the exams looked easy. And Jennie and Lee were anxious for me to take them so I could teach with Jennie. I took the examinations and thus, at sixteen, became a country teacher.

When I recall my first school at Hilda, in the southeastern part of Mason County, I think of Beaver Creek. I see it flowing across the roadbed of rocks to perch pools deep enough for boys to swim in. And wherever a bank cut steep, wild fern poked out of cliff crevices. Perhaps I see Beaver Creek because my sister Jennie and I crossed it each day going to and from school. Always its water carried a song—but you had to know the tune before you could hear it.

After leaving the two-storied stone house where Jennie and I stayed with Lee's parents, we crossed Beaver Creek and then walked between the big church of native stone and the cemetery, which lay north of it. We rounded Mr. Jim's house, also two-storied and built of cement blocks, and there it was: a two-room wooden schoolhouse facing south, with a cement porch spanning the front.

Even today this community is German. Most of its ancestors came to Texas around 1844. They were a part of Prince Solms-Braunfels's German Emigration Company. All but perhaps the very old speak English today. During that period of country schools, however, when any two got together, they invariably broke out into German.

Most of their homes were built of native rock, for those early Germans were excellent stonemasons. Their two-storied, square-built homes boasted no latticework or gingerbread trim, for the Germans were a sturdy, self-sufficient people, and their homes reflected their characters.

A three-year drought had ended the fall with rains so heavy there seemed to be no bottom to the mud. The people now were beginning to drive new cars, but the country roads had become so impassable that folks housed their treasures on wooden blocks in tight garages. They kept the dust wiped off them and went to church in team-drawn hacks, buggies, or wagons.

When I came to help Jennie teach, she moved into Lee's room, and I took over her primary grades. Jennie couldn't teach algebra, though. The trustees decided that the three boys taking algebra should come to my room for algebra after my primary grades had turned out at three.

They were so polite and lovable, my fourteen pupils from grades one through four. They had the broad foreheads and apple cheeks so typical of German children. They were handicapped, however, because the German language came first with them, not English. Since neither Jennie nor I spoke German, the trustees decided that no German should be spoken on the schoolgrounds.

I understood why this rule had to be, but it grieved me because of my two first graders, Selma and Margaret. They read beautifully, but they had no idea what they read. Selma and Margaret couldn't speak a word of English. At recess they stood around smiling politely but with pained expressions in their eyes.

Something had to be done. One morning before school I took Selma and Margaret to the farthest corner of the schoolyard. There against a northern backdrop of bee brush and live oak, I helped them build a playhouse. By making signs, I encouraged them to bring dolls, doll beds, and toy stoves. The next day they brought them to their playhouse, and I slipped away. As they stood in line at the close of each recess, I studied their happy faces. Those faces told me that, in that out-of-the-way, off-the schoolgrounds playhouse, Selma and Margaret really did *sprechen Deutsche!*

A week went by. I had been given that period of time to acquaint myself with the primary grades before I began the algebra classes. I had become so engrossed with the little boys and girls that I had all but forgotten that session assigned to me from three to four, when I would be teaching algebra to those older boys.

Algebra with the Boys

The first afternoon they came to my room, I realized just how big those three boys were. Why, they were grown men, older than I. With my primary grades I hadn't felt any embarrassment at being only sixteen, but those boys — why hadn't someone told me that they had ceased being boys?

They wedged themselves quickly into the small seats and laid their papers and books neatly on the desks. Then they waited. As I talked, they never took their eyes off me and answered my questions quite mannerly. And yet, every time I turned around to write an equation on the board, I had the uncomfortable feeling that a back button was missing from my blouse.

For four weeks I watched them squeeze their big bodies into those tiny seats. Every time they did, I was reminded of a group of ladies wedging their feet into shoes three sizes too small.

Finally the month was up. I put my first test on the board. Maybe it was too hard; I had no way to know. However, we had covered every problem. When the three boys got settled that afternoon and read the test I had written on the board, I saw their eyes widen, the first expressions I had caught on their faces. They read, then read again, the work on the board. They looked down at their papers. Still they wrote nothing. The hands on the wall clock moved toward four. Still they sat. Other than filling in the headings, they left their papers blank.

Four o'clock. Jennie breezed through the middle door and dropped the house keys on my desk. Then she was out across the playground, heading for the post office almost before her pupils had broken line. It was mail day. Jennie was hoping for a letter from Lee.

Five o'clock. At the edge of the playground, insects droned around a late-blooming bee myrtle. The sun left the baseball field and moved through the south door. Teddy wrote something on his paper. Rylie chewed the stub of his pencil. Willie looked at me once, a world of misery in his brown eyes. That did it.

"Boys," I said, "this is my first test. Maybe I've made it too hard. I wouldn't know. But I do know that I'm going to help you. Now pay close attention while I read and explain the first problem: A hound takes three leaps while a rabbit takes five; but one of the hound's leaps is equivalent to two of the rabbit's. The rabbit has a start of 120 of her own leaps. How many leaps will the rabbit take before she is caught?"

Silence. Not even a shifting in the tiny seats. The sun crept across Willie's left shoe. I went on: "Now let $3x$ equal the number of leaps taken by the hound, while $5x$ equals the number of leaps taken by the rabbit."

Three heads bent; three pencils scratched.

"Also, let a equal the number of feet in one leap of the rabbit. Then $2a$ equals the number of feet in one leap of the hound. So, $3x$ times $2a$ equals the distance in feet. Therefore, $6ax = (120 + 5x)a$. Divide through by a and you have $6x = 120 + 5x$. $x = 120$. $5x = 600$. Now, don't you see? The rabbit will take 600 leaps before she is caught."

On went my explanations, until six o'clock. Then three polite and obviously grateful young men turned in their papers and departed.

I hurried across the stepping stones in Beaver Creek. I did so hope that Jennie would not ask questions about the time. She didn't. Jennie was rereading a long letter from Lee—probably for the tenth time.

That night I went to bed without my customary feeling of fright brought on by having to teach three boys older than I. Those boys would never, never forget what I had done for them. Of that, I was sure. Outside, the gusty winds had stilled. A pale moon shone in the window. In the distance I could hear Beaver Creek running between the stepping stones. I lay there listening to it. Truly that night I knew its tune, for I was at peace. I slept.

Willie's older brother destroyed my peace. Those three algebra students were laughing and boasting all over the community. Look, they were telling everybody, how they had hoodwinked that little teacher. Now they wouldn't have to study algebra for the rest of the term;

10

they would only have to look pitiful, and she would melt.

I thought the next month would never pass. On the evening before I gave them their second monthly exam, I sat up half the night. I was determined to give them the trickiest, hardest problems we had covered. Oh, I'd explained these problems in great detail when we came to them, but none of the three listened. To be sure that they understood them, I had asked after each explanation, "Do you understand the problem?" They assured me politely that they did.

I had the test on the board when they came in. They squeezed into their seats, then frowned at the problems. Then they looked expectantly at me. However, I was quite busy with some reading questions I was making out for the fourth grade. Four o'clock came. Teddy wrote something on his paper. Rylie chewed the stub of his pencil. Willie looked up at me once, a world of misery in his brown eyes. I took up the papers. Teddy made 5. Rylie and Willie each made 0. It must be true indeed that hell has no fury like that of a woman scorned.

World War I Ends

October came and went, a bleak month of heavy rains and sodden country roads. It was agony for the people of the Hilda Community who had boys Over There. Often they received no mail, for the mail hacks and teams could not cover the soggy roads and swollen creeks. There were country lines for telephone service, but these wires were fastened to trees, and at times both trees and telephone poles gave way in the watery ground and blew down.

Other trees fell on the lines. The grim war across the Atlantic seemed far away indeed.

November began. A big V of wild geese went over. Jennie and I heard them honking as we crossed Beaver Creek on our way from school. I stopped on the middle rock and shaded my eyes as I watched them wing southward. I thought of the troop trains coming through San Marcos during the summer I was at school there. When would it all be over, and how many would not come back?

There was no letup to the rains, and November made it more uncomfortable by bringing in colder weather. Often clumps of grass crackled with ice along the road as we walked to and from school. Sometimes it was hard to see the stepping stones as Beaver Creek rose with an extra flow of water.

The night before November 11 was to be emblazoned across the world, I went upstairs early to prepare the next algebra lesson. Soon it would be November 27, and I would be seventeen. And seventeen was so much more dignified for a teacher's age than sixteen. I finished my lesson and went to bed. I was tired, for I had played baseball every recess with my primary pupils. I lay there thinking how funny it had been when I got trapped between the second and third basemen. They did a fine job of catch until I caught my heel under a root and fell.

The next morning I woke early, but I lay in bed listening to outside sounds. It seemed to me that Beaver Creek was making a strange sound. I drifted off to sleep, and then I came wide awake. I wasn't hearing Beaver Creek; off somewhere there came a distant *boom-m-m*. Guns were firing! That unusual sound was being punctuated by heavy blasts of dynamite. Somebody was blowing the Texas Hill Country to bits! I jumped out of bed.

Then I heard the church bell pealing wildly. I don't remember whether or not Jennie and I ate breakfast. All I do remember is the way Jennie and I hurried across Beaver Creek until we came to within sight of the stone church. The big bell fairly danced in its steeple. The ringing—I couldn't define it. Those tones were not a summons to church. They were not tolling a death, for the sound of that bell was the most joyous pealing I had ever heard. The War was over!

Mr. Jim dropped the bell rope when he saw us. He ran out and fairly crushed our hands in his powerful grasp. He was a big man and ordinarily shy. However, he wasn't shy that morning. Mr. Jim had a boy Over There.

We went on to school. Even though it was too early for pupils to come, we were not first. Sam, a good-natured boy who could learn anything but spelling, was ahead of us. Sam had wood fires roaring in both rooms, and all the blackboards sprawled with this glorious message: "Peas on Earth!"

In early spring, while the elms and pecans along Beaver Creek were uncurling their leaf buds, Lee came home. He took over the upper grades, and Jennie went back to her primary room. I moved on. I was sure that never again could I love any pupils as much as I had loved these rosy-cheeked little boys and girls. Also, I knew positively that never again would I be caught teaching boys older than I.

I returned to my parents' home at Mason to do some thinking. Perhaps now would be a good time to enter college. But I needed a few days to rid myself of the memory of my adorable little pupils at Hilda. And that was when Shakespeare's divinity stepped in again.

The Judge in Mason County learned that the little one-room school at Fly Gap in the upper northeastern reaches of Mason County was suddenly minus a teacher. Would I take the school? Oh well, I suppose I could. After all, I still was young enough to enter college later.

2. Fly Gap

The Fly Gap Community squatted among the craggiest hills in northeastern Mason County. It was a region so wild in its beauty that, the first week I spent there, I was afraid. At night the hoot owls took great pleasure in calling each other, their cackling laughter echoing from one hill to the next. I boarded near the school with a family who had four boys and one girl. Everybody called the couple Uncle Jim and Aunt Mollie.

I was dating a persistent young cowboy whose spread lay farther northeast in the county. His name was Pascal, but everybody called him Jack. He had a new Model T, which had to contend with muddy roads as wild as the hills. When he wanted to drive me to Fly Gap on that first date, his Model T was useless. We went in his buggy with a leather curtain fastened across the front to keep out the rain, which poured down in buckets.

The schoolhouse sat deep in the hills. They were smooth hills, sloping gently, as Texas hills are wont to do. The one-room house measured some sixteen by twenty-four feet. A stove, summer rusted and shaped like a sausage, divided the double desks, forming an aisle. My table in the west end was of unpainted pine, the nails evidently driven in impatiently, for some of them pierced the planks. My chair boasted a slatted back and a raw-hide bottom.

Part of the house had been built with boxed planks stripped with laths. However, the west and north walls were made of post-oak logs, unpeeled and laid horizontally. Often when I stood up to teach, a rusty-colored lizard would peek out from under a loose bark, terrifying me.

I was almost eighteen now. There were twenty pupils, ranging from seven years to eighteen. All but four of them rode horses to school. The live-oak thicket north of the schoolhouse, where the children tied their horses each morning, resembled the makings of a Texas rodeo.

The Musicians

On that first day of school I passed out my song-books. When I opened the singing with "America," I all but lost my tune. It wouldn't have mattered, though, for these children were singing without my help. Most of them sang a pure, joyous soprano, but a few altos and clear tenors chimed in. Where had these children learned to sing like that?

We spent several moments in song — that is, they sang. I was too surprised to join in. This, I realized, was going to be an unusual school. Not only could they ride horses, they could sing.

I was soon to learn that they were equally as proficient with stringed instruments. Here was a community tucked away in the hills and caring little about travel; they had what they wanted at home — comfortable

houses, plenty of good food to eat, and the capacity for
enjoyment. When some family gave a dance, the furniture was moved from one room, and the floor waxed with
paraffin shavings. Everybody from the grandpas to the
two-year-olds danced. They loved square dances, and the
musicians fiddling those hoedowns could set anybody's
toes to tapping:

> Round and round the room you go,
> Change yer partner, do-si-do.

Uncle Monroe was the caller. He had apple cheeks; his
hair was white and curly, and it bobbed up and down
on his head as he fiddled, stamped, and shouted.

Mr. Edd, the only German in the immediate community, declared in his mixture of German and English that
these people were "born a-dancing!" One night as I
watched both old and young bob and bounce, Mr. Edd
sidled up to me and remarked that "them couples, for
sure, wouldn't go to hell for dancing."

"Why?" I asked, puzzled.

"Hell, they ain't dancin'," he said and moved on.

When the dancers grew tired, or while they waited
for the hostess to sweep the pine floor before a second
round, they sang such songs as:

> Go tell Aunt Betsy,
> Go tell Aunt Betsy,
> Go tell Aunt Betsy,
> Her old gray goose is dead.

Sometimes I felt a bit lost among these happy people. I had not been brought up to dance. I was merely
a passable singer. I played no instrument. I couldn't even
ride a horse.

17

Cousin Audie's Donkey

One day Cousin Audie came to school. I say "Cousin" Audie because this was an isolated community of kinfolk. Even those living nearby were apt to be kin.

I never learned just where Audie lived. He simply appeared over the hill one day, riding a mouse-colored devil of a donkey as big as a mule. Lunch, ordinarily eaten leisurely on the south side of the house, literally was swallowed whole the day Audie came. Nobody said a word to me, but I knew by a kind of a sixth sense that, as soon as I went inside to grade papers, every child meant to ride Audie's donkey. I hurried inside and opened my grade book, which always was bloated with papers.

I heard a loud bray and looked through the north window. Bess was on Audie's donkey, her black braids whipping her back. Though I had no particular rodeo sense at that time, I knew that that donkey was bucking. I should have stopped the show then and there, but it was too fascinating. I would have given a month's salary just to have been able to sit in a saddle the way Bess sat.

The rodeo went on. Arch got a skinned cheek when the donkey ran under a post-oak limb. When I saw them bringing little Danny to ride, I knew it had to stop. I rang the bell.

I pretended not to see Arch's cheek when he came in. I saw Bess slip him a tube of Mentholatum from her purse. Orlie gave Arch his handkerchief to wipe off the blood. For tomorrow's lesson I assigned a review of the parts of speech to the four upper grades. The parts of speech — although I still was speechless over that donkey rodeo.

18

The next day Arch was absent. His mother sent a long note explaining how Arch had stumbled on the way from school and skinned his cheek. "That first gate after Arch leaves school," she wrote, "is so hard to open that Arch has to get off his horse to unlatch it. That was where he fell." I laid the note aside, wishing that Arch showed the same imagination when he wrote a theme.

Orlie and His Violin

That year the winter seemed unusually long. When it wasn't raining, it was drizzling. The children and I spent many recesses inside that little room of part log and part lumber. Noon hours were lightened by much lunch trading. I never had the feeling that any child got gypped, for this was a community whose women prided themselves on their culinary arts. I often wondered as I watched roasted yams traded for apple pie, home-cured ham for home-cured sausage, if those mothers didn't plan on such trades as a means for showing off their cooking ability.

On such days fourteen-year-old Orlie would bring his violin, carrying it lovingly in its case between him and the saddle horn. Sometimes he played happy tunes the children and I didn't know. I often wondered if he made them up. As he played them he made his bow dance, bringing forth little rills that made us tingle with happiness. Other times he swung into a haunting waltz, evoking a sadness that was both sweet and yearning. Always as he played, he laid his left cheek lovingly against his violin. His brown eyes reflected the tunes as

19

they dreamed into the future, with no knowledge of the tragedies which that future was to bring him.

Then it was spring. Bluebonnets blossomed in huge patches over the pastures, and sweet williams laid blankets of pink in between those patches. Blackbirds hopped about in the live-oak thicket where the horses were tied, waiting for every grain of corn that dropped from the feed bags hung around the horses' necks.

Johnnie's Haircut

Some of the younger children now came barefoot. But regardless of how they dressed, they came clean, their hair brushed and shiny. All but little Johnnie and his clan. They were a sore trial to this immaculate community of people. There was no hope that eventually they would move on, for Johnnie's people were landowners.

I overheard Orlie and Pete talking it over. It was warm now, and Johnnie's long, matted hair had to be cut. The next day Orlie brought his clippers. Pete brought his barber scissors. Trips from this community into town and to the barbershop were few and far between. Consequently, most families kept their own barber tools.

Pete and Orlie set a chair on the south side of the house and went to work on Johnnie's hair before school took up. By the time I rang the bell and the children came in, Johnnie's hair resembled a two-toned saddle blanket—one side trimmed, the other still shaggy.

Noon for the amateur barbers brought a hurried lunch. Then the hair cutting began again. Since neither of the three had lessons immediately after lunch, I left them outside to finish.

When they came in, Johnnie's blue eyes were dark with excitement, but Pete and Orlie were shaking their heads. Johnnie's blonde, sun-baked hair was well cut, but around his head where the trimming had taken place, there was a solid two-inch bank of caked dirt. I heard their lessons, then hunted up a cake of homemade lye soap which I kept to scrub the schoolroom floor. The three — Orlie, Pete, and Johnnie — took off for the little creek running south of the house. Before closing time they were back, Johnnie's eyes bigger and bluer than ever. And his hair was so clean that it positively shone. Instead of being matted now, Johnnie's hair was beginning to curl. I watched Johnnie's clan trudging homeward, the only children who walked. How proud his mother would be when she saw Johnnie!

The next morning even I hurried to school, but Pete and Orlie were there before me. Something was about to unfold. I think all of us sensed it. Pete and Orlie sat on the front step, their eyes glued to the trail which Johnnie's bunch would walk.

At last we saw them coming. Hedy was first, peering nearsightedly at us. Wiesie followed, her big front tooth shining in her smiling mouth. Frankie was next. He was the wild one. Sometimes Frankie got claustrophobia from being shut up in the schoolroom, and with a frenzied yelp he would dart out the door and head for a hole in the house underpinning. I had pulled him out so many times that I knew exactly which arm to fold and which leg to bend. Johnnie came last that morning, shoulders thrown back. He was not walking; he was marching. I'm sure that somewhere in Johnnie's mind a fife and a drum were playing.

Pete's voice was urgent: "Johnnie, what did your mama say about your haircut?"

Johnnie looked at me and sniffed disdainfully. Then he plowed into his benefactors. "Mama said," he told them, "that it looked just like them old fools Pete and Orlie."

How I Caught Mr. Jesse

A high hill spanned the front view I had from my desk. It sloped gently on both ends. Right in the middle two trees stood side by side, uplifted against the sky. When the pupils were busy with written assignments, I would sit at my desk and look at those trees. Somehow, they represented my future, a future when I would be married and making a life of my own.

During the third and last year I taught at the Fly Gap school, many were the mornings when I looked at those trees and began my dreams. However, on this particular morning something unpleasant obscured my view. That something was Mr. Jesse driving his wagon team to town.

He had moved into the community as a renter because Widow Gant was to old to farm her little strip of land and too contrary to let her children farm it. She couldn't have chosen anybody more suited to her temperament than Mr. Jesse. And to make matters worse, he was put in as a school trustee when Mr. Metz's term expired.

Most school trustees were cut from the same pattern. They were farmers and ranchers, who left the judge's office hurriedly as soon as the contract with me was drawn up and signed. Evidently it was embarrassing to do business with a woman. To them, hiring a teacher was a necessary evil.

It did no good to question trustees as to their preferences. "You just teach the school," they would say; "we want to plow." Usually I saw little of them. When the month was up, I'd send my voucher to them by their children. Though the signatures of two of the three trustees were sufficient for me to draw my pay, I always made it a point to try and get all three signatures. I did not want to show favoritism.

Mr. Jesse, however, was a breed apart. Mr. Jesse carried more than the proverbial chip on his shoulder – he shouldered the whole tree! Mr. Jesse wore grudges the way other men in the community wore their hats. He had a good, hard-working wife, whose face looked as if it were permanently creased. He had sired a whole passel of boys and girls.

He was thin, sandy haired, and held his pants up with galluses. When he stalked into the county judge's office on the day he was to sign my contract, he took a seat between the fireplace and the window. He never looked at me once.

He made one parting shot after signing his name to the contract. As he walked stiffly by me on his way to the door, he looked over my head and remarked sourly that he aimed to make teachers out of his kids. "That way," he said, "they won't have to do no work."

I let him get by the first two months without signing my voucher. Oh, I'd sent it to him by his children the last week of those two months. Always it came back

23

unsigned. Papa was too tired to sign it, or Papa said to send it to him sometime when he had more time. I got the other trustees' signatures and let it go.

Fall cotton picking was late that year, as a spring drought had caused a delay in planting. Mr. Jesse kept his children out of school most of those first two months. It was said that on good days the Jesse clan could pick a bale a day. On the morning that Mr. Jesse hauled the bale to the gin, the children got to come to school. That last week in November I saw him hauling a bale by the schoolhouse, and I rushed out with my voucher. However, when he saw me coming, Mr. Jesse whipped his mules and beat me over the hill.

It got to be a kind of obsession with me. I didn't have to have Mr. Jesse's signature, but I meant to get it. On the last Friday of the next month, the Jesse children came to school, which meant that Mr. Jesse would be hauling a bale by the schoolhouse. I got my voucher and stood by the front door while I handled my classes. That way, I could watch the road.

I heard him coming in time to have run out and blocked the road, but I was too proud. That would look as if I were begging for his signature. I waited for him to get even with the schoolhouse, then I walked out.

He saw me coming and began whipping his little mules until they fairly raced up the slope of the hill. He had to plow through a sandy hole before he reached the top. That's where I caught him. Something within me had snapped. I knew I would stop that man, if I had to chase him all the way to the gin. Right in the middle of the sandy hole I climbed up the front wagon wheel, and before he could say "scat," I had him covered, with my personal "weapon" – my pencil. There was nothing left for Mr. Jesse to do but sign my voucher.

When I walked inside the schoolroom, I knew that my pupils had sensed my triumph. They didn't say a word; neither did I. However, I knew there would be many chuckles and side slappings that night around the lamp-lit supper tables, for the whole community had been watching and waiting.

That evening I worked late grading papers. For some reason I had felt drained and exhausted all day. I put down Tessa's English paper and sighed. I had been teaching the principal parts of a verb. As usual, I had departed from the wording of the textbook, hoping that I could bring the rule down to the level the children could understand. "Try learning the rule like this," I told my two seventh graders: "I *see* the sun today; yesterday I *saw* it, and I *have seen* the sun before."

Tessa had applied my rule to the verb *burst:* "I *burst* my balloon today; yesterday I *bursted* it, and I *have bursten* it before."

I shoved the papers inside my grade book and slipped a rubber band around its swollen sides. I wished that I had been given some kind of power that could cause the Tessas to learn. Power.

That night at home, the moon swelled over the tree-tops and shone into my room. I thought of the day just past. I thought of Mr. Jesse, and I felt a kind of a pity for any human being so soured and twisted. That word *power* came to me again. What of the strange power which had gripped me when I saw Mr. Jesse whipping his mules up the hill? I had been gripped by it until I got his signature. Only a few times in my life had I felt such a sensation. I always had shunned anger. A pale moon climbed above the window. The hoot owls were quiet for a change. I turned over on my pillow and slept.

Lulu and Her Mother

During my tenure at Fly Gap, Governor Hobby began setting better standards for rural schools. The scholastic apportionment grew from $7.50 to $14.50, and free textbooks were provided.

However, the State Board of Education meant to see that those funds were not wasted. Therefore this new standard was to bring its influx of inspectors to those little one-room schools, each set in its own cup of Texas hills.

If I had looked long enough and objectively enough at the situation, I might have foreseen what was coming, but I was too busy teaching, too prone to put down my textbook and resort to my own determination to bring the meaning to everything, whether reading, history, math, or grammar — especially grammar.

I never learned what the inspectors' reports were. They remained hidden between the inspectors and the State Board of Education.

Also that year, Lulu started school at Fly Gap, and her coming precipitated all kinds of problems to my peaceful little Fly Gap school. Lulu came from a home which by no stretch of imagination should have been termed home. She and her mother lived in a tumbledown shanty with her half-blind grandmother. Lulu's father? No one knew. Her mother simply came to the community with a ten-year-old girl after an absence of some

26

fifteen years, during which her own mother had never heard from her.

I never went to Lulu's home, nor did anyone else. Lulu's mother was a big, rawboned woman with eyes glaring fiercely out of a face like wrinkled leather. Many were the speculations and tales about her, running wild throughout the community. Lulu's mother could outcuss any man. She cooled her butter in the washpan. Lulu's grandmother was said to have ruled her husband with a red-hot poker from the fireplace . . . I finally stopped listening.

I wanted to be kind to Lulu, but I couldn't. She never joined in the games. She never spoke to any child except to unleash language so vile, so filthy, that it left the child gasping and me stunned. One day I kept her in at recess, hoping I could talk to her and make her understand that I wanted to be her friend. I no more than started when Lulu called me a name I could not have dreamed up had I wanted to. That did it. I went outside and cut a keen little hackberry switch, which I used on Lulu. All the next week she was so sweet that I wondered why I hadn't used a switch before.

I had persuaded the trustees to build a basketball court with the money the community had made at a recent box supper. By adding a bit of my own money, we had enough left over to buy a ball. At the morning and afternoon recesses I trained the girls in basketball rules. At noon I coached the boys.

One afternoon we were in a hot game for the girls when Lulu's mother rode up. She wore a divided leather skirt and bestrode a mean-looking mustang pony. I was glad to see her. Maybe by talking to her I could convince her that I wanted to be Lulu's friend.

She didn't seem disposed to talk but just rode around and around the basketball court, popping her leather quirt against her skirt. The game went on, and it was a close one. When it came time to ring the bell, I went up to Lulu's mother again. I told her that, if she would come in, I would hear Lulu's lesson first and she could listen. She made no reply, just kept on wheeling her mustang around the court and popping her quirt. Maybe, I thought, after she had tied her pony she would come in. I got busy with the sixth-grade reading and never knew when she left.

The pupils were scarcely out of sight after school that day when Mr. Metz galloped up, riding bareback. Judging from the pony's lather, I knew Mr. Metz had left home at full speed. "Is she gone?" he shouted.

"Who? Oh, Lulu's mother. Yes, I tried to get her to come in and visit school, but she didn't."

I thought Mr. Metz was going to choke. "My God, girl," he sputtered, "you must a been behind the door when the brains was passed out."

I was shocked. Mr. Metz had always been so polite. "She, Lulu's ma, rode by the garden where my Amy was a-picking beans. Said she was a-going over to that school and horsewhip that — well, I won't say the word — little teacher. My Amy, she ran all the way to the field where I was plowing. I unhooked the team from the cultivator, straddled old Nellie, and rode hell-for-leather to get here. Thought for sure you'd be quirted to death by now." He stopped for a breath then went on. "Girl, you just don't know that woman. When she gets her dander riled, she's mean enough to step on little chickens." He turned Nellie around and sat looking at me. "Don't know what you've got," he said shaking his head. "Just don't know what saved you from Lulu's ma, but whatever 'tis, you'd sure better hold on to it."

I watched him ride off until he was lost in a gap of the hills before I realized what a fool I had been. Mr. Metz didn't know that all that had saved me from the horsewhipping was a big overdose of ignorance.

Mr. Kane and Jason

Mr. Kane was a wealthy landowner. His son August shared the fourth grade with Jason, whose father owned a few hilly acres. Mr. Kane's family lived in a two-storied house in rural luxury, as compared with Jason's family, who existed in dirty confusion in an unpainted shack.

I was a bit surprised when Mr. Kane came to school one morning, for he never had evinced any special liking for me. "August says that Jason stole his knife." Mr. Kane looked around the suddenly still roomful of pupils until he located sandy-haired Jason, who always sat with one suspender dangling between seat and back.

Nobody seemed shocked, for it was customary to blame all thefts on the so-called community trash. Still, I was surprised, for Jason never had shown any inclination to steal. I looked at Jason. He met my eyes in surprise. I asked, "Jason, did you steal August's knife?"

Jason's eyes flashed. A hot, red flush covered his face to well behind his big, dirty ears. "I didn't, I didn't," he said hotly, "but August he got mine yistiddy, before school taken out."

Mr. Kane took one long step and all but raised Jason

from the seat by his one good suspender. "Don't you dare accuse my boy of stealing anything of yours," he shouted, "you dirty, filthy scum!"

Jason stood his ground. "He did. I seed it this morning. Look in his left hip pocket. It's there!"

Mr. Kane shook Jason again, but from the corner of my eye I saw August's hand move toward his left hip pocket. I said, "August, stand up." Terrified, August stood up. I walked past the formidable Mr. Kane, who was still shaking Jason. I reached inside August's left pocket and drew out Jason's knife. Every child – even I – knew that dirty little white knife. It was one of Jason's prized possessions.

Mr. Kane let go of Jason to point the finger of God at me. "You forget I'm your trustee," he yelled. "I'll have you fired."

Finally I broke in on Mr. Kane's babblings. "Mr. Kane," I said, "I realize that you control the other trustees. I realize, too, that this is the last month of school and that more than half of this month is already gone. If you fired me today, I still could draw my salary. Also, there is a law governing teachers, protecting them from such dismissals. If you tried to fire me, you'd have to tell in court that you aided and abetted your boy in a theft."

Mr. Kane stalked out. He never spoke to me again. I didn't reapply, for I realized it was time to move on. It hurt to leave the children, but by now schools and schoolhouses had lost much of their individuality. All that really mattered to me now was that I teach and that I reach as many children as possible with something which they could hold on to for as long as they lived.

Mr. Jesse moved away with his clan; some of the

older pupils would be going into the Mason high school; Jason and his family went to California to pick fruit, so there wasn't enough money to hire a teacher for another term. The Great Depression hadn't struck yet, but it was not far around the corner.

After a small program that last day, I closed the schoolhouse door behind me and walked across the yard. A little black rubber ball, nicked from bouncing on too many jagged rocks, lay half hidden by a clump of pasture grass. I picked it up and thought of our happy games of ante over. Those days were gone. I dropped the little ball where I had found it. Again I was positive I'd never care that deeply for another group of children.

A wind came down from the hills, sweeping through a gap and breezing over the little schoolhouse. Still, as I'd told myself before, there would be a challenge when I moved on to the next school, a chance to see what lay over the next hill.

3. Husband Jack

On Christmas Eve, 1921, Jack and I were married at Mason. Two young people so different in upbringing, so deeply in love. How lightly said the marriage vows.

We began our lives together on Jack's ranch, ten miles northeast of the town of Mason, land he'd bought through the Federal Land Bank. Jack had done more than purchase our ranch land — he'd bought an old vacant country schoolhouse, moved the sound lumber, and was building our bungalow. We began our housekeeping with the kitchen wall wearing some schoolboy's jackknife carving of *XYZ*. During the following ten years, when I did not teach, I had that carving to remind me of country schools.

We hadn't been married many weeks when we had a falling out. I wish I could remember what it was all about, but that was so long ago.

We had gone to Mason, then we took what today is Highway 87 to Brady. It was a rough country road then, winding around granite boulders, bypassing clumps of live oak, and finally reaching the unpaved streets of Brady. We were barely speaking to each other when we drove around a house-sized granite boulder. Evidently a wild turkey hen was nesting atop the boulder. She flew off, barely skimming our heads, as we had the top of the Model T laid back.

Something about the incident caused Jack to stop the car and put his arms around me, and I was glad he did. We didn't see the wagon with two men in the spring seat until one of their mules snorted. The men yelled as they passed us and threw their hats in the air.

We sat there like two stones. Presently Jack started the car. As we drove down the rutted road, finally he burst out, "Damn, I wouldn't a minded it so bad if we hadn't a been married."

Though the Great Depression had not yet arrived, it hovered over us like a dark shadow. However, we had no time for it. We were too busy fencing our land, setting out an orchard, planting our garden, and laying out a yard. Money was scarce, so Jack often left home to ride the ranch for some older cowman. It was rather a lonely time for me when he was gone. I did not know then that life was teaching me how to live with myself. But in those days we learned a need for each other that was to mold our years to come.

Goat ropings were a popular pastime for cowboys, and Jack had no trouble winning. A twenty-five-dollar prize was money then.

One roping stays with me yet. It was held along the banks of the Comanche Creek, which separated the business section of Mason from the northern dwellings.

I can see Jack yet as he was that day, getting ready in the chute as the next roper. When he swung into the saddle, he always looked as if he were molded into it. The curve of his back and the slump to his shoulders went with his horse, Alkali, all seeming somehow to blend with the slope of the horizon. "I was born in the saddle, Miss Stell," he always told me with a grin.

I watched him tuck the end of the pigging string under his belt and clamp the loop end between his teeth. He shook out a bigger loop to his roping rope and rode into the starting arena. I could sense the excitement building in Alkali, for a good roping horse always feels the same tension as his rider. The gate swung open. The goat dashed across the score line. The flagman's hand dropped. Jack crossed the line, and horse, goat, rope, and Jack blended into one — poetry in action.

He swung the loop over his head once, then forward. As it slipped over the goat's horns and settled around its neck, Alkali dug in his hind heels, settling in the moist dirt. Before the goat had reached the end of the rope, Jack was down and had flipped it on its side. He bunched its feet, made two quick wraps with the pigging string, and finished with a quick tie. Then he threw up his hands to stop the judges' watches.

Seven seconds! A great win. A gasp ran along the spectators, then a wild cheering.

"Jack," I said as we sat under the yard oaks, "you really made an enemy out of John. His score was only twelve seconds."

He leaned over and unbuckled his spurs. "Look, Miss Stell, I don't want no trouble with nobody, but when I beat a man fair and square, I've a right to."

It was time to send some of the cattle to market. That next week Jack, his father, and his two older brothers drove their herd some twenty-five miles to the Brady stock pens to load on the freight cars going to Fort Worth.

34

Jack's enemy John and his cowhands were driving their spread from below Mason to Brady. The two herds were shut up in adjoining pens until loading the next morning. Nobody knew what happened in the night; possibly bulls shoved the gate open, allowing the herds to mix. It took most of the next day to separate them.

"We were all tired and cranky," Jack told me when he got home. "I was out by Alkali, tightening my saddle girth, when John stalked over and accused the Polks of trying to steal his cattle."

"Oh, Jack, how awful. What did you do?"

"I blacked his damned eye."

"Oh, no. Respectable people don't have fights."

I was washing the dishes then, and Jack was drying. He turned on me and said, "Miss Stell, I've told you I don't want no trouble with nobody, but when a man looks me in the eye and calls me a thief, well, he just oughtn't."

I was mortified when the sheriff's notice came, fining Jack ten dollars for his participation in the fight. Jack's cowboy buddies paid his fine, but I burned the notice in our little four-eyed cookstove. How I wish now I'd kept it, for it was the only fight he ever had while we were married.

While he was attending the University of Texas, the older of my two brothers, Fred Gipson, began bringing one of his friends to our home. He was Joe Small. Many were the hours Joe and Fred spent on our porch dreaming their dreams of the future. Two young men in their early twenties. Neither knew that Joe Small's future would culminate in his founding of *True West* and *Old West* magazines, which would bring years of pleasure to those who loved to read of those olden days.

As for Fred, he wrote other books. His most famous effort, however, was *Old Yeller,* a little story he told me he dashed off in about three months.

Fred loved coming to our home, loved the give-and-take camaraderie between Jack and me. "Jack, you old rascal," he would say, "for sure you're no pretty boy, and you murder the King's English every time you open your mouth, but you could stalk into New York's elite society wearing your cowboy boots and that devilish grin and captivate the whole crowd. I envy you."

4. Baby Jackie

On October 29, 1929, the stock market crashed. We didn't feel its effect at first, for we were used to rather lean times.

Then on November 17, 1930, Jack Gordon Polk was born, at the Brady hospital, the baby we had wanted so very much. The nurses declared Papa Jack walked the hospital halls like a king.

I shall never forget the first time he held his baby. For nine months he'd talked of the horse, saddle, and spurs he'd buy his boy.

"What if it's a girl?"

"It won't be, Miss Stell." So that was that.

As he held Jack Gordon, I listened for him to begin talking horse, saddle, and spurs. Presently he uncurled that little fist from his finger. "Let's don't ever tell him a lie," he said. . . .

By now we began to feel the Great Depression. On March 11, 1931, a late snow had begun melting. Coming from riding the pasture, Jack saw a ewe sheep running between the house and barn, with a bucket bail tightening around her throat. He shook out his rope, rode Alkali forward, and roped the ewe.

Alkali slid on some wet maize stalks and fell, break-

37

ing Jack's leg. Mason had no hospital. The Brady hospital had patients even out in the halls, an outbreak of late flu. A doctor from Mason came out and set Jack's leg. So now I had a baby and a bedfast husband.

By 1933, the nation was in the grips of the worst depression people had ever known. Wealthy men jumped out of windows when their wealth disappeared. Even some staid ranchers committed suicide.

I got a job teaching the little Behrens school, some six miles down the road, some six miles between our ranch and the town of Mason. This was merely a temporary school set up for ranchers who could not buy gas to drive their children to the Mason school. I drove my car and was paid thirty dollars a month.

Jack put Baby Jackie in front of him when he rode the pasture. We were not farmers, but we did have a little patch of droughty grain. When he had to plow the grain, Jack built a box on the cultivator between him and the mules, Kit and Jude, for Jackie to sit. He always said Jackie loved sitting there and looking around — that is, until it was time for me to come from school at 2:30, and then he began asking for his mother. "He was like a time clock," his daddy declared.

When Jack got a job for a dollar a day riding on some ranch, a friendly couple of neighbors kept Jackie until I could come home. So now we had a happy little boy who knew nothing about depressions, and I was back in the schoolroom again.

5. Behrens

The Great Depression was everywhere while I was
teaching that little Behrens school, which was merely
a stopping place for children in the surrounding area.
If times ever righted, they would be going to Mason, but
the little school could answer until there was money to
buy gasoline and tires. I was glad the school turned out
so early, for, like Baby Jackie, I began getting restless
to go to him.

In the Behrens school, the depression had brought
the elite down on the same grounds with the poor. Nobody had money; nobody saw any way to make money.
It was a dangerous situation. Many wealthy landowners, faced with poverty for the first times in their lives,
committed suicide. The poor were better equipped to take
it. They had always tightened their belts; now they simply drew in another notch.

With a few of the elite, however, snobbery at school
still was there. Each recess I sternly took the stick from
some child who did not want to touch another child's
hand in "Ring around the Rosy."

It was noon on that particular day. The sun glared
down on the parched countryside surrounding the little
schoolhouse. Even the donkeys tied under a grove of half-

dead live oaks were restless and stamping, fighting flies and red ants. Since practically all the boys rode donkeys, the school bore the nickname "Donkey School."

I think everybody was relieved when I rang the bell to go inside. It had been too hot to run and play, and since the schoolhouse had been set within a clearing, there were no trees for shade. The reading class droned on and on. I scarcely could keep awake. A few flies flew disconsolately about the room. None of the children seemed inclined even to whisper.

Mrs. Hart and the Kerosene

I shook myself awake and looked through the front door and to the sandy lane east, leading up to the schoolhouse. Somebody was walking that lane in this terrible heat. As the figures drew nearer, I made out Mrs. Hart carrying her year-old baby boy, bending her head and shoulders above its inert form to provide some shade. Two preschool children were trudging along behind her. The Harts were a family of poor renters. It was the children of this family that the elite pupils had tried not to touch. They had held sticks between them in games in order not to touch the dirty hands of the Harts.

I knew something was wrong when Mrs. Hart left the lane and turned toward the schoolhouse. I put down my reader and went out to meet her. I thought the baby was dead, and I judged from the mother's almost incoherent babbling that it had drunk some kerosene which she had set in the corner of the kitchen after using it to light a fire in the cookstove.

There were no telephones anywhere in the area because nobody could meet the monthly bill. I called back to the schoolroom for Maisie to take over the lessons while I was gone. Then I hurried Mrs. Hart and her brood into my car. I had no idea that a doctor could help now, but I had to try. I drove my old rattletrap car too fast, and as I drove, I prayed as I hadn't prayed for some time that my threadbare tires would hold out.

The doctor's office was up a narrow flight of stairs. When we started up, I saw that Mrs. Hart was not going to make the climb with her chubby baby, so I took him. Bubbles were wreathing his mouth, each bubble reeking with kerosene. It was all so frightening, so nauseating, that I was afraid I was going to be sick there on the stairs.

The doctor was in and went to work immediately with a stomach pump. Strange how the sight of that doctor's open mouth with his tongue folded back between his teeth made such a lasting impression on me. The smell of the room filled with the scent of kerosene was too much. I ran to the window and was sick on the overhang below.

Later, after the baby had been revived, I drove Mrs. Hart and the two little Harts, as well as the baby, up the sandy lane to their hovel on the right side of the fence. Going back to school, I wondered if, after paying the doctor's fee, my husband and I would have enough money between us to buy groceries at the end of the week.

Patty and Prejudice

That afternoon recess I walked down to where the children were playing "Squat, Little Josie." A breeze had risen, and a thin cloud now obscured the sun. I was glad that at last it was cool enough for them to play.

I got a little closer. There was that inevitable stick between Patty and the oldest Hart girl. A revulsion bitter and equally as sickening as the previous smell of kerosene rose up within me. I grabbed that stick and threw it as far as I could send it across the dusty school ground. The children stood there amazed. They had never seen Teacher show temper before. Then I let them have it. I laid down the law as I should have done when I first began the school. I told them that if ever I saw any child hold a stick between him and some other child, I would switch him good. And that rule held good for girls as well as for boys.

The term ended. The school system in town made provisions to take this little school in with them. I never bothered to learn the details. I drew my last salary and spent that thirty dollars buying a hundred pounds of sugar, a hundred pounds of flour, and clothes for myself, my husband, and my baby boy. There was a little left over. I added that to Jack's pay. He had helped another rancher round up but had had to furnish his own horse in order to do the job and get paid. With what remained of Jack's earnings and mine, we bought a barrel of gas. I signed a contract for another one-teacher school, Ranch Branch, for the fabulous sum of eighty dollars a month! I taught there for the next six years, with Jackie there daily as a pupil.

Gone were dreams of going to college. To receive eighty dollars a month during those depression years was too much. Husband Jack and his neighbor built a little one-room shack near the schoolhouse where four-year-old Jackie and I stayed until Jack could manage enough gasoline to come for us over the weekends.

6. Ranch Branch

During the six years I taught at Ranch Branch, there were six Christmas programs. The Christmas of 1934 lives with me, possibly because four-year-old Jackie was old enough to appreciate that Christmas. The Ranch Branch schoolhouse, as usual, sat in the middle of some Texas-sized pasture. My little shack looked so odd, its stovepipe capped with a black cover poking up above the roof, looking for all the world like an old lady with a long neck, wearing a black hat!

When the weather permitted, Jackie and I drove the eight miles of country road from our ranch east of the Ranch Branch community, but with two turbulent creeks to cross and a rocky hill to climb, often we stayed in our little cabin near the schoolhouse, set in the corner of Mr. Ernest's pasture. We still were in the Great Depression, so with those six years of poor roads, few and undependable telephones, and little money, Christmas in that little isolated community was a great event.

Christmas Pageants

Two bachelor brothers, Sam and Tom, always helped when the community called. It was left to them to provide the school Christmas tree. A sprinkling of cedar still grew on the ranches, even though ranchers fought all forms of the juniper, because it furnished no feed for the livestock.

The old Ranch Branch schoolhouse was built of lumber so hard that it was difficult to drive a nail into its walls. And those walls were ten feet high. When Sam and Tom brought the cedar Christmas tree through the front double doors and set it up on the stage at the north end of the room, its top branches pressed against the ceiling.

As usual, I wrote my own program, and we began practicing. I always had a two-part program, the first part religious, for the people missed church services. Quite often the only service they had was when some friendly pastor preached at the schoolhouse on Sunday.

The trustees stretched a double wire through the stage curtain running east to west. The pupils and I covered a large pasteboard star with gold paper sprinkled with glitter I had bought at Mason. We fastened a flashlight to its back and hung it from one of the curtain wires, ready to make its slow journey from the East.

At noon I sent the boys for dead sticks of Spanish dagger out in the pasture. We twisted several strands of wire, bent them to a proper crooked shape, and fastened them to one end of the dagger stick. Covered with brown crepe paper, they made credible shepherd staffs. We wrapped dagger sticks with gold paper for angel wands. Then we wrapped wire-shaped wings with gold paper for the angel wings.

Wire was no problem. Ranchers ripped it off bales of hay during winter feeding. In fact, Rancher McWilliams, who fed a sizable herd of cows, named his spread Baling Wire Ranch!

Most of the mothers were skilled in making do with nothing. Worn white sheets created angel garments, and rugs, thin from many washings, became shepherd robes. Truly, necessity must be the mother of invention.

A star-studded blue sky of crepe paper floated over the stage backdrop. The wise men's star, lighted by a single lantern (the star looked better in dim light), hovered over Mr. Elliot's real straw-filled manger, on which Sara's big doll slept on the hay. (*Slept,* because Sara informed me right away that her doll had open-and-shut eyes.) Angels flocked in the background near the kneeling shepherds. Elroy as Joseph stood by the cradle, while Sara, her little face peeping from out a blue mantle, sat at the head of her cradle. Behind the curtain I moved the lighted star slowly west as I sang:

> Star of the East,
> The hope of the soul. . . .

When the star came to rest above the manger, Sara's sweet voice took over my song with her version of:

> Go tell it on the mountain
> Go tell it on the mountain,
> Go tell it on the mountain
> That Jesus Christ is born. . . .

The Christmas Elephant

I don't know why, but one year I wanted a Christmas circus, including an elephant. I had an old used bedspread about the color of a rusty elephant. From it I made the elephant's head, floppy ears, long trunk, and stubby tail. I stuffed it all with cotton Darrell brought from home, since his father was a cotton farmer.

I showed it to Husband Jack. "What do you think about it?" I wanted to know.

He grinned and tweaked my ear. "Tell you what, I'd sure hate to meet a thing like that on some dark night." I poked my tongue out at him.

I put the elephant's tail on top of the books in the closet so I wouldn't misplace it. The remainder of the bedspread would cover the elephant's body.

The night of the program I had been afraid Mr. Strack would forget his guitar, but as he twanged "Under the Double Eagle," the procession moved slowly across the stage — first the tumblers, then the dancing girls in their red crepe-paper finery, then the bouncers.

Last but certainly not least, the elephant lumbered across the stage. Two boys bent their bodies at the waist, the front one carrying the elephant's head. Sometimes the front and hind legs moved in unison, but often one set of legs moved one way while the hind legs wobbled the other way. From the audience came shouts of laughter. My elephant was a knockout!

Then from across the room came Connally's shrill voice, "Hey, Teacher, that elephant ain't got no tail!"

Oh, dear, I'd left that tail on top of the books in the closet! Can't anything ever be perfect?

Santa Claus bounced in and jigged while the bigger girls took the presents off the tree. They had to use the stepladder to reach Granny Vance's gift to me: a gift-wrapped pound of yellow butter!

Going home, Jackie said, "Me and Travis lay down on the floor so we could see what was under Santa's suit.

Know what we saw? Rancher Marion's brown pants."
So long, Santa Claus days. Kids grow up too fast.

The Inspector (We Think)

By the time I had begun my next term of school at
Ranch Branch, the depression had lightened. Still its
aftereffects lingered on in this community. The State
Board of Education was beginning to increase salaries
again, and the men governing that board decided it was
time to investigate these one-teacher schools and see if
those higher salaries were justified. Thus began the period of inspectors.

The inspector from Austin was to come on Friday
that year. The pupils and I had exactly one day to get
ready, since the county judge hadn't notified me until
Thursday. One whole day in which to sweep, dust, wash
blackboards and windows, and clean the closet. I had
been at Ranch Branch now for two years, and already
I had come to dread these visits. Inspectors were well-
mannered young men, but why couldn't they notify us
at least one week ahead? They were all cut from the same
cloth. They did their jobs efficiently and always wiped
their hands when they finished inspection. The way they
saw it, inspection was merely a rather unpleasant but
a well-paid job. To them, education was confined to
catered lunches, waxed floors, and single desks. There
was no way of getting around it – one-teacher schools
were on their way out.

I straightened my desk and wondered about it all.
How would Joseph, who lived with his blind grandmother, go to school then? And little Lupe, product of

47

a Mexican shearing camp – what would become of her schooling? I thought of Homer, of the tiny dark freckles dusting his cheeks. Homer's widowed mother worked in the cotton fields and carried her wash water from a creek. If consolidation came now, how would she scrape together enough money to pay for Homer's school lunches, his workbooks, or suitable clothing?

I smiled a bit as I rose from my desk. I was remembering the gentle way Homer touched his books, the neat manner in which he stacked them. I recalled the way his eyes glowed whenever I brought him a storybook to read. Homer never asked for my books. Homer never asked for anything. He was of those rare, proud people who asked nothing from anybody.

Something like a white cloud drifted in from the east door. I hurried out to the back of the house. Dorothy and Susan were dusting the erasers and chasing each other in a fog of white dust. Back in the room again, I sent Leroy and Raymond to repolish the windows for the third time. Even then, when they had finished, smudges of Bon Ami lingered on the panes.

We had been in the middle of making eight posters, one for each part of speech, when the judge sent us news by Mr. Parker that the inspector was coming. I went back to where the girls were working on the posters. Everybody in the school, from first grader through eighth, had contributed toward the making of those posters. We had closed the grammar books and coined our own rhymes:

> A noun is the name of a person,
> A place or a thing.
> It can be a city, a girl,
> Or a diamond ring.

Sara, my fifth grader, was doing the decoration. Sara could draw a rose so perfectly and color it so exquisitely that just looking at it made one want to smell it. I rang the bell for the afternoon recess ahead of time. There was the closet to clean, and I wanted to do that myself.

It was a corner closet housing all unused textbooks on its two top shelves. The shelf below held library books. If only box suppers had brought in more money, there might have been two rows of library books instead of one. I stopped my cleaning long enough to reread some of the titles. There were Hawthorne's *Tanglewood Tales* and *The Stories of Greece and Rome,* which recounted the heroic deeds of Achilles, Ulysses, Aeneas, and Horatio, prefaced by a quotation from Goethe: "One cannot always be a hero, but one can always be a man."

I made myself leave the library books until I had finished the rest of the closet. Below the library shelf the floor held a conglomeration of paintbrushes soaking in kerosene, a can of red paint for the two peeling outhouses, and two brooms. Each broom had its straws twisted to a sideways point because every sweeper in the school swept right handed. I finished and went back to the library shelf, which was my pride and joy.

Ruskin's *King of the Golden River* looked a bit thumbed, for every child in the school loved it. When I first began reading it to them, they had worked diligently each afternoon so there could be a period left over from their lessons for my reading. Now when some older pupil had the time, he or she led an assorted group of listeners to the reading table set up in the far corner of the room and, in mumbling tones, reread to them that fascinating story.

Poetry. I couldn't resist it. There was Kipling's "If,"

49

Kilmer's "Trees," Browning's "Pied Piper of Hamelin," Longfellow's "Psalm of Life," and Whittier's "Barefoot Boy." If an older pupil stood up to recite these or similar poems and stumbled, some second or third grader often prompted the one reciting before I could.

I brushed the dust from George Eliot's *Silas Marner* and closed the door. These meager little libraries which I always left behind me in every school were my *paso por aquí*, my trademark.

The day the inspector was due was cold and drizzly. A shrill north wind shook the walls of the dilapidated schoolhouse. I had hoped that the day could be warm. Now it would be necessary to draw the desks along either side of the stove until the room warmed up.

We sang "The Star Spangled Banner" and repeated the flag pledge. Perhaps I could get through the first four reading classes before the inspector showed up. If only he could arrive while Sara read, for Sara read as beautifully as she drew and painted.

Classes droned on as usual. I stopped them long enough to break up a punching contest between Darrell and Steven. Also, I had to remove the long, dangling earrings which Dorothy wore in honor of the inspector's coming visit. What did Dorothy's mother mean, letting a child like that wear such jewelry? I dropped the earrings into my desk drawer, pretending not to notice Dorothy's angry looks. Perhaps she had taken them from her mother's jewelry and put them on as she walked the mile to school.

Again the north wall shook from the whipping winds. I lifted and filled the firebox with chunks of blackjack. Blackjack oak made such good fires. Maybe the inspector wouldn't come until noon. By then, the room would be warm, and we could move the desks back to their orderly rows.

The pot of beans simmered and gave off tantalizing odors. Usually I supplied the beans, but occasionally parents sent a bag of dried pintos from their garden, a hunk of bacon, or peppers and onions. Our meals in this one-room shack weren't exactly catered, but hungry boys and girls could study quite well following a steaming bowl of thick juicy red beans.

"Teacher, can I go out?"

"Connally, please say, 'May I be excused.'" I watched him dash for the front door and struggle against the winds sweeping around each side of the house. I sighed. How many, many times over the years had I made that correction?

Morning recess came. I didn't go out and play baseball as usual. The pupils looked at me strangely. I was too nervous. When the inspector came, would Connally ask to go out? Would Dorothy be working on another hateful blob of bubble gum? I must remember to brush Walter's hair as soon as the children marched in. I must caution Susan not to giggle, and I *must* watch carefully that the beans on the stove didn't boil over . . . oh, dear! I rang the bell.

The children stopped their game and ran for the front door, bringing the ball and dragging the bat. They always formed two straight lines at the beginning, but if I did not ring the bell in a hurry, the ones on the ends got impatient and made a kind of an arc out of the lines as they fanned around, watching me.

Now it was reading time again through the primary

grades. I was determined that the clean blackboards should stay clean, so the other pupils had to work their history questions on their tablets. A few drops of rain fell, or was it sleet? Why didn't the inspector come and get it over?

"Teacher, can I go out?"

"Connally, you go out, and this time you make sure you stay out until you finish. Do you hear?" The pupils looked at me in surprise. I hadn't realized it before, but I was getting cross.

Noon came. Still no inspector. A drizzly rain was falling. Already the country roads were full of bog holes. Certainly we didn't need any more rain just now. The chili beans still simmered, and even I was succumbing to their aroma. I had a surprise for the children. Ordinarily I supplied white paper napkins to spread over their desks, but today I had brought napkins depicting a circus. A gasp of pleasure went over the room as I passed them out. It was Lupe's turn to ask the blessing. I always urged the children to say what was in their hearts when they said grace. Lupe's background of sheep camps, combined with this her first year in school, hadn't prepared her too well for the English language. But Lupe tried. She stepped out in the middle of the aisle, her oversized, hand-me-down dress bulking about her thin little hips. Clasping her little brown hands, Lupe murmered, "Gracias, Gracias," and sat down.

I began dishing beans into each child's bowl. It was then I realized that every circus napkin had disappeared. I opened my mouth to question, and then I knew. The pupils had put away their napkins to take home to some little brother or sister. Without a word, I brought the white napkins from the closet.

Lupe's Armadillo

Two o'clock. The wind had died to a whisper, and a pale sun broke through the clouds. I was deep in the seventh-grade English when I heard Lupe at the front door. I always let her out at two, and she played around until four when I drove her home. I said, "Darrell, open the door for Lupe."

She came in hugging the biggest armadillo I had ever seen. Its horny tail whipped the floor, but Lupe held it hard against her little flat chest. Her eyes were shining. "Muy buena para comer" (very good to eat), she said happily. "Muy buena para comer."

Up the road I could hear a car. The inspector! "Lupe," I said frantically, "you can't keep that armadillo here in the house, not with the inspector coming. Take it outside. Hurry!"

"But Teacher, outside she vamoose."

So it would, for the armadillo was almost as big as Lupe. But I couldn't help it. With that car coming, I was bereft of thought. I knew that, if the inspector found that armadillo inside my schoolhouse, it would be the end of this little school.

On came the car, barely crawling in the mud and weaving drunkenly around the bog holes. I looked at Lupe. Her eyes were shining now with unshed tears. That armadillo meant tamales for Lupe. I thought of the scanty spread of pounded meat inside Lupe's tortillas.

Suddenly I knew that I couldn't do it. "Lupe," I said, "sit on the back bench by the front door. Put the armadillo on the floor and hold it hard by its tail. Do you hear me? I said *hold it hard!*" My voice cracked. The pupils looked at me strangely.

53

The English class dragged on. The clock on my desk ticked loudly. The armadillo made scratching sounds on the floor. A car stopped before the closed door. I opened it. Bachelor Sam stood there worrying with his hat. "Evenin', ma'am." He cleared his throat. "Thought I'd stop by and sort of report." Report what? I waited frantically. "You see, ma'am, there's that big bog hole right at the corner of my field, where the road makes that bend. Well, that inspector he got to it and 'stead of taking roundings like a body ort, he just busted right straight through it. Couldn't see nothing of the wheels but the tire tips."

He stopped long enough to turn his hat around and start from the other side. Then he went on. "I was a-puttin' some stays in my fence, and I had my block and tackle with me, too. I drove around the bog hole and pitched the hook to him to tie on to his bumper. Then I tied the other to my car and yanked him across. Threw mud all over him and clean to the tail of his car. On top of that, I sort of pulled his front bumper out of kilter." Sam shook his head.

"Then what did that blamed inspector do? Be dogged if he didn't turn around that bog hole and head for town. Said as far as he was concerned we could keep this hick school for the rest of our natural lives." He went down the steps and opened the car door. He got in, shut the door, then put his head out the window and said, "Thought I ort to report." He left in a splatter of mud.

After school I drove Lupe to her father's sheep camp just around the bend. She still held on to the armadillo, which by now had become either tame or tired. I was grateful, for I knew its claws could easily rip my cushion.

At the camp I stopped the car and helped Lupe out

with her armadillo. What seemed to me like a dozen little childen ran up in silent surprise. A late sun shone down upon Lupe and on her blue-black hair, parted in the middle. Inside her red hair ribbon was tucked the circus napkin. She looked up at me, a wealth of happiness shining in her dark eyes. "I have the good, good Teacher," she said.

The Inspector Arrives

I still was enjoying my escape from the inspector when I took my voucher to town for the judge to sign. There I received a jolt. The judge had a letter from the State Board of Education. Austin would be sending another inspector to my school in the near future.

In the near future. Would that mean sometime next week, beginning with Monday? Or would it be the following week? And when he came, would it be in the morning or the afternoon?

I comforted myself. Lupe's armadillo was coming to school now in the form of tamales. I had broken Connally's habit of asking to go out. Also, I had bought a new red dress which fit me perfectly. Certainly I would wear it when the inspector came—that is, if I could know ahead when he was coming. But of course I wouldn't wear it until he came.

Little girls always looked each morning to see what Teacher was wearing. They held long discussions as to which of her dresses they liked and why they liked them. I went to school on Monday morning wearing a rather faded gingham dress because I meant to clean the schoolroom from top to bottom.

I always had math classes the first thing in the morning. My theory was that both teacher and pupils had clearer minds then.

It always did vex me when I couldn't get a point across to a class, and the arithmetic book that came out new that term was a bogey. On this Monday morning, while the sun came through the east windows and made mote rays across the room, I set out to explain a problem which the seventh grade couldn't solve: A water trough is constructed with triangular ends and two rectangular sides of the same dimensions. How many gallons of water will it hold if it measures twelve feet long and three feet wide?

My three seventh graders shook their heads. "Let me show you," I said finally when I couldn't make them see the solution in words. I took a stack of books from my desk and knelt on the floor. I used a part of the books for props. With the rest I constructed a replica of the trough. Still on my knees I began to explain: "Using your formula for the volume of a triangular prism, get your cubic measure for volume first. Then figure your gallons of water, and remember that you are figuring a triangular, not a rectangular trough."

The whole roomful of pupils had crept up and was crowding the recitation bench. I talked on, picturing to them a flow of cooling water, cattle coming down the hill for a drink. They sat, fascinated.

A man cleared his throat in the open door. I knew from past experience that it was the inspector.

How long I knelt there paralyzed I don't know. Across the baseball ground came the *clack*, *clack*, of Mrs. Essie's stalk cutter in the field beyond. For some reason, community gossip came to me then as clear as a bell: Mrs. Essie always got up before dawn, cooked a breakfast of ham and hot biscuits for her husband, who suffered from poor health. Then after she'd fed the team of horses, she went back and washed the dishes. She always had her team hooked up and going in the field by good daylight. Now why did I have to think of all that now?

The books collapsed and lay in a heap on the splintered floor. My desk clock ticked loudly and impudently. The inspector was in the room now, picking up the clutter of books. I got up and brushed at my knees. He stacked the books neatly on my desk beside the saucy clock. Then he turned to me, a smile working at his mouth. "If the problem had been a water tower," he asked, "would you have climbed the wall?"

I stood there helplessly, for I could think of nothing to say. Why did I have to be like this? A teacher always should be neat and dignified. I thought of Miss Sallie, my favorite teacher. I could see her now, standing before the roomful of pupils, hands clasped, shirtwaist crisp, hair neat and shiny. Miss Sallie was reciting:

> Bobby Shafto's gone to sea,
> Silver buckles on his knee.
> He'll come back no more to me;
> Pretty Bobby Shafto.

Never would Miss Sallie have gone down on her knees and built a water trough of books. . . .

Across the crowded recitation bench came Connally's piping voice, "Teacher, can I go out?"

I never learned what the inspector's report was. I

57

never cared to know. All I could remember about that day was the ungraceful figure I made as that immaculate young man helped me to my feet.

And I never cared for that red dress!

Bonnie's Sex Books

That particular morning at Ranch Branch was a wintry one. I had the fire going and the room fairly well warmed by the time Bonnie got to school. Bonnie was my third grader, tall and thin with a carrot-colored thatch of hair. Her pinched little face, always too sallow, was sprinkled with pale freckles. However, I couldn't see Bonnie's features too well that morning, for Bonnie carried an enormous stack of books.

I wanted to take them from her, but they swayed back and forth in her arms until I was afraid to touch them. "Bonnie," I gasped, "where did you get so many books?" I had never been in Bonnie's home, but my teacher's instinct told me that Bonnie didn't come from a reading family.

She eased the books onto her desk. Then she turned to me, her eyes shining. "Twenty books," she told me, "one for every kid in school."

"But you still haven't told me where you got them."

"Oh, they belong to Mr. Fergus. He lived with us the year I started to school. Mama said she reckoned he was a book peddler or something. Anyway, all he did that year was to pay us board and read. When he left, he didn't take his books, and he never did send for them. Mama said she guessed he died or left the country. She said she wanted to be shet of them, for they wasn't nothing

but dust catchers. So I brung them over to the kids."
She stepped back and dusted her hands. "The kids'll
be tickled," she said happily. "I'll give the littlest books
to the littlest ones and the biggest books to the biggest
ones." Ordinarily I would have been anxious to look at
the books, but my desk clock said nine, so I rang the
bell as Bonnie laid a book on each child's desk.

A cold wind blew in from the north, so I ran over
lesson time in order to cut short the morning recess. That
way, if the weather got too severe, I could let the children out early yet still get in teaching hours. I promised the children, though, that if the weather cleared,
I would add extra time to their lunch hour.

By the time lunch was over, the sun shone out and
the wind had stilled. I told them I would keep my promise. Twenty happy children dashed out to the baseball
field. Usually I went with them, for I liked to think that
I was a pretty good ball player. But with that extra fifteen minutes, I decided to stay in and straighten the book
closet.

I don't know why, but when I walked to Connally's
desk I glanced down at the book which Bonnie had given
him. It was a small book, gold in color with its title
printed in black. Idly I picked it up. The title fairly
jumped out at me: *What Every Man Should Know about
Sex.*

Horrified, I glanced over the room. Most of the gift
books lay on top of the desks. However, I noticed that
the older children had put theirs inside their desks. That
meant they had hidden them. I began my search. Every
book in the room was about sex! Why, that Mr. Fergus
must have been a sex maniac! What was I to do? I looked
uneasily through the window. The baseball game was

going strong. I slid open the long stove lid and began gathering gift books.

How many could I burn at a time without running the risk of flames shooting too high up the stovepipe? I laid four books on the red coals. The coals licked them up without too much roaring. I dropped in four more. After they had burned down, I ran to the window, praying that the children would still be busy with their game. They were. When I came back to the stove, the book which Bonnie had given Margaret was turning and twisting and curling within the stove. For a moment its title mocked me: *A Time for Bed Fe____*; the rest of the title had burned. As I laid in more books, I wondered if that unfinished word had been *fellows* or *feathers*. I punched the books with the poker. Now I would never know. Why hadn't I read the title before I threw it in?

The pupils got an extra ten minutes so I could burn all the books. Then I had to wait a few minutes more in order to punch down the evidence. Finally I was able to ring the bell. The pupils marched in, exclaiming how hot the room was. Before they settled down to lessons, they had opened every window and were fanning with their tablets.

Afternoon classes droned on. Black clouds scudded low above the horizon. The wind had risen again. "Watch the weather," the trustees had warned me. "We want our young'uns to learn, but we don't want no cyclone blowing them around."

That was one of my major worries. If I saw the makings of a cyclone, what should I do? I had chosen in my mind a long, ditchlike gully on the west side of the schoolyard. I would take them there and have them lie down. The weather that day, though, did not show any sign of a cyclone. Still, it did look rainy. Before we'd finished with lessons, the sky grew overcast, and a few sparse needles of ice fell. I had to get those children home before it grew worse. The pupils began getting their coats and books together.

I went to the blackboard to write tomorrow's assignments. Suddenly I was aware of a commotion. I dropped chalk and eraser into the chalk trough and turned around impatiently. "Look," I told them, "the weather's getting worse. Get your things and hurry."

Dorothy spoke up. "Teacher," she said, "I can't find the book Bonnie gave me."

A chorus of disappointed cries sounded from all over the room. What was I to say? I never had been a good liar. That fact had nothing to do with either my morals or my sins; I simply had never mastered the art. A spatter of hail sounded on the tin roof, and then it was gone. Thin patches of blue showed in the north. If they went on now, the children would be safe from the weather.

The commotion had turned into a riot. Twenty books had disappeared. Dorothy declared some traveler got them while I cleaned the closet. Maisie accused Bonnie of hiding them to take home again. Little Connally was the worst stricken of them all. "Maybe Sandy Claus got them and is gonna bring them back at Christmas," he quavered.

I finally got them marched through the schoolyard gate. Then I went back to the schoolroom and leaned weakly against the door. It was over. The mystery never would be cleared up. But then quite often, mysteries never are. I locked the front door and put the key under the root of the big live-oak so any child getting to school ahead of me could go inside. Then I headed for my car.

Mysteries. Even I was plagued with one. That word after *bed* on Margaret's book — could it have been *fellows* or *feathers?*

On the Oregon Trail

There were days when history or reading lessons became so interesting that I made no effort to separate the classes. Such a history lesson was the one about the Oregon Trail.

As long as the chapter dealt with the location of Oregon Country west of the Rocky Mountains and between the forty-second and fifty-fourth parallels, nobody in the room came up to sit on the extra bench. Even Delmo and Vhonda yawned throughout their class. However, as the story moved on, a pupil here or there crept up to listen. I knew that I had to make that story more interesting, for I wanted every child in the room to share in this experience.

"Each spring," I said, "emigrants would gather on the Missouri River. Here they camped until May or June, then they would 'jump off' into the great western prairies."

I caught a gleam in Connally's eyes. Then he raised his hand from the back of the room. "Teacher," he asked, "did they jump off in the river and swim across?"

Dorothy, the ever wise, answered for me. "Why, no, silly, they had to take grub and bedding along and some of them had kids they wanted to take along."

"Children," I said, "everybody come to the extra bench so I can answer you." There was a big "jump off" in the room for that extra bench.

"Now," I went on, "as I talk I want questions – from anybody. Just raise your hands quietly. And, Connally, as to your question – no, the people would gather at different points on the river. The term *jump off* extended all the way from Independence, Missouri, to Council Bluffs, Iowa."

The little ones began to fidget. I had to bring the story nearer home. I said, "Let's pretend we're at Independence, Missouri. There are a dozen other families traveling with us in covered wagons, called prairie schooners. I shall be a grandmother; Delmo and Vhonda are the parents. The rest of you are the children.

Connally stopped wriggling and forgot to ask if he could go out. I put Delmo on an imaginary roan horse to help drive the herds of cattle and horses. I let Dorothy be a big daughter. She could ride with the men. Here Dorothy's imagination so exceeded mine that I let her take over. She rode a sidesaddle and carried a bright red umbrella over her head. The rest of us rode in the wagon. I drove the team. "Remember," I cautioned them, "we are embarking on a long, slow, and perilous journey. Our wagon is drawn by two big, lumbering oxen, and they are pulling a heavy load."

We spent almost an hour and two spelling lessons on this trail. Then it was night. We watched the wagons being drawn in a circle, and we helped with the chores, cooking and spreading out the bedding. I noticed that Dorothy wasn't helping with the night work, so I questioned her. It developed that Dorothy's pinto pony, Strawberry, was lame, and she had to bathe her ankles with turpentine.

These lessons went on during the history periods for four days. We followed the banks of the Platte River,

through the center of what now is Nebraska and Wyo-
ming. As we traveled, all the route was marked with
crayola on the big, roll-up Rand McNally map. We crossed
the Rockies, then turned northwestward through Idaho
to the Columbia River. Every time I called on Dorothy
to discuss something in class, that paint pony of hers
had gone lame again.

I explained to the children why our trail had to follow the banks of creeks and rivers whenever possible.
Then I brought them face to face with the frightful truth
that during summer heat these streams often went dry.
At such dreaded time, Papa Delmo had to leave the cara-
van to help hunt out the widely scattered water holes.

We had Connally get sick from thirst; we let Debbie
be pierced through the shoulder by an Indian's arrow.
But when little Arthur offered his scalp to the Indians,
I drew the line. This was getting a bit serious.

Eventually, though, we sighted the blue Pacific, but
not before we had lightened our loaded wagon by throwing our Great-Aunt Prudie's claw-footed dining table,
Grandma Beam's bureau of carved oak, and Vhonda's
hope chest of polished cedar. The boys didn't seem the
least bit disturbed by all this loss of gentility, but when
Dorothy dramatically announced that her strawberry
pinto had birthed a colt and that it died from the heat,
they set up loud ejaculations.

Personally I wondered how the pinto, in foal and
starved until every rib showed, could have concealed her
condition for that long, but I said nothing. We had
reached the Pacific. Next week we would settle California and begin the overland mail. Besides, I was a bit
travel weary.

"Well, children," I said as I closed the history book,

"we have come a long way from that day in Independence, Missouri, where all we could hear in that town was the hammering and banging as wagons were being repaired, and the constant 'whoaing' as blacksmiths shod the horses and oxen."

Charlie's Big Grandpa

Up went Charlie's hand. "Teacher, how did the blacksmiths shoe the oxen?"

That question was a stumper. I realized all too sadly that books didn't supply all the answers. I had to admit to the children that I had no idea how to shoe an ox. This was a blow to them, for Teacher was supposed to know everything.

Finally Charlie raised his hand again. "Teacher, I bet Big Grandpa knows."

I had forgotten Charlie's great-grandfather, who lived with Charlie's family. Or rather, Charlie's family lived with him. "Charlie," I said, "you be sure and ask your grandfather tonight so you can tell us in the morning."

The next morning as I drove to school, I was well aware that it was spring. Up in the neck of land jutting south from the Robles' field, buttercups had massed until no ground showed. From the live-oak thicket in the middle of the main field, a mockingbird sounded so many different notes that finally I stopped the car and counted them. Thirty calls in all — a tumultuous aria.

When I got to school, Big Grandpa and Charlie were sitting in the east doorway. Big Grandpa was dressed for the occasion. He wore a suit of gray plaid, a yellowed white shirt, a bright blue tie, and a purple vest which sported cowboys in their various actions. I hurried in and rang the bell. Big Grandpa was rarin' to talk!

He talked till well past the morning recess, and I was as interested as the children. He told how the blacksmith first shod the oxen with horseshoes and then, using a sharp rasp, cut the shoes in two and fitted them to the animals' hooves. I never knew whether or not this method actually was used, but it served the purpose that day.

Big Grandpa left just before I rang the bell. He walked through the schoolyard gate and down the sandy lane as jauntily as if he had been eighteen instead of eighty.

After he was out of sight and the children had come in from recess, Charlie sat with a puzzled expression covering his face. Finally he shook his head and said, "Big Grandpa can't even read and write, but he knows more than the Teacher does."

Agarita Berries

By the last of March, Mr. Echard's pasture north of the Ranch Branch schoolhouse was yellow with agarita blossoms. They gave off a dusty, pungent smell that somehow was pleasant to inhale. Every north wind brought their sweetish odor into the schoolroom.

The ranchers hated the agarita brush, which they called algerita. With the exception of their berry crop, these bushes, covered with prickly leaves, had no rangeland value. Some of the community women dug the roots and made an excellent yellow dye by boiling them. They canned the berries or made jelly from the fresh ones. The red berries were rather small and hard to pick because

of the prickly leaves, so usually families would go on picnics and take along canvas wagon tarps. They would lay
a tarp beneath a bush which had extra-juicy berries. With
sticks for beating, they soon had a goodly supply of berries. After lunch, they could sit under a big live oak and
pick out the sticks and leaves. When they boiled these
berries, the juice had to be dripped later, not squeezed.
If some housewife got hasty and pressed her bag of berries and juice, she could count on bitter jelly.

May came. The agarita bushes now were covered with
an unusual crop of berries. It was more than the children could bear. When recess came, they climbed the
fence separating the bushes and the schoolyard. Besides,
they knew those berry bushes as well as most folks know
their neighbors. For instance, the big bush by the fence
in the northeast corner of the schoolyard had huge berries, deep red and juicy. But those berries were bitter.
The bush behind the girls' outhouse had a sweet-tasting
crop, but its berries were always small and dried looking. The bushes on the side of the hill farthest (naturally) from the schoolhouse had the sweetest-tasting
berries of them all.

The bushes on the other side of the hill — those farthest from the schoolhouse. That same old story — the
farther the hill, the greener the grass. I had to do something about this situation. This was rattlesnake country, with not a telephone nearer than two miles of the
schoolhouse. I always tried to see that my car stayed
in top condition, but who can tell about a car? Besides,
it was becoming increasingly harder to ring my hand-
bell loud enough for the children over the hill to hear.
I had been sending the little children out to bring in the
big ones until I suspected that they made no effort to

come in until they were thus notified. This thing had gone
far enough. When recess ended, I rang my bell so fast
and so furiously that all the pupils, even those over the
hill and no telling how much further, came on a run.

"Children," I told them when they were seated, "beginning tomorrow, there will be no more berry picking.
Everyone stays in the schoolyard."

They looked at me blankly, their chins dripping red
juice down the front of their clothes. Finally Darrell
raised his hand. "But Teacher—"

"I know, Darrell, and I'm sorry; but I have the responsibility of you pupils. What if you got a rattlesnake
bite off among the berry bushes? Or what if you fell and
broke a leg?" I knew that my reasons sounded far-fetched,
but this thing had to end.

Vhonda's Broken Leg

The ball game that next morning was halfhearted.
Frequently I'd catch the basemen staring disconsolately
across the fence to those berry bushes, red now against
the sun; but Teacher had said no, and they had to mind.
I tried not to notice when they grouped and threw bel-
ligerent glances in my direction.

Afternoon recess came. Dorothy ran to tell me there
was a red wasps' nest in the girls' outhouse. I got the
spouted can of kerosene from the corner closet and went
to get the wasps.

When I came out of the outhouse, I was met by the
whole baseball team. Vhonda, they said, was running
from second to third base and fell and broke her leg.

Vhonda with a broken leg! Where was Vhonda? In

the schoolhouse, they said, lying on the floor of the stage. Darrell and Tessie had carried her in. I ran so fast the kerosene bounced from the oil can spout and marked a greasy trail. So I had kept Vhonda out of the berry pasture only to have her break her leg on the baseball field!

The stage floor was built across the front, or north, of the room. Vhonda lay full length, Tessie kneeling at her head, Darrell kneeling at her feet. Her eyes were closed. Her hands were folded across her chest. I stopped inside the front door and looked at her. I should have been terrified still, but something about the scene looked too theatrical. All she needs now is a lily in her hand, I thought irreverently, and I immediately was horrified at my thought.

What was I do do? Why hadn't I left these children free to roam the berry pasture at will? Why hadn't I let them wander all the way over the hill as far even as Bachelor Echard's house? Why did I have to shut them up on the school ground and force them to play baseball?

"Vhonda," I quavered, still in the front doorway, "is your leg really broken?"

"Yes, ma'am," Vonda answered faintly.

"Where is it broken?"

"Just below the knee."

Something about this tableau still didn't make sense. The scene was too perfect. I kept staring at Vhonda's closed eyes and folded hands, and I couldn't get that lily thought out of my mind. I'd try to call their bluff. If it didn't work, then I'd face the worst; if it did work . . . "Vhonda," I said, "Come here and let me look at your broken leg."

Sure enough, Vhonda got up and limped down the middle aisle to where I stood at the front door. I sat her on a bench and rang for the children to come in. I gave Darrell permission to hear the fifth grade reading, while I drove Vhonda and her "broken" leg home.

School Plays

School plays were a must in those country communities. Some of them, especially the two-and-a-half-hour performances at school closings, were acted by grownups. Always, though, regardless of time, age, or place, Teacher had to coach the plays.

The plays put on by the adults, in some ways, were easier to coach than those for children. At least, for grown-ups I could order the plays according to the cast of characters. Many community men and women made excellent actors — that is, if the play was a comedy. Something about a serious play embarrassed these people. They were quite reticent when it came to emotional display. But comedy? Every community had its clown. I learned early that farce was what the people wanted.

Then began the frustrating hours of pure and simple technique. Mr. Silas was a first-rate comedian, but Mr. Silas didn't always bother to face the audience with his act. That took hours of patient directing.

Mr. Dan loved to sing. He loved hearing his voice roll out across the stage. Mr. Dan, however, couldn't sing. How do you go about taking the starch out of a man without wilting him, I'd ask myself over and over. I learned by accident that Mr. Dan could play a guitar. I went to Mr. Dan and told him how very much I needed someone in the third act to accompany the songs with a guitar. Then I asked him if he knew of anybody in the community who could play a guitar. Mr. Dan could. After that, though, I had to convince Mr. Dan that he couldn't sing as well as play, because he'd have to stand behind the curtain and accompany female voices. Mr. Dan cheerfully confined his act to music alone because Teacher was in a spot.

Now for the stage and its settings. In the book of plays which I had ordered, the stage settings ran like this: Act 1. (Mrs. Vanderbilt's living room. The window curtains are a rich damask, the settee a soft pink brocade. A garden shows through the open window. Pink roses climb the garden wall. There are trees and shrubs in view.)

I found the community women quite versatile; and though damask curtains had to be changed to dyed muslin and the brocaded settee to a bolstered bench sitting on sheep boards, it was surprising what those ladies could create from pasteboard and crepe paper. Even their husbands caught the spirit, and the fences and stone walls they built across the stage were quite effective.

Night was the only time the men and women could practice. There were evenings when frustration took over, throwing everybody on edge. Still, there were other nights, especially as practice progressed, when the labor was fun filled, climaxed by generous servings of Miss Cordie's fresh coconut cake.

I was adamant on only one issue. After the third practice I took away the actors' books and prompted them. I had known too many situations where the actors held on to their books until they began to resemble a little child learning to walk: they didn't recessarily have to read from their books; they just had to hold on to them, the way babies walk by touching their mother's skirt.

Finding plays for the children was a job, for I had my own rigid rule: no child could be left out of the play. Finally in exasperation I had declared that I would start writing my own school plays.

Word spread like wildfire. Teacher was going to write the school play herself! What began as an idle threat ended in the children's greeting me each morning with, "Teacher, did you write the play?" What do you do when you are cornered by the faith of children? I wrote the play.

Each successive play became a bit easier to write, for I had the previous play to evaluate, compare, and criticize. In time I became capable of viewing my own plays objectively. Then, too, I knew the character and the ability of each pupil. It was an excellent opportunity to write parts for them.

In the end, after making a few changes upon seeing the performance, I began marketing these school plays. I rarely received more than twenty-five dollars for any play.

Leon and His Father

This was to be my last year at Ranch Branch, and it was November. I got to school earlier than usual that morning, for I wanted to have the schoolhouse warm by the time the children came. I had a good fire going in the woodstove when Leon opened the door. He stood there defiantly, a newcomer. Snow swirled about him, and big lazy flakes settled on his shock of dark hair. I

72

judged him to be about fourteen years old but small for his years.

I confess that I was disappointed. I had been two months arranging a schedule for handling twenty children and eight grades. With this new pupil, I would have to rearrange things. I put him in the seventh grade with two other boys. They were cheerful, outgoing lads and had little patience with Leon's moodiness.

At recess everybody except the three first graders played baseball. With me on the team, that made nine players on each side with no umpire. Our school was so isolated in its customary Texas-sized pasture that we never bothered about baseball rules and regulations. Now Leon would unbalance the team. I would have to umpire, and I hated to umpire.

Leon, however, solved the situation himself. "Never did like baseball," he said sullenly and squatted on the sideline to watch.

The week before Thanksgiving we made construction-paper posters which the children were to take home. I had drawn my own pattern: a white country church on grass-covered ground, with a fringe of bushes separating it from a blue sky. Four white clouds floated toward the steeple, bearing this message: *Thankful to Be Americans.*

I noticed that Leon wasn't using the paper which I had issued him. "No need to make it," he said flatly; "Pa would just laugh at it."

I had heard rumors about Leon and his father. Country gossip had it that Leon's mother had run off with a salesman when Leon was just a baby.

"Leon," I asked, "would you like to make a poster to put up in the schoolroom?"

He looked at me, and the look of moody worship in

his dark eyes made me uncomfortable. "I'll make it for you," he muttered, "and you can put it where you want to."

I grew increasingly aware of Leon's adoration. He never studied; consequently, his work was poorly done. Wherever I stood in the schoolroom, I was acutely conscious of his watchfulness. Finally he made so many failing grades that I felt I had to talk with his father.

It was the first week in December when I drove Leon home after school. Winter was on the land, and the hills showed bleakly through naked trees. I felt its stark beauty, and I wanted Leon to feel it too. "Leon," I said impulsively, "out there do you get the feeling that everything is waiting until spring comes along and wakes it up?"

Leon never took his eyes off my face. "It's all right, I guess," he said.

I stopped the car in front of an unpainted shack. For once, I caught Leon not watching me. I was wearing a dress made of a colorful silk print, and where a fold of the pleated skirt had escaped my coat, Leon was holding it between his hands. He touched it so gently that a lump caught in my throat. "Leon," I said, "you do love pretty things."

He dropped the fold and shoved both hands inside his pockets. "It's all right," he said again. And then, "There's Pa standing in the door."

The house was one of a number of such squalid cabins which at that time dotted the countryside: a high-walled room slipping from a peaked roof to a low shed tacked on behind. I got out of the car.

Leon's father could not have been old, but he looked old. I could see where Leon got his defiance and his moody brown eyes. "Don't bother to come in," he said harshly; "talk where you are." Leon had disappeared.

"I wanted to see you about Leon's grades," I began, but he stopped me.

"You're his teacher. Don't you know enough to teach a seventh-grade boy?"

"But Leon is failing, and he shouldn't be. It's as if a spark has gone out of him. He needs somebody to care about his grades at home, somebody to love him."

I understood then why Leon didn't want his father to see the Thanksgiving poster, for the man's laughter was more like a bray, carrying with it a combination of hatred, scorn, and obscenity. "Love!" he scoffed. "His ma used to cuddle him before she run off with that sugar-talking peddler." He came so close to me that I stepped back, half in fright, for the fire smoldering within his eyes was terrifying. He looked me over for what seemed like an eternity. Then, "You're the spittin' image of Leon's ma," he shouted. "Now, get!"

I drove home slowly. I understood now the tense quality of Leon's worship. He had been taught to hate his mother's memory. Yet an intangible something had lived on within the boy. My resemblance to his mother had brought it out. I lay awake that night. I could understand why Leon's mother had run away from his father, but how could any mother desert her baby?

Christmas that year was a repetition of Thanksgiving. Under my supervision, the pupils made gifts for their families. But not Leon. Finally he did cover a matchbox messily with glitter. "Here," he said, shoving it toward me where I sat at my desk. "You can have it." I thanked him, and once again I felt that queer lump which I had come to associate with Leon.

Mother's Day was the worst of all. I had brought small squares of glass to school which the pupils laid over colorful pictures. Then they painted these pictures on the glass. Next we turned the painted glass over on bright backgrounds and framed the pictures with tape. I was thrilled when I saw Leon painting his glass, but I pretended not to notice. It was not neat, for Leon was notoriously messy. At least, though, he was making a picture. Nicky, my second grader, held up his neatly framed print. "Mother's going to like this," he said happily.

I saw Leon's body jerk and then grow rigid. He sat for a moment looking down at his picture. Then he dipped his brush into his water colors. "Mother," he muttered, swiping the dripping brush across his work. "Mother!" He made the word sound like an obscenity.

During the summer Leon and his father moved away.

My last year at this school had been filled with talk of countywide consolidation, but as yet it hadn't come.

Before we knew it, we were in World War II. One Saturday morning as my husband and I drank our breakfast coffee and listened to the grim news coming over the radio, Leon opened our kitchen door. The radio had drowned out the sounds of his Model A car.

I knew him instantly, although he was in soldier's uniform and looked quite manly. I made a quick calculation. If he had given his correct age when he started at my school, Leon now couldn't be more than sixteen. How, then, had he managed to get into the army?

I recognized all too well that familiar look of adoration in his moody brown eyes. "Leaving Fort Hood next week," he said with his usual abruptness. "Going overseas. Just dropped by to say hello and goodbye."

Again I felt that pesky lump. "Leon," I said, "you're so young to be going off to war."

An eagerness replaced his moodiness. "Want to go," he said, waving off my efforts to give him breakfast. "Going to be fun stabbing Nazis."

I swallowed my revulsion. "Do you have to hate them so much?" I asked.

He looked at me, his eyes opaque now from some indescribable filtering out of color and expression. "What do you want me to do," he asked in exactly his father's tone of voice, "kiss 'em before I stab 'em?"

I heard from Leon occasionally, but my life as a wife, a mother, and a teacher was more than full. I always answered his letters, but I confess that I thought of him only occasionally. Mine was a selfish corner, filled merely with what was dear to me.

In February of that year I received a valentine from Leon. It came from Somewhere in France. It read, "For my teacher who was more like a mother to me." I put away the little card. Why was I always too busy to think of that boy? Why had his moodiness, his crudity, even his adoration always exasperated me? I went back to my own busy little corner.

His next letter read, "Gunning them down like hell. Haven't had my shoes off in ten days." It was by accident I read that Leon had been killed in France, still manning his machine gun.

Today, when I hear affluent youth complaining about inequalities, I remember Leon. Talk about inequalities! As far as I know, Leon's short life had held only two realities: his bitterness and me.

Time to Leave

That year, toward the close of school, I asked the Ranch Branch trustees for a raise in salary. The trustees refused. "You're getting eighty dollars a month," they told me. "We never made that kind of money in our lives."

At that time, in the early 1940s, eighty dollars was an accepted salary, equaling that paid to many teachers in the town schools. Somehow, though, after teaching for six years in this school, I felt that I deserved a raise. The community ranch land brought in quite a sum of money. I resented being turned down.

The next day, while I was in the middle of a noon ball game, a trustee from the neighboring Ten Mile school drove into the schoolyard. He offered me $140 per month to teach the little school in his community. This was an unheard-of salary for a country teacher in a little one-room school. I lost no time in accepting his offer.

Again, it hurt to go. Some of those pupils had started school under me. Now, as sixth graders, they had never known any other teacher. Perhaps there is no greater thrill in the teaching profession than to take beginners who can't read a word and within three months have them trying to read everything that came within their grasp. Still, going to a new school is a challenge, another chance to see what lies on the other side of the hill.

That last day after a short program, I closed the doors of the Ranch Branch school and laid the keys under a root of the big live-oak tree. Who would reopen the schoolhouse doors that coming fall? And would the live-oak tree be full of acorns ready for the boys to chunk the girls when I wasn't looking? But I wouldn't be looking. Who would be their next teacher?

7. Ten Mile

The Ten Mile schoolhouse also sat in the middle of a proverbial Texas-sized pasture. However, this schoolhouse was neither lumber or logs. It was stucco. It faced east, with a side door on the north. The south wall was all windows. Behind my desk, the west wall featured a long row of slate blackboards. There were twelve pupils, ranging from the first grade through the seventh.

Jimmy and Billy's Present

On that first morning, nine-year-old Jimmy and his seven-year-old brother brought Teacher a present. It wasn't an apple. Having grown up in the country and in tune with all nature's creatures, they came in proudly bearing a Coke bottle inside of which writhed a baby snake—a spreading adder!

I couldn't bear to see it writhing and wriggling there on my desk, even if it couldn't get out of the bottle. Besides, I was nervous. I always was nervous when I opened a new school. I explained to Billy that the little snake was afraid up there in front of the room. I persuaded him to take it back to the sandbox and partially bury

79

the bottle in the sand where it wouldn't turn over. I didn't bother to explain to him that if that snake got out and began wriggling toward my desk, the pupils might well be minus a teacher.

Billy carried it lovingly back to the sandbox. That afternoon when school let out, I talked him and Jimmy into turning the snake out in the weeds by the roadside, explaining that it might die shut up all night in the Coke bottle. They did so reluctantly, and as I watched that tiny reptile wriggle away to freedom, I had the uneasy feeling that two little boys were already disappointed with their teacher.

Life in the Schoolroom

I brought to this little school all the experience and the technique for dispensing knowledge which I had acquired over the years, beginning at sixteen and lasting from World War I to World War II. I had acquired this knowledge for teaching country schools by the trial-and-error method. My previous pupils had borne the brunt of my mistakes.

Again I set an extra bench beside the recitation bench facing my desk. Once more I set out to train these twelve students; anyone in the room was welcome to come and sit on the extra bench and hear any lesson, provided they did not neglect their own lessons. That last rule was one of my stern stipulations: each student had to know his or her own lessons.

I trained this new group to tiptoe and to whisper. Each pupil was welcome to walk quietly about the room in this manner without permission, provided he or she had a purpose for walking. I explained to them that any group had free access to the worktable in the back of the room as long as that group worked together constructively.

As it was in my other schools, such newfound freedom seemed boundless. However, when a few began drawing foolish pictures on the blackboard and consequently lost board privilege for a week, they learned, and in the learning, education took on a new meaning for them.

All twelve loved the blackboard. Though the smaller children used the board more, my seventh graders, the oldest group, sometimes would push aside their books and tiptoe quietly to the blackboard to depict there what they had just read while preparing a lesson. And every Monday morning when I got to school, I could read from the drawings by early pupils just what had taken place over the weekend. Their best drawings were Texas rodeos, the grandstands filled with men wearing Stetson hats, Levi's, and boots and spurs. Out in the blackboard arena some daredevil stunt was taking place – a bulldogging, a barrel race, or a bronc ride.

Any giggling or pushing meant no board privileges for the rest of the week: the same rule applied to the worktable. Strange how thirst for knowledge grows. I never had a schoolroom so quiet I could hear a pin drop. Too many projects were going on at the same time. I always argued, though, that when machinery is working, it makes a noise – but a machine is in working order only when its noise is a constructive hum.

No matter whose lesson or what subject was recited, somebody drew it on the board. The word *hibernation* in the fifth-grade science held a peculiar significance to the first and second graders. They hurriedly tiptoed to the board to portray various beasts in their winter caves — all of them hibernating standing up. Only Grandma Moses ever came anywhere near to capturing that special something which little children draw into their pictures.

When the sixth-grade history class recited that ever-exciting story of the Pilgrims coming over in the *Mayflower*, Ken, my first grader, broke a stern rule; he interrupted the class by bursting out with, "Teacher, did the book say the Pilgrims came over in the Maytag?"

One day I found Jimmy and Dale spending the recess catching butterflies and idly pulling off their wings. I lifted out the butterflies which they had captured in a pencil box and were keeping to pull off the wings later. I showed them the intricate patterns and colors in each pair of wings. I pointed out the dogface butterfly, whose wings depict a dog's head, nose, and eyes. They became interested in the Texas monarch butterfly. I took the little insect into the schoolroom with me, and when it came time for the two boys' English lesson, everybody in the room had a hand in fashioning this poem:

Monarch Butterfly, as you follow the Texas trail,
Flitting from yellow flowers to those of gentian blue,
Has anybody ever told you that without fail
Boys and girls in Texas schools love to read about you?

The worktable in the back of the room was a wonderful place to explore the world through the pages of an encyclopedia. Some of the children were too young to read all the words, but the pictures were there; also the older pupils were there to pronounce those words for them.

They knew they could go to the bookshelf anytime and select any book they wanted while at the worktable. When it came time to go to their seats, the books had to go back on their shelves.

Perhaps my own love of books infused these pupils. However, it took time and patience to teach the children how to handle them and appreciate them. It opened a new experience for them. I imposed one important rule on each pupil: learn something new every day.

What a wealth of interest that rule invoked. Their knowledge ranged from the number of petals on the face of a common field daisy to the weight of warships' anchors. It was a fascinating game, but for me it posed problems.

We had come in one day from playing baseball. Billy set the bat in its accustomed corner by the side door. Then he asked, "Teacher, what kind of wood is a baseball bat made out of?"

It took three days, with everybody from the first grade on up searching and asking. Finally Curtis found the answer in a *Nationl Geographic:* a real baseball bat is made from the wood of an ash tree.

On it went, every day. My schoolroom became a humming beehive. Certainly nobody had time to punch somebody or steal another's pencil. Boredom? There was none. Besides, we had already located the only spot where boredom grows: in the human head.

A Final Exam in Spelling

Toward the end of the last semester of that first year, I began giving finals. My three second-grade boys hur-

83

ried back to the worktable for a whispered consultation. Finally all three of them came up to my desk. They knew they were not supposed to take finals in the second grade, but they wanted to. Please, could I give them a final in spelling?

"Well," I told them, "you will have to take the final over the whole speller; you see, you didn't take a midterm exam."

They assured me it was all right, as they could spell any of the words. I promised to give them a spelling final the next day, and they hurried back to the worktable to bone up on the test.

Their preparation back at the worktable all the next day was something. Finally by three o'clock that afternoon they closed their spellers. They were ready. "Just give us any word, Teacher," Billy said confidently, "we can spell it—just any word."

Something prompted me to have a little fun. "Did you say just *any* word?" I asked.

"You bet, Teacher," they chorused, "just any word."

I pretended to search the pages of the speller. Finally I called out, "Czechoslovakia."

I wish I could have photographed the expressions on their faces, pencils poised like runners lined up for a race, then blank faces and open mouths. There was a long pause. Finally Billy unscrewed his face and said, "Teacher, don't you have the wrong speller?"

By now World War II was deep in savage fighting. My two seventh graders were studying current events. While we discussed the latest troop movements, firstgrader Ken tiptoed to the board. He set his reader in the chalk trough, then began slashing marks all the way across the board. I was shocked and angry. I said sternly, "Ken, you know the rules for using the board. You are to *draw* something, not just make silly slashes with your chalk."

Ken's blue eyes flashed. "That's not silly slashes," he said hotly. "That's the Road to Tokyo!"

8. Consolidation

The year 1945 had been momentous. That was the year when consolidation began all over the county. Many were the speeches made at night in the little schoolhouses. "Your children are not getting a proper education. Close your one-teacher schools and let us bus your children to town." By 1947, all the little schools had come in. The children now rode buses to town. I had gone into town to teach.

Just as the word *secession* long ago had become a fighting word between the North and South, so was the word *consolidation* between town and country. It had become all too apparent why: the ranches had tax money the towns needed.

There were advantages, of course, when buses began carrying the children to town. Also, in the beginning there had been disadvantages. For when consolidation finally was effected, it came too swiftly. However, ambitious parents saw a dazzling future for their Susies and Johnnys: pep squads for Susie, football for Johnny. And instead of being unable to see the forest for the trees, the situation was reversed.

They had failed to see schoolrooms so congested with pupils that teachers had to adopt a form of an eenymeeny-miney-mo system of placing children. Tempers flared. Parents rebelled when they saw the situation, but it was too late. The day of the one-room school was over.

The first time the elementary school where I was teaching decided to turn out an hour earlier than usual, I went to bat for those living out in the country. "You can't," I argued; "these rural children won't be able to contact their parents."

"They can telephone. Surely they have telephones."

"But how many ranchers sit under their telephones at three P.M.?"

"Well, what if they can't get their parents? Can't they sit at home alone an extra hour?"

"But you don't understand. Some homes are three miles from the bus."

I was getting a bit riled. I remembered the time I made a government survey: Our crew leader began by showing us a movie of how to make a rural government survey: A nattily dressed young man drove his car down a paved country road. Houses were set equidistant on either side of the road. The handsome young man got out at the first house and rang the doorbell. Immediately a dressy lady appeared and answered his questions prettily. Then he drove to the house equidistant on the other side. Same scene.

I recalled when, in order to get a survey from a Mr. Itz, I had to drive five miles down a rocky road, turn around a hill, and then drive four miles to his house . . . Oh well, no use reminding anybody; people see what they want to see.

Eventually changes were scheduled ahead, extra rooms were added to accommodate the influx of pupils.

Buses were lined up before schools turned out, eliminating the danger of children being run over.

It was a difficult time also for the teachers in town. They had material programmed from one year to the other. Suddenly their rooms were overflowing with new and bewildered pupils. It meant different regulations, even on the schoolgrounds. Small wonder everybody connected with school grew aggressive.

Most town teachers were kind and cooperative. However, when the rural-school furniture began to come in, one fastidious marm refused a teacher's chair from a rural school. It had a little crack in the seat. "I wasn't about to sit on it," she complained; "it might have bedbugs." I did another of my slow burns as I asked myself, were bedbugs really able to distinguish between rural hides and town hides?

I was given a section of the third grade, thirty-seven children, all about the same age. No older ones to pronounce words for the smaller ones. The sameness, the crowding, and the noise got me. I was pining for a little one-room school set in a Texas-sized pasture. Gone were the days when the schoolhouse became a church house and the two-and-a-half-hour plays when school closed. The barbecue pits which once sent out tantalizing odors at school picnics had fallen in now from disuse. Wild morning glories covered them in the summer, and beady-eyed skunks sheltered there in the winter. Consolidation had brought two changes: it built up city education, while it destroyed community life.

The day my worktable was brought in from my Ten Mile school, I choked up. Ken, Curtis, Billy — where are you now, and where have the days gone when you sat around this little worktable and explored the world through the pages of an encyclopedia?

I picked up my third-grade reader. Outside, bees hummed about a bee brush that had been overlooked on the trim school grounds. The courthouse clock struck. I would go on. I have never been one to sit on the tail of progress and holler whoa. I had divided my thirty-seven third graders into three reading groups. Now it was time to hear the slowest readers. . . .

Epilogue: The Voices Now... and the Hills

I was substitute teaching in Mason's high school that year of 1958, Mason's centennial year. Kurt Zesch was already at work building the props around the football field which would portray the town of Mason in its frontier days. My brother, Fred Gipson, was to write the script for the centennial pageant. He had begun jotting down a few notes when Walt Disney telephoned him to come to Hollywood to write the movie script for *Old Yeller.* I hadn't seen too much of Fred, as he was married, with two boys. Also, he was completely wrapped up in his writing.

I had ridden the school bus home from school that afternoon when he came. He told me of his predicament, then laid his notes for the Mason pageant in my lap. "You'll have to write this pageant," he said as casually as if he were discussing the weather.

I was stunned. Write the script for Mason's pageant? Why, there'd be thousands of people to see that performance. "But, Fred, I can't write this pageant. I never wrote the script for a pageant in my life!"

He grinned. "Time you learned," he laughed as he left, gunning his car as if he was afraid I'd run him down.

I wrote the pageant. Our pageant was held that summer for a two-night performance and was a sellout. I give the greatest credit to the actors, for I still say I did not know how to write a pageant script.

Jack and I traveled some in the 1960s — Yosemite and Sequoia national forests, the Petrified Forest, the Ozarks, Nashville, Tennessee, Padre Island — always ending up at San Diego, where Jackie now lived with Pauline and their little daughter, Patricia.

I was writing and selling now, *Mason and Mason County: A History, Glory Girl* (fiction), and many features. There were autograph parties, much public speaking at Mason, Brady, Kerrville, Llano, San Angelo, and Fort Worth. I enjoyed it all, for public speaking was never any particular problem for me. However, my most rewarding moments came when my husband and I sat under our yard oaks and watched a wagon-wheel moon rise majestically over the treeline, watched a doe deer bring her twin fawns to the house pond, snort and paw the ground, so she and her babies could frolic.

In 1971 we celebrated our golden wedding anniversary. "You must have it catered in town," our sophisticated friends and relatives told us — but we didn't. Our house had weathered us for fifty years. We meant it to share this great event.

Pauline, Jackie, and Patricia came in their plane from San Diego, landing on the home strip. Two of my Fly Gap pupils, gray-haired grandfathers now, Orlie with his violin, Clarence with his guitar, played old-time songs:

> Come put on your old gray bonnet
> With the blue ribbons on it,
> While I hitch old Dobbin to the shay,

Epilogue

Through the fields of clover
We'll drive in to Dover,
On our Golden Wedding Day.

Best of all, though, was ten-year-old Patricia's tucking her violin under her chin and playing "Silver Threads among the Gold." Some three hundred guests registered that afternoon.

And then they were gone. The old house settled in the twilight and grew still. Pauline made fresh coffee for us and hot chocolate for Patricia and heated the ham sandwiches she took from the freezer.

I saw them all—my husband, my son and wife, my granddaughter Patricia. Then something like a premonition came over me. *Oh God, let it be, let it be....*

"Give us a year," the children said, "and then we're coming home to build on the ranch."

My dear brother, Fred Gipson, died in 1973. He is buried in the Austin State Cemetery near his old writer pals. His simple headstone bears this inscription: "His books are his monument."

Then Husband Jack became ill. The doctor's diagnosis was quite plain: cancer. "I guess you know what you have before you," the doctor told me.

I told him I did—but I didn't. Four years from one hospital over Texas to another, while the children built their home of the lovely blue-gray flint they hauled from the hills and cared for the ranch. Jack and I tried hard to hold on to that crust of reality, tried not to discuss what was ahead, but once I couldn't contain the longing I had for the old days. "Jack, do you still love me?"

His broken words will live with me always. "I love

you, Miss Stell. I loved you the first time I laid eyes on you, and I've loved you ever since."

Jackie sat by me during Jack's funeral at the Methodist Church in Mason. He held my hand while the organist played softly the fluting tones of "I'm Heading for the Last Roundup." Not a church song, to be sure, but Cowboy Jack loved it.

Do you take this man . . . in sickness and in health . . . till death do you part?

Three months later, one hot September afternoon, Jackie's plane crashed in the field by my house. The doctor let me out of the hospital for Jackie's funeral at the same church in Mason, but only bits of the sermon came to me, the pastor reading "High Flight," by John Gillespie, Jr.: "And while with silent lifting mind I've trod the high, untrespassed sanctity of space, put out my hand and touched the face of God." They flew from everywhere for his funeral, for Jackie was one of the four directors of the National Antique Airplane Association.

"Mother, you don't know what it's like up there above the clouds, all alone . . ."

It was very difficult for sixteen-year-old Patricia, who had never known death and who within three months lost the two men she loved. After graduation from the Brady High School, she went back to her hometown of San Diego, California. Today, as one of the supervisors in the U.S.A. Credit Union, a glassed-in building overlooking lovely San Diego, she has found an anchor at last.

Daughter-in-law Pauline, who had come from Mississippi and who came to Mason with a degree and a pilot's license, has taken to ranching like an old pro. She has an excellent job at Mason with the Agricultural

Stabilization and Conservation Service office. She is proud of the engraved plaque the conservation committee awarded her for her ranch practice, though certainly her Mississippi and Alabama upbringing had not equipped her for Texas ranch life. Each of us still lives in our separate homes, some quarter of a mile apart.

I sold my horse and saddle as well as Jack's horses, but Pauline and I kept Jack's saddle for Patricia, a memento of the days when she rode with her grandfather. She still keeps her father's banjo.

I have laid my pen aside and lifted the last page out of my clipboard. It is finished, this tableau which I have played out these last few months. The voices are gone, back into that oblivion out of which I called them. I stood up and the present took over. Shakespeare, Hemingway, Kipling, Edna St. Vincent Millay — did you feel like this when you had finished?

A car comes down the country road between my yard and barn, trailing a swirl of dust. The wild ducks are diving in the lowering house pond, heedless of this Texas drought. I think they are mallards, but they won't let me get close enough to tell. The sun sits atop the western hill; the whitetail deer are closing in now behind the house, crowding their deer run before shadows darken their trail.

The land stretches out around me — land Jack and I worked for and which, according to the deeds, goes to Pauline and Patricia. I am glad to have it pass on to them. Sometimes, though, I wonder if anybody ever really owns this land. For land is a heritage to be passed on and on to countless generations yet unborn.

From my west window the hills close in. How many

millennia before they change, or will they someday flatten in one vast nuclear blast? Still, they are here today and look as changeless as when I came over sixty years ago—the land and those blessed, everlasting hills.

For All Those Pupils Whose Lives Touched Mine was composed into type on a Compugraphic digital photo-typesetter in eleven point Century Schoolbook with three points of spacing between the lines. The book was designed by Jim Billingsley, typeset by Metricomp, Inc., printed offset by Thomson-Shore, Inc., and bound by John H. Dekker & Sons. The paper on which the book is printed carries acid-free characteristics for an effective life of at least three hundred years.

TEXAS A&M UNIVERSITY PRESS : COLLEGE STATION

For Emily, Sean, and Gabriel
my three grandchildren—so far

Contents

Sections of photographs follow pages 82, 146, and 210.

List of Illustrations

ACKNOWLEDGMENTS

The illustrations in this book are reproduced by kind permission of the
following: Bettmann Archive: 4–9, 10, 15; Beverly Wilshire Hotel: 35, 47;
Phototeque Archive: 2, 11, 12–14, 16, 17, 19, 25–30, 32, 37, 42–45.

AUTHOR'S COLLECTION: 1, 3, 18, 20–24, 31, 33–34, 36, 38–41, 46, 48–54.

Acknowledgments

MY THANKS TO THE FRIENDS in New York and California who jogged my memories as we reminisced about the great years of my time in Hollywood. And to my son, Robert Westbrook, who contributed his car and tape recorder; to my son-in-law, Donald MacRae Fairey, who helped organize the material; to David Shipman in London, who searched for factual errors; to Alison Burns, my British editor. And above all my thanks to Tom McCormack, the President of St. Martin's Press in New York, who took time out from a busy schedule to work with me on the American edition of this book.

A Note to the Reader

My LAST VISIT TO Hollywood was in October 1982. There have been a few changes since then. Some stars are no longer with us—the charming Richard Burton, the austere James Mason. Since 1982 there has been a big upturn at the box office with added profits for Hollywood from home video. Top executives have been indulging in a new kind of musical chairs, dashing from one major studio to another. There are more women in important jobs. Some stars have dimmed, others have risen.

Among other changes Elizabeth Taylor, the glamorous paragraph for the gossip columnists, has fooled us all by losing weight and dyeing her black hair a reddish blonde! But basically the Hollywood of 1982 is the same as the Hollywood of today. So with these thoughts in mind, I hope you will turn the page and read on.

Prologue

THE YEAR 1985 IS an important anniversary for me. It was fifty years ago, in 1935, that I first went to Hollywood. "I will go there for three months," I told my new boss, John Wheeler. With two brief interruptions I remained a Hollywood columnist for almost forty years.

In the early 1980's, after having been away from California for several years, I kept hearing in London and New York that the Hollywood I used to know was disappearing at a fast rate. So I felt it was incumbent on me as the last of what I called "The Unholy Trio"—Louella Parsons, Hedda Hopper, and me—to take a final look at the extraordinary city where I had spent more than half my life writing a syndicated gossip and news column for the North American Newspaper Alliance (NANA), and where I had raised my two children and been in love with a man who had changed the whole course of my life.

Louella and Hedda are long since gone. And so are Clark and Carole and Gary, Bogey, Duke and Roz, Ty, Errol, Robert and Spencer, and so many of the shining stars of the last half century. And I thought, if the Hollywood I knew *is* disappearing, there may be some interest in my getting down on paper just what Hollywood was really like: the Hollywood of a gossip columnist whose day-to-day work was recording the professional and personal doings of the most famous people in the most glamorous business in the world.

My publishers agreed, so I took the assignment. I would revisit Hollywood and remember what it was like then, and describe what it is like now in the eighties. And perhaps this would help my readers decide if in fact Hollywood is totally dead. Well, I can assure you that it is not dead. It is different. I didn't say it was better. And that is where the interest lies. What has changed? How and why? I'll try to answer those questions. And I think the best way to start is by trying to convey just what it was like—the town, the people, the industry, the state of mind, and the life style that was my Hollywood when I arrived there five decades ago.

Book One

Chapter 1

Going There

On the plane to Hollywood the night before Christmas Day, 1935, I was escaping from a love affair with a married man. He had told me that he wanted to divorce his wife and marry me. I never quite believed this. Besides, I too was married then, to a man I always called The Major. The Major was handsome, twenty-five years older than I, lovable, but rather a weakling. It was he who urged me in the early thirties to go to New York and make a fortune for us both. He would remain in London until I had made us rich.

After nearly two years in New York, working as a reporter for the *Daily Mirror,* then writing a column on the woman's page for the *New York Evening Journal,* I heard that the person writing the Hollywood column for NANA was leaving and I asked for the job. I realized that the situations with both the Major in London and the married man in New York were leading nowhere, and I felt that a migration of another three thousand miles to the west was the sensible thing to do.

It would mean a drop in income. In New York I'd been earning about five hundred dollars a week, from the column, special stories for King Features, occasional pieces for magazines, and some appearances on radio. In those days five hundred dollars a week was a lot for a young woman, but I was not worried about coming down from such a crest. I have always been an optimist and I was sure I would soon be making more than the $125 a week the new job was offering.

It was only when I was on the plane to California that I experienced some qualms about the momentous step I was taking. I was leaving a city where I was successful, enjoyed myself, and had many friends. Among them was Quentin Reynolds, newly returned from Germany, where he'd been interviewing Hitler and "Putsy" Hanfstangel—the future Führer's press agent—for *Collier's* magazine. Quentin had been in love with Margaret Lane, an English writer who had gone back to London, and he assumed that I was to be his next English girlfriend—oh how he begged me to stop seeing the married man.

Quentin had introduced me to the Gene Tunneys—Gene had retired while still the world's heavyweight boxing champion. We had spent a weekend at their lovely house in Connecticut. I was surprised that Gene was more interested in quoting Shakespeare than talking about the thrilling fight when he had beaten Jack Dempsey for the second time. I had also met the famous theatre critic George Jean Nathan, who was in love with Lillian Gish; the composer Deems Taylor; and Edwin James, the managing editor of the *New York Times;* and their wives and other women they went with.

There was dancing on the St. Regis Roof, and lunches at the Colony, then the most fashionable restaurant in New York; and, in the summer, dining in the garden at the Ritz Hotel on Park Avenue, and afternoon drives to the Atlantic Beach Club on Long Island. Baseball games too—I still smile, remembering how I shocked Bill Corum, the sports editor of the *Journal,* by saying that baseball was much slower than cricket! And, in the autumn, the races at Belmont Park, football games, and chrysanthemums.

And I was leaving it all to go a continent farther than the ocean's width. I had already come from my home and friends in London, for a place that was only a name to me, and where I had no close friends at all.

Before leaving New York, I had asked Roland Young, the popular character actor—he was in the *Topper* films—"Will I like it in Hollywood?" He gave me a quizzical look. "You will if you enjoy sports and open-air life." I did. In what I called my "social period" in England, after I had left the stage, I had learned to ride horseback at the Cadogan School in Belgravia, and a rich friend had given me a membership at the Queen's Club, where I had progressed to a fairly good game of tennis. So I comforted myself with the thought that perhaps this new life might not be too bad.

In the thirties, all flights from the East to the West Coast left from Newark, New Jersey. The non-pressurized TWA DC2 plane had a seating capacity of twenty-one passengers and took nineteen hours for the trip that takes five hours today. There were four stops on the way for refuelling. I remember it was snowing hard when we came down in Kansas City, but in the early morning the sun was shining in Albuquerque. As we bumped into the landing at the Los Angeles airport, then in the suburb of Burbank, the sky was cloudy because of the spiralling smoke from the smudge pots that protected the vast citrus groves on cold nights.

I was met by a member of the Metro-Goldwyn-Mayer publicity department. Why MGM? Shortly before I left New York, the lawyer Fanny Holtzman had given me a letter of introduction to Louis B. Mayer, who was visiting his office people in New York. I was a bit cautious about using it because Fanny, in 1934, had won a million-dollar libel suit in London against MGM for her client Prince Youssoupoff. He had claimed that *Rasputin and the Empress* suggested that his wife had been raped by the Mad Monk. But as I needed all the help I could get, I presented my letter to Mr. Mayer in New York.

He scrutinized me carefully. He then demanded, "Do you dance?" My God, I thought, he wants to offer me a contract. It wasn't that. Mr. Mayer was a dedicated dancer and exhausted his partners at a rapid rate. As it happened, I was never asked to dance with him, although he arranged for me to be met in Los Angeles.

I was dropped off at the Pasadena estate of the rich Earl C. Anthonys. Before leaving for the coast I had turned over the lease of my New York apartment to their son, Kelly, whom I remember for three reasons. In making a last search in the drawers of the chest in my bedroom, I had seen a gun: Kelly's. At that time he was engaged to the beautiful blonde actress Anita Louise—Titania in Max Reinhardt's 1935 film *A Midsummer Night's Dream*. I was told later that he had used that gun to kill himself.

Kelly had invited me to spend Christmas with him and his family. I was too tired to remember anything of that day although I am sure there was the usual turkey and trimmings. In fact I fell asleep in front of the blazing fire in the great hall.

Up at eight the next morning—I have always been a "day person"—I waited for Kelly to recover from the night before's too much champagne. He was still somewhat under the weather when he appeared at noon. "I know of a home for you," he told me. His friend, the actor Cesar Romero, lived at the Andalusia apartments, as Spanish-looking as their name, on Havenhurst Drive, on the western side of the Garden of Allah complex. There was a vacancy. Everything was overwhelmingly Spanish, from the tiles in the bathroom and kitchen to the multi-coloured stone fireplace in the sitting room. I took it on the spot, with the mental reservation that I would soon look for something more to my (simple) taste.

Going into the courtyard, Cesar and Kelly were accosted by a short, unprepossessing man. I caught the first name, Nate, and said, "How do you do?" Kelly advised me to be sure to buy the two trade papers every day—*Daily Variety* and the *Hollywood Reporter*—"or you won't know what is going on in Hollywood." The next day I was annoyed to read in the *Hollywood Reporter* that a Mr. Nate Stein was showing me the town. It was my first experience of phoney Hollywood gossip and I wasn't sure I was going to like this new world.

Kelly had also warned me not to have affairs with actors: "They all have a social disease." I thought he was joking, but he was serious. Whenever I see Bob Hope he still explodes with laughter over those two frightening words. But the warning made me more careful than I might have been.

I had already interviewed some of the stars and celebrities during my time as a reporter and columnist in New York. "If ever you come to Hollywood," said Carole Lombard, "look me up." Merle Oberon, then in love with Leslie Howard, told me of her Sunday brunches in Santa Monica. I had found Claudette Colbert as charming as when I had seen her with Clark Gable in the 1934 film *It Happened One Night*.

I had also talked with the twenty-nine-year-old Howard Hughes at a cocktail party on Park Avenue. He would soon be spending nine years making and remaking *The Outlaw*. Jock Whitney, the multi-millionaire owner of the *New York Herald Tribune* and later the ambassador to the Court of St. James, escorting me to the lift, mentioned he was arranging the financing for *Becky Sharp*, to be the first Hollywood feature film in the new three-tone Technicolor system. I had dined with Charlie Chaplin at Quaglino's in London, as the guest of Randolph Churchill and one of his sisters. And they had all said, "Be sure to look me up if ever you come to Hollywood."

As soon as I had unpacked in my new home, I searched for the telephone numbers of Miss Lombard, Miss Oberon, Miss Colbert, Mr. Hughes, and Mr. Chaplin. They were not in the book. Had they all left? I dialled the operator. They were unlisted and, no, she could not give me the numbers, and hung up before I could tell her that they were all so anxious for me to call them. I phoned Kelly. "Forget it," he said. "No one in Hollywood has a listed telephone number." He meant the celebrities.

Life looked better when I presented my letter of introduction to Robert Benchley, who lived at the Garden of Allah. It was drinking time, and the imbibers there would often include Ernest Hemingway, S. J. Perelman, John O'Hara, Dorothy Parker and her husband, Alan Campbell, Marc Connelly, and Eddie Mayer.

Robert accepted me immediately into this charmed circle and poured me a drink combining whiskey and gin. I have never been much of a drinker, and I asked: "Are you sure they will mix?"

"Don't worry," he said. "God takes care of drunks and children." I wasn't sure which category I was supposed to be in, and God must have been busy elsewhere, because I became violently ill.

I was surprised when Miss Parker referred to our host as Mr. Benchley. I knew they had worked together in New York on the old *Life* magazine and later on *Vanity Fair*. There was some talk that they had been lovers but Bob assured me that he had not smoked a cigarette or kissed a woman until he was thirty-one.

The conversation in those early years was of the Civil War in Spain. Hemingway was a frequent visitor to Hollywood to raise money for the Loyalist cause. I remember one time how he laughed when telling us that Errol Flynn, so daring in his films, had had sudden pressing business elsewhere when the hat went round at the home of Lillian Hellman. There was also talk of the battle between the Left and the Right to represent the screenwriters of the Guild that had been founded in 1933. Robert, who described himself as "a confused liberal," was actually apolitical, but he sympathized with his leftist friends.

I was to see a lot of Mr. Benchley and his group, but apart from the Marx Brothers and W. C. Fields, whom he admired above Chaplin, I don't remember meeting many actors there, although later Errol Flynn was an on-and-off resident of the Garden, as were also

Frank Sinatra and Humphrey Bogart, when he was hoping to hide from his rampaging wife, Mayo Methot. Bogey became friendly with Bob, who would run interference for him from Mayo.

The writers from the East, all of whom seemed to detest their producers, who were paying them large sums of money to write mediocre scripts (one of them called the studio Metro-Golden-Merde), were not in evidence at the party I attended a week or so after I arrived, at the Marion Davies beach "cottage" at Santa Monica. It was a few days before the start of my Hollywood column on 6 January 1936.

At the beginning, to gather news from the glamorous stars, I tried to get invited to what they called the A parties, and I would call up the host or hostess and make the excuse of wanting to see what a Hollywood party was really like. Or I'd mention that someone important was in town, and shouldn't he or she be invited? With me, of course.

I remember Raoul Fleischmann, the owner of the *New Yorker* magazine, phoning and saying, "Marion Davies is giving a party. *Everyone* will be there, and I'd love to go." I thought, "Good, he'd love to go." I called up Miss Davies' secretary and said, "My name is Sheilah Graham, and I'm calling for Raoul Fleischmann. He's in town and would love to go to the party." That's the way I got in. Later I would realize that because of my syndicated column I was more important to these people than rich men or even publishers from the East.

Everyone who mattered *was* at the Davies party. They all seemed to know each other. Loud greetings. Boisterous hugs. And drinking. Gary Cooper, tall, beautiful, was trying to seem detached. Chaplin was with Paulette Goddard—he had obviously forgotten our meeting in London. Paulette was showing off the diamond necklace she had managed to extract from her tight-wad lover. Ronald Colman, his hand bandaged heavily, was sombrely listening to Ernst Lubitsch—I heard someone say that Ronald's wife (his first) had hit him with a telephone; Joan Crawford was in intimate conversation with her ex-husband, Douglas Fairbanks, Jr.; Louella Parsons —Hedda Hopper was still in real estate and not yet invited to the A parties; Merle Oberon, not with Leslie Howard, who was there with his wife, but with her new love, David Niven, whom I had met in New York at the "21" Club in December 1933, on the night Prohibition was repealed. (David was then a liquor salesman for Jack and Charlie, the owners of the club.) And of course, the hostess, Marion Davies, somewhat intoxicated, and the host, William Randolph Hearst, smiling benignly over the heads of his guests.

Mr. Fleischmann, his objective obtained, had wandered off, leaving me embarrassingly alone. William Powell took pity on me. He strolled over with his girl, Jean Harlow, her platinum-dyed hair like burnished silver under the clusters of bright chandeliers. "We've been watching you," he said. "Why is such an attractive lady all alone?" I mumbled something about having lost my escort. He asked my name and immediately dubbed me "Gams" Graham—I was wearing a dark blue short evening dress and my legs have always been my best feature.

"Why don't you sit with us at dinner," said Miss Harlow. But I could not join them. At the long table in the dining room you sat where your name plate was. I found myself next to the twenty-four-year-old Maureen O'Sullivan and her fiancé, John Farrow, the Australian writer and director. They politely asked me why I was in Hollywood and Maureen invited me to the jungle set at MGM, where she was playing Jane with Johnny Weissmuller in *Tarzan Escapes.* We became friends and the following year I attended their wedding reception in the garden of Loretta Young's sister Sally Blane, the new Mrs. Norman Foster.

I wrote about Marion's party in my first Hollywood column. The glamorous names filled a lot of space. At the end I added an observation. What I couldn't understand, I wrote, was that with all those magnificent Gainsboroughs and other eighteenth-century masterpieces on the walls of the dining room, why did she have those awful paintings in the entrance hall?

Jock Whitney called me. He was laughing. "Those awful paintings," he said, "are of Marion in her movie costumes!" It was a long time before I was invited again to that beach cottage. And by then Miss Davies and Mr. Hearst were both dead and it had been converted into a hotel, which gives you an idea of how large this "cottage" was. I remember there were *two* swimming pools.

The Douglas Fairbankses, senior and junior, invited me to dine with them at their nearby home in Santa Monica—at that time Santa

Monica was the "in" place at the beach, though later it would be Malibu and later still Broad Beach Road at Trancas, ten miles farther north, where $50,000 homes are now selling for $3 to $5 million.

As usual when I am nervous, I talked a great deal, and on this occasion I tried to be amusing. I was pleased with my performance and was sure they had found me fascinating. Afterwards I heard from another guest that when I left the Fairbankses' home, young Doug had said, "She's the most conceited woman I have ever met!"

Howard Strickling, head of MGM publicity in Hollywood, thought it would make a good story for me to dine with William Powell. Stars in those days were all under contract to the major studios, and no matter how important they were, they did as they were told. I hoped Mr. Powell wouldn't mind. Miss Harlow was in Washington with a contingent of movie stars, an annual custom for President Roosevelt's birthday. (Jean was to die the following year of cerebral edema, at the age of twenty-six.)

After an exquisite dinner when I was vaguely preparing for the worst—surely *he* didn't have a social disease—Mr. Powell produced a slim volume, titled *The Wild Party*. Ah ha! Opening the book, he told me to make myself comfortable and started to read. I was nodding long before he reached the end and, sitting up with a start, I heard him telling his driver to take me home. Some wild party!

Another dinner was arranged for me with three young bachelors, Henry Fonda, Jimmy Stewart, and Josh Logan, then a dialogue director, who was later to direct Marilyn Monroe in *Bus Stop* and Henry Fonda in the stage version of *Mister Roberts*.

They were not long in Hollywood—they had all arrived in 1935 —and were sharing expenses in a somewhat broken-down hillside home. After dinner, during which they were elaborately polite— "Miss Graham, would you like some bread?" "Or some salt?" "Or this, or that"—and not quite knowing what to do with me, Jimmy announced, "Let's go out and shoot some bobcats." It was my cue to leave. Many years later, in a rare communicative mood, Mr. Fonda told me that before my arrival they had drawn lots as to who should have me. He wouldn't tell me who had won. In any case, I would have remembered Kelly's warning!

I preferred these small get-togethers. At the larger gatherings, where my sole objective was to gather news for my column, unless I arrived early, when the guests were still sober, it was a waste of time. I could do better at the studios. I bought a pale blue second-hand Ford and drove to a different one every day, usually lunching with a star or a director, and afterwards visiting the sets.

In 1936, as indeed from then on until the advent of television, every studio was bursting with activity. It was the Golden Age of Hollywood, and as the columnist for a powerful syndicate, I was treated with eager co-operation. MGM couldn't do enough for me, at first. Andy Hervey, the press agent who had met me at the airport, was deputized to introduce me to the publicity directors at the other major studios, the first of many mistakes I was to make.

So I met Harry Brand, at the recently formed Twentieth Century–Fox—I soon learned that he siphoned the best stories to Louella Parsons and therefore gave him up as a bad job; Perry "Friend of Everyone" Lieber, at RKO (though he was cannily vague when asked for information)—Howard Hughes later took him with him when he left for Las Vegas; Charlie Einfeld, always rather worried but always helpful, first at Warners, later at Fox (much later he had a disastrous session with his own independent company, managing with two bad films, *Joan of Arc* and *Arch of Triumph*, to throw the discouraged Ingrid Bergman into the arms of Roberto Rossellini); and Robert Gilham at Paramount.

They all thought that MGM had me in its pocket. When I became aware of this and believed I had been taken advantage of, I decided to tell MGM where to get off. Oh foolish girl, to take on the most powerful studio in the world!

Clark Gable was Metro's biggest money-maker. He had been my idol in England before I came to the United States in early June 1933. Mr. Strickling introduced me to him on the set of *Love on the Run*. I was disappointed. He was heavier than I had imagined. The following day I wrote in my column, "Clark Gable threw back his handsome head and exposed a neckline on which a thin ridge of fat is beginning to collect." Of course he was furious. (P.S. He did go on a diet.)

When Joan Crawford cancelled an interview date with me, and later deigned to see me in her dressing room surrounded by her hairdresser, wardrobe woman, make-up man, and half a dozen oth-

ers, I wrote, "I would never have recognized the sallow-complex-
ioned woman as the glamorous Joan Crawford of the screen." And
if that weren't enough, there was my unsolicited critique of *Suzy*,
starring Jean Harlow and Cary Grant: "I can't understand why
MGM, which has the best stars, the best writers, the best directors,
could make a film like *Suzy*, which has the worst acting, the worst
dialogue, and the worst direction."

War had been declared! Howard Dietz, the New York publicity
head, sent a letter to every newspaper taking my column, asking why
MGM should advertise *Suzy* in their paper, when I had ruined it in
advance in my column? I received an anguished call from my boss.
"Take it easy," he advised.

The top people at MGM, East and West, called a meeting with
the heads of the other studios. Who was this Limey who was trying
to destroy their billion-dollar business? If they all united in refusing
me admittance to their studios, it could result in my having to leave
Hollywood. The only problem was, like the OPEC members of
today, they found it difficult to agree. If one studio refused, another
might let me in. Meanwhile, I had proved that MGM did not have
me in its pocket.

So the only result of my foolishness was that I was barred from
Mr. Gable's sets. I soothed Miss Crawford's ruffled feathers with
another, nice, interview. In fact thereafter she was always charming
to me and a regular at the parties *I* was to give. But I had come to
Hollywood determined to be honest—to write a column about the
way things were, not how they wanted me to write. However, I soon
realized that if I wanted to remain a columnist in Hollywood I must
not be *quite* so honest. Although God knows I tried, which put me
constantly in hot water.

Every decade or so, there is usually a scandal that rocks Hollywood. There were two big ones in 1936. The first was a running
story in *Daily Variety*. Willie Bioff, the leader of IATSE, a labour
union, was caught making a deal with Joseph Schenck, the head man
at Twentieth Century–Fox, to pay him X thousands of dollars every
year. In return, the studio would be safe from strikes. They both
served prison sentences.

Scandal Two was more fascinating for the general public: the
patrician actress Mary Astor's affair with the unhandsome but bril-

liant playwright George S. Kaufman. The intriguing details might never have been known if her husband, Dr. Frank Nolan, had not found her Dear Diary. And when Mary sued him for the custody of their twin sons he produced the diary in court.

What a field day for the scandal-loving press! One much-quoted sentence in the diary was: ". . . thrilling ecstasy. He fits perfectly. . . . Many thrilling moments. . . . Twenty, count 'em diary, twenty—I don't see how he does it. He's perfect!" If anything, the revelations enhanced Miss Astor's career. She made movies almost every year until her retirement in 1965 and also managed to write a couple of novels. She is still remembered for her classic performances in *Dodsworth* with Walter Huston, *The Maltese Falcon* with Humphrey Bogart, and *Meet Me in St. Louis* with Judy Garland.

You can find the now seventy-eight-year-old actress happily riding her bicycle at the Motion Picture and Television Lodge, in nearby Woodland Hills. Norma Shearer, who, alas, was then blind, also lived there for several years before her death.

The idea for such a place was born sixty-three years ago around a luncheon table at the Los Angeles Brown Derby. Mary Pickford, Charles Chaplin, and Douglas Fairbanks were discussing the financial plight of some of the ageing men and women they had worked with. They put together a benevolent fund to give them a home where they could live in dignity and comfort. Those who can afford to pay, do so. For the others it is free. The Lodge, as it is today, was founded by Jean Hersholt, who died in 1956. In 1939 he was the first recipient of what eventually became known as the Academy's Jean Hersholt Humanitarian Award.

The romantic headline of the day was the 1935–6 New Year's Eve elopement of Claudette Colbert and Dr. Joel Pressman. Claudette was married previously to Norman Foster, the actor and director. Her marriage to the nose and throat specialist (they met and fell in love when he cured her sinus trouble) was seemingly successful. There were some hints of problems in the marriage, but they remained together until his death in 1968.

Claudette, an acknowledged expert in lighting for the camera, was obsessed with the idea that the left side of her face photographed better than the right. The left was also Charles Boyer's best side, and it was a battle of the Titans when they co-starred in *Tova-*

rich (released in 1937). At Claudette's insistence, all the scenery and furniture had been moved so the camera would favour her good side. The word *Tovarich* means "comrade" in Russian, a misnomer for the two battling stars.

Some important films were being made and released during my first year in Hollywood: *King Kong,* with Fay Wray; *Mary of Scotland* at RKO, starring Katharine Hepburn and directed by John Ford; *The Petrified Forest* at Warner Brothers, with Leslie Howard, Bette Davis, and Humphrey Bogart; two beauties from Sam Goldwyn— *These Three,* starring Merle Oberon, Joel McCrea, Miriam Hopkins, and Bonita Granville as the schoolgirl brat; and *Dodsworth,* from the Sinclair Lewis classic, with Mary Astor, Walter Huston, and Ruth Chatterton; *Camille,* with the incomparable Greta Garbo and the young, handsome Robert Taylor, her "Armand, ah Armand," for MGM. At the same studio, Norma Shearer, Leslie Howard, and John Barrymore were in *Romeo and Juliet.*

Chaplin was making *Modern Times* with Paulette Goddard, to whom he was reportedly married, but no one knew for sure; Marlene Dietrich, Charles Boyer, and Tilly Losch were in *The Garden of Allah,* from the Robert Hitchens novel of 1904. And busy David Selznick came up with another blockbuster in the same year, *Little Lord Fauntleroy,* starring the twelve-year-old Freddie Bartholomew, who had portrayed David Copperfield for Selznick the year before. What a time for a new columnist to arrive in Hollywood!

Nineteen thirty-six was not only a good year for films, it was also a vintage year for marriages. Douglas Fairbanks, Sr., married Lady Sylvia Ashley (whom I had known in London as plain Sylvia Hawkes) two months after his divorce from Mary Pickford. Lord Beaverbrook had tipped me off to the romance in November, 1934, when I was in London to cover the wedding of the Duke of Kent to Princess Marina of Greece. Sylvia, the cool blonde model type, had previously married Lord Ashley, the Earl of Shrewsbury's heir. She was always known as Lady Ashley no matter whom she married thereafter. Even as the wife of Clark Gable—who eloped with her in the mistaken belief that because she resembled his late wife, Carole Lombard, she would be the same outdoor-loving girl. That marriage did not last long.

In 1936 Fred MacMurray, who made several comedies with

Miss Lombard, felt secure enough to marry the pretty actress Lillian Lamont. Carole was masterminding Fred's career; despite two leading roles with her, he was receiving only two hundred dollars a week. "Go to Palm Springs," she urged him the day after they started *True Confessions* at Paramount, "and wait there."

A week passed and Fred was getting nervous. Then Carole called him with the good news. "You can come back now. They will give you a new contract." And what a contract! "From $200 a week to $2,000 a week," he called to tell me. Fred still has most of it. His friends had to pay for the lighting when they played tennis at night on his court.

Every decade or so, Hollywood has splurged on musicals. They are costly and difficult to make. But when they are good they are very good.

I am sorry I did not get to know Busby Berkeley. He was always too busy rehearsing, or shooting those song-and-dance extravaganzas, with hundreds of girls photographed in all sorts of complicated patterns, sideways, backwards, and from the ceiling. He had emerged at Warner Brothers in 1933, with *Footlight Parade,* starring Ruby Keeler, Dick Powell, and Joan Blondell. They were also the leads in Mr. Berkeley's *Gold Diggers of 1933.* But the best for me in the year that I crossed the Atlantic to live and work in the United States was *42nd Street,* with Ruby Keeler tapping away to Dick Powell's singing. There was also a small role for Ginger Rogers.

And while we are retrogressing, the two lovely musicals that started the trend in 1929 were, first, *The Jazz Singer,* the first talkie, with Al Jolson singing on his knees to his Mammy (I saw it in a cinema in the Strand after a long wait in a long line), and then *The Love Parade* from Paramount, with Maurice Chevalier wooing Jeanette MacDonald—"Every Little Breeze Seems to Whisper Louise"—directed by the whiz kid director from Europe, Ernst Lubitsch.

In 1936, Alice Faye was crooning "Sing, Baby Sing" to Shirley Temple at Twentieth Century–Fox. Alice, a blue-eyed blonde, had been discovered by Rudy Vallee in a chorus line in New York. I liked her better in *Alexander's Ragtime Band* with Don Ameche, who a year later would play Mr. Telephone, Alexander Graham Bell, in that film biography. And Deanna Durbin at the age of fourteen would be saving Universal from bankruptcy with her first musical for them, *Three Smart Girls*. How different from the musicals of today—*Hair*, *Jesus Christ Superstar*, and John Travolta in *Saturday Night Fever* and *Grease*!

In 1933, Fred Astaire had taken a chance on Ginger Rogers as his dancing partner in *Flying Down to Rio*. He had liked her bit in *42nd Street*. What if he hadn't seen the film! He himself had been discovered for Hollywood—although he had been a star on Broadway—when Joan Crawford consented to have him for her partner —it was just a few minutes—in her 1932 *Dancing Lady*. At first sight Mr. Astaire was not promising material for the screen. The comment after his film test: "Can't act, slightly bald, can dance a little!"

When the fifteen-year-old Scottie Fitzgerald visited her father in the summer of 1938, I offered to take her with me to the studios. "Which stars would you like to meet?" I asked her. She chose Errol Flynn, then starring as the gallant man who stole from the rich to give to the poor in *The Adventures of Robin Hood*. Scottie was pretty, although a little plump at that time, but Errol liked girls of all shapes, sizes, and ages and he stood still for a photograph with her which I sent on to her boarding school.

But even more than Mr. Flynn, Scottie wanted to meet Fred Astaire, who had been her idol since she had swooned for him in his 1935 *Top Hat*. Another photograph, interrupting Fred's rehearsals for *The Story of Vernon and Irene Castle*. This visit started a friendship between Scottie and me that has lasted to this day.

Eleanor Powell, who had landed at MGM in 1935, brought a new excellence in tap dancing to Hollywood films. When it went out of fashion (to be resurrected later by Ann Miller), her popularity declined, and she was ready for marriage in 1943 with the Canadian-born Glenn Ford, who was then serving with the Marines, after a brief career as a juvenile leading man.

Actually, Miss Powell's career had received a small dent in the star-filled cast of *Broadway Melody of 1938*. The fifteen-going-on-sixteen Judy Garland stole the show when she sang "Dear Mr. Gable" to his photograph. I remember that as we spilled out of the preview showing at the Westwood Theatre all the talk was of Judy. The following year, her performance as Dorothy in *The Wizard of Oz*, and the sad song "Somewhere Over the Rainbow," would clinch her claim to the title "superstar." I am glad that none of us at that time could foresee Judy's tragic ending.

It was mostly all singing in the Jeanette MacDonald–Nelson Eddy musicals at Metro. But here and there, in between calling to yoo hoo, the choreographer managed to get in some dancing—oh, not with the two stars; the only heavy breathing was in their love duets, "Rose Marie," "Maytime," "Rosalie," "Girl of the Golden West," etc.

I found Jeanette more animated than Nelson, but their combined popularity brought millions of dollars to the MGM coffers. And they are still remembered with fan clubs in America and England. Gene Raymond, a star of B pictures whom Jeanette married in 1937, abandoned his career after directing the unsuccessful *Million Dollar Weekend* in 1948. He became a businessman, whatever that means. But once an actor, always an actor, and in recent years I have seen him on television playing small roles. I have not heard of Gene marrying again after Jeanette died in 1965.

I was told that some of the stars were unreachable. Chaplin never saw *anyone* when he was working, and very few people when he was not working. And now he was working. I wrote a letter reminding him I had met him in London with Randolph Churchill. It had annoyed me then to see the famous comedian almost falling into his soup, awed by the great name of our host. At Randolph's prodding, he even did his little tramp walk as we had left Quaglino's. I doubt whether Chaplin received my letter. In any case there was no reply.

"Who is close to him?" I asked around Hollywood. Several people mentioned Harry Crocker, the poor relation of the Crocker banking family in San Francisco. He was working as an aide to William Randolph Hearst. Harry was easier to contact. Reacting to my pleading expression, he suggested that we should meet the next day outside Chaplin's studio gate "when he finishes work around six-thirty."

January in California can be cold when the sun goes down, but I was shivering as much from excitement as the weather when Charlie finally emerged near seven o'clock. "We were just passing," said Harry, innocently slurring my name in the introduction. To my delight, Chaplin invited us to have a drink with him at the Musso

Frank restaurant—a popular place for the movie people—on Hollywood Boulevard. The filming had gone well that day and he was in a mood to celebrate.

I reminded him of our dinner in London, and he said, "Oh yes," but vaguely. After a couple of drinks Harry mentioned that I was a reporter, but it didn't seem to matter. Like most egotists, Charlie was oblivious to any conversation but his own. I wish I could remember what he said—they didn't have tape recorders in those days and I didn't dare take notes. It was almost nine o'clock when he looked at his watch and said, "My God, Paulette has some people coming for dinner. She'll be furious with me for being late." I also had a dinner date, but I assumed that John O'Hara had long since given up waiting for me. I wasn't too disturbed because I knew I had a scoop that Louella would have given a great deal to get.

CHAPTER 2
STAR CHASING

BEFORE I WENT to Hollywood, Ward Greene, who ran King Features, gave me some valuable advice: "Write only about the celebrities. No one cares to read about the unimportant people, unless it's something outrageous." I soon learned that it was not easy to pin down the big names. But the twenty-year-old girl who had said "Yes" to C. B. Cochran when he asked her if she could do ballet, and had done so at the prestigious London Pavilion when she had not even taken any ballet exercises, was not going to be intimidated by a loud "No" from a Hollywood star.

THE LADIES

Katharine Hepburn had come charging into Hollywood like a wild gazelle in 1932. No one was going to tell her what to do. And the one thing she would *not* do was to give interviews. Her private life, and even her working life, was her own business. And before she started her first film, *A Bill of Divorcement,* she informed the unit man assigned to publicize the film, "If you want to get on with me you will keep the press off the set when I am working." He was taken aback. It was not as though she was the star of the film. John Barrymore was, and the publicist expected enough trouble from that quarter, without problems with this skinny, twenty-five-year-old girl wearing men's trousers.

Shortly before his recent death, I talked with George Cukor in his hillside home on the edge of Beverly Hills. George had directed

Miss Hepburn in that first film. "You have been quoted as saying that Katharine was terribly opinionated, usually about things she knew nothing about." "I didn't say that," he replied. "I wouldn't talk that way because she has always been very intelligent." His young male secretary interposed: "But you always said she had a lot to learn." "Oh she knew that, in the beginning."

"What did she have to learn?" I asked the eighty-three-year-old director. "Because she is very clever, she knew she had a lot to learn. But let me tell you about her impact on John Barrymore. First of all she was dressed in a rather eccentric way." She still is. (She almost bought a new outfit for a recent television appearance but when she heard the price she said, "This old one will have to do for another ten years.") "She was dressed up wrongly for this thing," said Mr. Cukor, "so I talked to her and this snooty college kid was inclined to be argumentative."

We were interrupted by his butler bringing in tea and home-made biscuits. He was reprimanded severely for serving the wrong cups and saucers. Mr. Cukor continued: "Anyway, I took Kate up to the make-up department and we did her hair in a certain way. She didn't argue about that. The first day on the set, she had to cue Jack Barrymore off camera, and he looked at me and made a sign, in-dicating that he thought she was going to be very good. But she knew she had a lot to learn about the movies. This was her first. Over the years I made ten movies with her, including two television things, one with Larry Olivier." (*Love Among the Ruins* in 1975.)

"When did you realize that she would be a star?" I asked. He told me that in *A Bill of Divorcement* when she said goodnight to her mother, Billie Burke, she stood at the door and waved and smiled. It was the first time they had seen her smile and they all saw that she had a lovely face. Then she crossed the room and took a pillow and put it on the hearth and lay down on it. And they could see then that she had a beautiful figure and moved beautifully. "And that," said Mr. Cukor, "is when I said, 'She will become a star.' "

"Did she know it herself?" "No, although they always hope they will be." I wondered how she was discovered for her first movie. "I think someone cast her in New York, or rather suggested her. She had already acted in the theatre, starting with a small role in a stock company's production of *Czarina*. Previously she had appeared in several Bryn Mawr college plays. She was soon playing bits on Broadway, always outspoken and troublesome. Finally getting hired and then fired, then rehired for *The Warrior's Husband.* She was praised by the critics and that is when RKO brought her to Hollywood."

I knew a great deal about Miss Hepburn before I came to California. That she had been born in Hartford, Connecticut, one of six children to a well-known surgeon and a mother who was a fighter for women's rights. She had been distraught when a favourite brother had died at the age of fifteen. I had learned this from her brother-in-law, Sam Smith, whom I had met in London in the summer of 1932. He had said the usual thing, "If you ever come to America, let me know, and I'll meet you." And there he was at the pier in New York when my ship, the ss *Europa,* pulled alongside. Not knowing anyone else in America, although I had some letters of introduction, I was relieved to see his pleasant face.

Picking me up after going through customs, Sam drove me to the family home on the Main Line from Philadelphia, where I was welcomed by his parents, Judge and Mrs. Samuel Ogden Smith. Sam told me that his brother, Ludlow, was in New York "with his wife, the actress Katharine Hepburn." How kind the Smiths were to me. I was delighted with my room and the four-poster curtained bed, and the servant who brought me a glass of hot milk and what he called some "cookies"—biscuits in my native England. The Smiths became my good friends, and I often spent weekends with them as a happy change from my reporter job in New York.

I was with them in 1934 on the sad occasion when Kate announced that she was planning a divorce from Ludlow. She was now an important Hollywood star, and had won the Oscar for her movie *Morning Glory* in 1933 and achieved a triumph in the same year for her performance as Jo in *Little Women.* The Smith house was surrounded by reporters wanting a story. Some were even in the trees with cameras taking photographs of everything that moved. It was a distressing time for the Judge and his family. Ludlow was to marry again, but they remained friends all his life.

Perhaps I should have used some of this knowledge as a means of getting the interview I wanted with Miss Hepburn. But I have rarely used a social introduction for my work. At least I didn't then.

I might now, having been somewhat spoiled by my years in Hollywood. Instead I made a point of meeting Cliff Reid, the producer of her current film, *Mary of Scotland*. To my request he said, "Impossible; she will not give any interviews." "But I admire her so much," I replied. "I've seen all her films and I especially loved her in *Little Women*, taking care of all her sisters." He came up with an idea.

"Every day, Kate, members of the cast, John Ford" (the director), "Pandro Berman" (the executive producer), "and I have lunch together in the commissary. You can come with me as my guest." Hallelujah and sound the trumpets! We were already at the table when the star, some other members of the cast, and Mr. Ford took their seats. They were chattering away and my introduction was not heard. They accepted me as a friend of the producer. I was trying desperately to remember everything that was said (in the normal course of an interview I would have used my notebook) and then Mr. Ford, who was sitting next to Miss Hepburn, whispered something in her ear.

She immediately put down her fork and stared at me, then demanded, "What is your name?" Oh for the earth to swallow me up! I could think of nothing but the last name of my boss. "Sheilah Wheeler," I gulped. "Who do you work for?" she asked. If ever there was a rat in a trap. "John Wheeler," I replied. "That's funny," said the lady sarcastically. "Your name is Sheilah Wheeler and you work for John Wheeler." I could only nod miserably. She ignored me for the rest of the meal.

I was relieved when the assistant director called them back to the set, with Mr. Ford turning around and grinning devilishly in my direction. "Of course I will have to tell her who you really are," said Mr. Reid when we were alone. I agreed. He phoned me later. "If you had used your real name you would have gotten the only personal interview she has ever given in Hollywood. 'My God,' she said when I told her, 'she's a great friend of my in-laws. I would have been delighted to answer her questions.'"

Greta Garbo and Marlene Dietrich were the most glamorous stars in the Golden Age of Hollywood, or any other age. Marlene, born in 1901 in Berlin, was the daughter of a policeman. Greta, now in her seventy-ninth year, the daughter of a labourer, was born in Stockholm. Marlene played the violin in Mischa Spoliansky's composition for orchestra, and studied at the Deutsche Schule in Berlin. Greta earned her living in a barber shop, soaping men's faces, and later toiled in a department store before receiving a scholarship to the Royal Theatre in Stockholm.

They both had a Svengali who would bring them to Hollywood: Josef von Sternberg for Marlene, Mauritz Stiller for Greta. Over the years von Sternberg directed six of his Trilby's films in Hollywood. He would not allow her to move her face on camera without his approval, which rather stilted her performances.

Stiller, a well-known director in Sweden, had refused to come to Hollywood in the mid-twenties without his protegée, Greta Gustafsson, as she was then. For a reason lost in the antiquity of that time, he was not asked to direct *The Torrent,* her first Hollywood film, in 1926, and was removed as director from her second, *The Temptress.* He returned to Sweden in 1928 and died not long after. Garbo's third film, *Flesh and the Devil,* threw her into the arms, on and off camera, of the handsome leading man John Gilbert. King Vidor, who died recently, once told me that when he was directing that picture, their love scenes were so passionate, and their kisses lasted so long (mouths closed, of course) after the command to "cut," that everyone on the set would be embarrassed. (Compare that to the tongue gymnastics of today!)

For various reasons, the legendary actress has never married. King told me that his first marriage, to Eleanor Boardman, the silent-screen star, was supposed to be a double ceremony with Garbo and Gilbert. The latter turned up, but Garbo did not. Gilbert was understandably furious, and after downing a quantity of alcohol, he took off in his car with the avowed intention of killing Miss Garbo. Fortunately he was arrested for drunken driving before he could carry out his threat.

The marriage-shy lady did the same leaving-in-the-lurch to the famed maestro Leopold Stokowski, who was left at the gate with the plane he had hired for the planned elopement to Yuma, Arizona. Another unlegalized romance was with George Brent, a popular star of my early years in Hollywood. The affair had started during their picture *The Painted Veil* in 1934. But when George pressed for marriage, Greta took off for Sweden, stating she was through with George and Hollywood. Of course she returned. Later there was talk of close associations with George Schlee. I can assure you that the later was friendship only.

I remember reading of the apprehension at Metro when "talkies" emerged in the late twenties. Garbo was the most profitable asset at the studio, but could she talk? The studio where she had started at $350 a week, and where she would eventually receive $300,000 per picture, was taking no chances. A huge publicity campaign informed the public that Garbo would talk in *Anna Christie* (1930). After more than half an hour into the film, she did, huskily demanding a "visky."

I never did get to talk to Miss Garbo. Not even a President of the United States was as protected from the world at large as Garbo was. She did not say, "I vant to be alone." She didn't have to. At the beginning of her career in Hollywood, she had happily posed in a bathing suit, romping on the beach with lions, with anything. But with the overwhelming success of her first Hollywood film, she used the whip of power to dictate to her employers what she would do to publicize her films. Nothing. And she would reserve her off-camera conversation for her friends. Also, she would leave the studio at four-thirty sharp to go home, regardless of whether she was in the middle of a scene.

Sometimes around lunchtime when I was walking on the MGM lot, I would see Garbo emerge from the set and watch her take long strides to her dressing room suite. Or, if she were leaving the studio, see her enter her chauffeur-driven limousine, parked at the door of the sound stage, and be driven off the lot. It was one of my fantasies that I would chase after her and find out what was behind the facade of the silent Swedish actress.

It was Walter Winchell who started the canard that Garbo had big feet, size 11. When she refused to give him an interview he staked himself outside her suite at the St. Moritz Hotel in New York and followed her into the elevator. They were alone, just the two of them. What an opportunity for a chat! But to all his questions, Greta returned a blank silence. Downstairs, watching her walk away, somewhat clumsily, he decided to nickname her Miss Big Foot.

It was a young actress, Barbara Barondess, who had escaped from Russia during the Revolution, who revealed the actual size of Greta's feet. In 1934 she was at MGM in Hollywood playing the maid in Garbo's film *Queen Christina*. In one scene she had to kneel at the Queen's feet—Garbo was disguised as a man—and pull off her long riding boots.

Take after take and the boots would not come off. Afterwards, sitting with the star on the set, Barbara said, "I bet I could take off your shoes now in one take!" Garbo laughed, and said, "I was in a shoe store the other day on Hollywood Boulevard. The salesman brought me some shoes that were miles too big for me. 'These are like canoes,' I told him. 'Oh,' he said, 'I thought you were Miss Garbo.'" "When I took her own shoes off," said Barbara, "I saw they were size six-and-a-half."

You win some, you lose some. Garbo was unreachable. Miss Dietrich was not. Marlene was comfortable with people. Garbo was relaxed only with a circle of close friends: Salka Viertel, whom she insisted should write her scripts, the socialite Mercedes de Acosta, the nutritionist Gaylord Hauser, and the numerologist Carroll Righter. Also Clarence Brown, who directed many of her films—the two Annas, *Christie* and *Karenina*—and Bill Daniels, her favourite cameraman.

In London, during 1930, I had seen *The Blue Angel* with Lola-Lola, the overweight Miss Dietrich, huskily singing "Falling in Love Again." It was the film that brought her to Hollywood. By the time I arrived there, Marlene had evolved into a slender, chic woman of mystery, her now-visible cheekbones setting a fashion for feminine beauty. I heard there was a husband around but he was never seen with her in public. In fact they did not live together. It was thought better for her career that she should be regarded as a single woman. So Rudolf Sieber, who had been the casting director for her German film *Tragedy of Love* in 1923, was banished to a ranch in the San Fernando Valley where he raised chickens.

Her first Hollywood film, *Morocco*, was written by my friend Eddie Mayer. Eddie would have had happier memories of the film if von Sternberg had not continued to change his dialogue and if he had been less dictatorial with his leading lady. She was again singing in a cabaret, but instead of Emil Jannings as the older man she had Adolphe Menjou, with Gary Cooper as the handsome young French legionnaire whom, at the end, she would follow into the desert, dragging her high-heeled shoes and evening gown in the sand.

She continued to play shady ladies, in *Dishonoured, Shanghai Express,* and *Blonde Venus,* where she had the good fortune to be the mistress of Cary Grant. I suppose it would have been disastrous for her to play a *hausfrau* type, which is what she was in real life. One of her joys away from the camera was to bake bread. (Dietrich?)

An early gossip writer in a fan magazine had described Miss Dietrich as "cold and inhuman," which made me hesitate about interviewing her, but I have always gone through the motions of trying. David Selznick's public relations director for *The Garden of Allah* was Russell Birdwell, an imaginative former reporter. He knew the value of publicity in the columns. It was worth thousands of dollars. Readers believed us while being somewhat sceptical of the extravagant praise in the ads. "I will see what I can do," he replied to my request. Soon after, I was invited to Marlene's dressing room on the set of the film.

Mr. Birdwell left us alone and I was delighted with what I had expected would be a "cold, inhuman star." She was warm, friendly, and anxious to give me a good interview. When I asked, "How do you like living in Hollywood?" she replied, "The climate is wonderful, and life here is so easy." "What about American men, compared to those you knew in Europe?" She did not care too much for American men. "The European men are more polite." They knew how to treat a lady.

Afterwards Russell telephoned me to ask how the interview had gone. "Marvellously," I said and revealed all of what Marlene had told me. Later the same day I received a call from him. "Marlene assures me she did not make those remarks about American men. She adores American men." He had obviously persuaded Marlene that her frankness with me would hurt her in America, with the women as well as the men, and worst of all it would hurt them all at the box office.

I was in a quandary. If I sent the story as she had told it to me, Mr. Birdwell, on behalf of his star and Mr. Selznick, would deny it. They would say I had invented the whole thing to cause a sensation and would, at the least, insist on a retraction. At the worst, they would sue me and all the newspapers that carried my column. I had been in Hollywood only a few months and this could damage me permanently as a reliable columnist.

Angry and upset, I telephoned Walter Winchell, then the most powerful columnist in America. I had met him during my time in New York. I would see him mostly at the Stork Club, a night club for the rich and famous, where the owner, Sherman Billingsley, treated him like a king, giving him a private room upstairs with his own barber to shave him. But mostly Winchell could be viewed downstairs, cornering the celebrities for their news, and scanning the debutantes, who were dancing cheek to cheek with their young men, rear ends at a thirty-degree angle.

"What shall I do?" I asked Walter. "Was anyone else with you?" he asked. "No, we were alone." "Well, if it was me, I would write it the way it was, and add Birdwell's disclaimer at the end." But I was not Walter Winchell. I was the vulnerable new girl in town. After much thought, I sent the piece as I had written it. To my surprise, there was no reaction. As I have remarked, Mr. Birdwell was aware of the power of, and the need to remain friendly with, a columnist.

At that time I did not talk to Charles Boyer, who was Miss Dietrich's co-star in the desert epic. I was too annoyed with Mr. Birdwell. But I did visit Tilly Losch, who was playing an exotic dancer in the film. I had known Tilly since 1928, when she did part of the choreography for Charles B. Cochran's revue *This Year of Grace,* in which I had graduated from the chorus to be a featured player. I wrote a glowing piece about her and she was pleased.

Bette Davis was one of the most difficult stars I had to deal with in Hollywood. As a very young actress she had been fired from the Rochester Star Stock Company, by that same George Cukor who would go on to be one of the top directors in Hollywood. "And she does not let me forget it," Mr. Cukor complained to me. "She keeps telling the story. I find it a great bore."

There is the legendary tale of when she first came to Hollywood in 1930 and applied for a job at Universal. The boss, Carl Laemmle, called in Carl, Jr., and ran Bette's test for him. "Well, what do you think?" Pop asked his son, whom he was training to follow in his footsteps. The young man's instant opinion was that the lady left him cold, that she had no sex appeal. Nonetheless, she was signed by the studio with a salary of $300 a week. Her first film at Universal,

Bad Sister, was a dismal failure. No wonder: Bette was playing the *good* sister!

After a few bit roles in mediocre films, Bette dyed her mousey hair blonde and was seen by George Arliss in *The Menace*—that was more like it. He insisted that Warners should sign her and give her the lead opposite him in *The Man Who Played God,* and she was on her way, playing the bitchy roles that made her famous.

There was the time when Bette decided to leave Warners in defiance of her contract, which still had several years to run. She took off for England, where she had received some film offers. Warners promptly issued an injunction. She sued the company for preventing her from working. But she lost her case and, being a realist, she returned to the studio in Hollywood.

A clue to her personality can be found in her recent talk to the audience at the National Film Theatre in London. "If I had had a face like Elizabeth Taylor's," she said, "I would never have won my two Oscars." And, pointing to the screen showing an excerpt from one of her films, "That face up there is all I had," meaning that because she was not as beautiful as Liz she had to work harder to make the best of a plain job.

But Bette *was* pretty as a young actress. And her looks did not prevent her from winning those two Oscars, for *Dangerous* in 1935 and *Jezebel* three years later. Both awards were delayed appreciations for past performances, in 1934 as the cockney waitress in *Of Human Bondage,* and the Oscar for *Jezebel* was really for her excellence the year before in *The Petrified Forest.* This sort of thing happens all the time in Hollywood.

Bette's problem has never been her face, although as she got older she has cared less about how she looks. What a fright she was as the first Elizabeth in *The Private Lives of Elizabeth and Essex* with Errol Flynn in 1939. The problem has been her irritability, caused by her determination to fight for the meaty roles. She was often on suspension for refusing films, especially after winning her Oscars. And even when she liked the part, she was sometimes so difficult that Carl Coombs, an easygoing unit man on an early film at Warners, asked to be relieved of the assignment, which could have cost him his job. "I can't take it anymore," I remember him telling me at the time. Luckily he was a fine press agent, a fact appreciated by his boss, Mr. Einfeld, who had a word with Bette.

But she never stopped fighting for work in good pictures. It became a way of life, never giving up no matter what the discouragement. I remember when she advertised for a job during the film depression of the fifties. The great star begging for work!

Those early years of battling for her career seem to have embittered Miss Davis. Co-workers in her films have sometimes complained about her attitude towards them. Even kindly Celeste Holm told me of trouble during their *All About Eve* movie. "On our first day when I said, 'Good morning' to her, she snapped, 'Manners!' and walked away."

A young actor I interviewed in one of Bette's productions in London was unhappy because some of his scenes and close-ups had been cut. I told him that the star has to guard her role in order to remain the star. Roy Dotrice, before televising *Family Portrait* with Bette in 1981, was warned, "She'll grind you to powder." Apparently Roy held his own.

Recently, Bette was in a New York store autographing a record she had made. There was a line stretching around the block waiting for her signature on the record they had bought. I saw the scene on television, with the irritable superstar admonishing her admirers, "Come on, come on, come on!"

And of course there was all that publicized feuding with Joan Crawford in *Whatever Happened to Baby Jane?* Years later, when Bette was asked what she thought of *Mommie Dearest,* Christina Crawford's cruel biography of her mother, she replied, "I'm sure it's all true. Joan was not cut out to be a mother." Joan's husband, Al Steele, had been the principal stockholder of Pepsi-Cola, and on the first day of shooting, his widow made a big show of coming on the set carrying a huge cooler emblazoned with the Pepsi motto. The next day Bette walked in with a larger case of Coca-Cola! It all made for some fun in the columns.

But if rudeness has to come in the same package with great talent, who are we others to be critical? I recently saw Bette in a TV show playing the owner of a school for flying, hair drawn back under a baseball hat, wearing faded blue jeans, and looking all of her seventy-five years. And she was simply marvellous.

Whenever I take my young grandchildren to a restaurant for lunch or dinner, they always order a Shirley Temple, an innocuous lemonade drink, brightened with a cherry on top. They looked blank when I tried to tell them who Shirley Temple was. But in 1936, the year I started my column in Hollywood, the eight-year-old Miss Temple was the number one box office star in the world. And almost to the end of her film career, from which she retired in 1949, at the age of twenty-one, every important visitor to Hollywood, including King Olav of Sweden, was introduced to the dimpled darling.

Twentieth Century–Fox was the lucky studio that had this money-making treasure under contract. She was treated like a princess, with her own prettily decorated bungalow on the lot, a press agent whose job was to spread every happening in her life—what lessons she had with her tutor, what she said in her prayers at night, and how many thousands of fan letters she received every week. What the PA did not reveal to the waiting world was the method used to make her cry for the camera. I happened to be on the set when I heard someone telling her that her pet dog had had an accident. The tears flowed. After the shot, it was explained that the accident was not serious and her pet would soon recover. Something similar was used to make that other child star, Margaret O'Brien, shed the tears for which she was renowned. I thought it was rather cruel.

Shirley's father was a teller in a bank and he took good care of her salary and the vast industry—dolls, toys, games, dresses, furniture, books, puzzles, etc.—that brought a fortune into Shirley's account. On her eighth birthday she received 135,000 presents from all parts of the world! Mrs. Temple was paid to be with her daughter on the set at all times.

I was having my hair done one day in 1936 at Westmores, the beauty parlour for the stars on mid-town Sunset Boulevard. The Westmore brothers had cornered the hairdressing business in Hollywood. In addition to the places on Sunset, there was a Westmore in most of the studios.

"Guess who's in the next booth?" said the girl putting my hair into rollers. "Who?" I asked. "Shirley Temple!" "Really? Are they making those lovely golden curls?" "Yes, but the curls aren't golden." And whispering, "The natural colour is black." "How awful," said I, whispering back—those booths only had a curtain to divide them. "At her age to use a strong dye will surely ruin her hair." I saw Shirley on last year's televised Oscar awards and was glad to see that my dire prophecy had not come true for the child wonder, who is now in her middle fifties.

I remember when Scott Fitzgerald suggested Shirley to portray the child in the film version of *Babylon Revisited*, which Scott thought was one of his best short stories. He wanted Cary Grant for the rich Charlie Wales. After spending some time with Shirley he told me how impressed he was with her. "She was very intelligent. She actually reads *Time* magazine every week!" Lester Cowan, who had bought the story for $5,000, eventually sold it for $100,000 to MGM, which made it under the title *The Last Time I Saw Paris*, starring Elizabeth Taylor and Van Johnson!

Shirley was married at the age of seventeen to the good-looking, twenty-five-year-old actor John Agar. I was present with other members of the press and relatives at the Presbyterian church off downtown Wilshire Boulevard. It was a sugar-sweet ceremony with the small bridesmaids not much younger than the bride. An array of large cars took us to the hotel where the reception was held.

Growing up had become a problem to Shirley's career, which had started at the age of four with bits in the "Baby Burlesks" series, and really took off when she sang "Baby Take a Bow" in *Stand Up and Cheer* for Fox—it had not yet become Twentieth Century–Fox. Paramount then grabbed her for *Little Miss Marker*, the Damon Runyon story about an orphan who reforms the bad bookmaker, played by Adolphe Menjou. In *Now and Forever* Shirley reunited the lovers, Gary Cooper and Carole Lombard. By this time Mr. Temple, who was masterminding Shirley's career, had managed to raise her salary to $1,250 a week.

Back to Fox, and in *Bright Eyes* the world said "Ahhh" as she sang "The Good Ship Lollipop." After which every story that had a poor or rich child was resurrected and earmarked for the wunderkind. The Kipling story *Wee Willie Winkie* (1937), under the direction of John Ford, was even changed to make the boy hero a girl. *Dimples*, *The Little Colonel*, *Rebecca of Sunnybrook Farm*, and on, and on.

With adolescence it was more difficult to find the right properties for her. And Shirley's popularity declined. Her picture price in 1939 was $300,000, but the polls of that year no longer had her name at the top. She was eleven years old (although the studio, desperate to keep her as young as possible, gave her age as ten) when Mrs. Temple, reading the writing on the wall, stated that her daughter needed some proper schooling and, to everyone's relief, took her away for two years, ostensibly to further her education, but also to get her a contract at another studio.

When she returned it was never quite the same, although David Selznick, believing the public would be interested in watching Shirley grow to womanhood, signed her to a seven-year contract. She was to appear in only two films for him, *Since You Went Away* in 1944, where she was number three in importance to Claudette Colbert and Jennifer Jones, and in support of Ginger Rogers and Joseph Cotten in *I'll Be Seeing You.*

I remember the fuss created by the publicity department when Shirley was to receive her first kiss in *Kiss and Tell,* in which it was hinted that the kiss would lead to pregnancy. A first kiss from Robert Stack had worked for Deanna Durbin in *First Love.* But the box office signal was down for Shirley.

Also, I was told by the usual close friend that Shirley was having problems in her marriage, caused by the wrong kind of publicity Mr. Agar was receiving in the newspapers—an arrest for drunkenness.

A week after the item had appeared in my column, I found myself sitting at the same table as Shirley and John at a dinner function at Holiday House in Malibu. I expected them to be angry with me because there had been no announcement of a possible separation. They seemed quite friendly, and I wondered, had I been wrong?

To my relief, and surprise, Shirley thanked me for preparing the public for the future divorce. It is always hard for one of America's Sweethearts to break up her marriage. Mary Pickford suffered the same anxiety when she divorced Douglas Fairbanks in 1933. So did Deanna Durbin, who went through two difficult divorces. How wise she was to leave Hollywood when the ungrateful studio abandoned her in 1949, claiming public apathy; this for the girl who had saved them from bankruptcy with her early films. Deanna has been married for many years now to Charles David, a French director, and lives happily in Paris with him and their children.

Shirley has also been happily married for many years now. In the late forties she was on holiday in Hawaii with her mother, and she met Charles Black, who was stationed there in the army. They were married in 1950, and left Hollywood to live in Northern California and then in Washington, D.C. Later, President Nixon would send her to Ghana as the United States ambassador.

But before Shirley took off from Hollywood, I brought my then seven-year-old daughter, Wendy, to visit her in her home nearby in Brentwood. While I talked with Shirley, Mrs. Temple took Wendy into the playroom, to show her the collection of dolls that had been sent to Shirley from all parts of the world during the years of her fame. They were upright in cupboards, on row after row of shelves, protected behind glass and never played with. Mrs. Temple explained that they were too exquisite for a child to touch, a statement which amazed my daughter.

Merle Oberon, to my knowledge, never had an acting lesson in her life and yet she became one of the top stars in Hollywood. I doubt whether that could happen today, where the emphasis is on acting —even E.T. had to learn to say "Phone home" with proper pathos. But in the early years of my time in Hollywood, personality was more important. If you could act it could be a hindrance for the screen, as it was for Richard Burton until Elizabeth Taylor coated his ability with a sexy image.

Merle looked more like her Indian mother, with a high, oval forehead and slanty eyes, than her half-Irish father. One of my London acquaintances, a Colonel Thomas, remembered her as a young lady in Calcutta. He said he had been surprised when a fellow officer brought her into the mess for lunch. It simply wasn't done. If the then Estelle Thompson was embarrassed, it did not show. The cool behaviour of the seventeen-year-old typist was a quality that would guide her through the uneven road to stardom in England and Hollywood.

"She was sure that if she went to London she would make her fortune," the Colonel told me. "We tried to dissuade her but she was determined. Years later I was in a cinema and there she was on the screen having her head chopped off" (as Anne Boleyn in *The Private Life of Henry VIII*). "Just goes to show what determination can do."

I had first met Merle on a tennis court in London's Kingston

Hill. Or rather, *I* was on the court, sweating, while *she* was sitting, cool as she nearly always would be, watching the game. She had gone through several transitions since leaving India for London. Starting as a hostess with the name Queenie O'Brien at the Café de Paris, then changing back to Estelle Thompson as an extra and bit player in films. But when Alexander Korda groomed her for stardom, she was already known as Merle Oberon.

Henry VIII was about to be released. There had already been some publicity about Korda's new find, and she was treated like someone who would probably soon be very famous. But it was not until her discoverer sold half of her contract to Sam Goldwyn in Hollywood that she became an international star. I disagree with the critics who panned her Cathy in *Wuthering Heights* while praising Laurence Olivier's Heathcliff. I thought she was excellent. As for Olivier, it was the start of my long swoon for him.

The Sunday brunches at Merle's Santa Monica home were a magnet for the top echelon in Hollywood, and I was glad to be invited. It was a good place to pick up bits of information for my column. But one item I did not use. When she took me into her dressing room and removed her make-up, I saw that her face was badly scarred. "I had some X-ray treatment for a small bump and this is what happened," she explained matter-of-factly. With heavy make-up the blemishes were invisible.

Because of David Niven's association with Merle, it was easier, at the beginning of what would be a successful career in Hollywood, for him to meet the directors and producers who would be useful for his new acting career. There was no talk of marriage, from him at any rate, although the affair lasted for several years. I wondered if David, from an old Scottish family and an officer in a good regiment, was reluctant to take as his wife a girl who was three-quarters Indian. I was sorry to hear of his death last year.

Mr. Korda, a Hungarian by birth, had no such qualms. They were married in 1939, and divorced some five years later. After his death, his first wife, Maria, went to court to recover the paintings that she claimed he had given her, but were then still on the walls of Merle's beautiful Nash home in Regent's Park. The first Mrs. Korda lost her case. During my trips to England, I visited Merle and could see why she wanted to hang on to the masterpieces.

Merle was not the kind of woman to stay single for long. And I was not surprised to hear that she had married again, first to her cameraman, Lucien Ballard, then to the Mexican multi-millionaire Bruno Pagliai, who owned, among other properties, the fashionable race track in Mexico City, also a magnificent home in Acapulco overlooking the bay. But in spite of the fact that President Lyndon Johnson and Prince Philip had been guests there, Merle was not accepted by Mexican society. She was considered Jet Set and Jet Set was not quite quite. Rather like Jackie Kennedy, who, until she became the First Lady, was never quite accepted by Boston society —Irish Catholic, you know, not Boston WASP.

There were two stories about Merle that amused me. In spite of her stardom, the former typist was always somewhat in awe of her fellow movie stars. When she was having an affair with Jimmy Cagney during a bond-selling tour in World War Two, she interrupted the proceedings by saying, "Just imagine, I'm in bed with Jimmy Cagney!" As he told the male friend who told me, it somewhat diminished his ardour.

I had to laugh when she broke her engagement to Joseph Schenck soon after I arrived in Hollywood, on the grounds that she thought marriage to him would hinder her career. As the wife of the powerful boss of Twentieth Century–Fox, as Mrs. Joseph Schenck, Merle could have been queen of that studio, as Norma Shearer, the wife of Irving Thalberg, was at MGM.

And being married to Mr. Schenck had certainly not dimmed the career of Norma Talmadge, the great star of the silent films. Or her private-life flings with other men. She was in bed with my writer friend Eddie Mayer. When sex was over, instead of cuddling up and being relaxed, she turned on him fiercely and said, "If you tell anyone about this, I'll tell my husband. He's more important than you are and he'll ruin you." This was one of Eddie's favourite after-dinner stories. But I doubt whether he mentioned this when Merle was present.

I often envied Merle her trim figure. I learned how she kept it, from a masseur who told me she spent two hours every day pounding Merle's body and massaging her face. I was not surprised when late in life she married again, for the fourth time, Robert Wolders, an actor, who was very much her junior when they said, "I do."

When she died in 1979, she left him most of the fortunes she had accumulated from two of her marriages. (She had not been as lucky with husband number two, Lucien Ballard. When they divorced, he took her expensive beach house at Trancas as his share of their community property.)

In addition to her paintings, Merle had a great collection of jewels, a huge emerald necklace with earrings and bracelets to match, the same set for her rubies, and blinding diamonds. Not long ago, Mr. Wolders sold them all at auction for several million dollars —a forty-one-carat diamond bracelet went for $350,000, and the matching earrings for $450,000. The still-young Mr. Wolders then escorted Audrey Hepburn, who was fifty-three when she became his girl. I understand they have now parted. Nonetheless, I would like to find out why Robert prefers older women. As my granddaughter, Emily, reminds me, I'm not as young as I used to be, and you never know.

Claire Trevor was one of the few people I really liked among the acting community in Hollywood. Most of the people I saw on my own time were not usually performers. There was a doctor and his wife, a lawyer, Alan and Helen Hooker, who owned a restaurant in Ojai, seventy miles north of Los Angeles. Some press agents, Johnny Campbell and his wife, Joan, Walter Seltzer, and Orin and Laura Borsten. But mostly my non-work time was spent with writers who had jobs at the various studios. I remember when I was having dinner with Robert Benchley at The Players, and a reporter passed the table. "An interview?" he queried. "No," said Bob angrily. "Sex!" He was annoyed at the assumption that I was dining with him not because he liked me, but as a newspaperwoman getting a story.

With few exceptions, it was difficult to get friendly with the stars. Perhaps it was my fault. I regarded them as paragraphs for my column. Our relationship was one of caution. They were wary of me, while all I wanted from them was to extract a good story. Sometimes I was asked to a dinner party at their homes but I began to refuse, because even if they let slip a juicy bit of gossip, I felt that as a guest in their home I should not use it.

I preferred to talk to them on the set or lunch with them in the studio commissaries over a good steak. And sometimes we became almost close, but when the picture was finished I would not see them again until the next one, or casually at industry functions.

But Claire was different. There was a forthrightness about her. You did not have to talk to her about what she thought of her last film, and what she was planning for the next one. She was more interested in what was going on in the world outside of Hollywood, and books, plays, history, politics.

She had come to Hollywood with her mother in 1932 after a good career on Broadway and settled in a modest house on Sunshine Lane in the Valley. Until *Stagecoach* with John Wayne in 1939, and in spite of critical acclaim for her role in *Dead End* with Humphrey Bogart two years earlier, Claire was known as the "Queen of the Bs," making four, five, six, and once even nine films a year. Usually she was cast as a gangster's moll, or a floosie with the heart of gold, a "dese, dem, and dose" character. Actually she was better educated than most of the stars who played true-blue ladies. She had attended Columbia University and had studied at the American Academy of Arts.

The High and the Mighty won Claire an Oscar nomination, and *Key Largo* in 1948 gave her the actual award for the Best Supporting Performance by an Actress. She was always busy, always in demand. But she slowed down somewhat after her marriage to the producer Milton Bren, when they went to live at Newport Beach, some thirty-five miles from Hollywood, with her son Charlie from a previous marriage. (When Charlie was five and my daughter, Wendy, was five, they were sweethearts.)

I had met Mr. Bren several years before their marriage. He was always easy to talk to, and when he saw me standing unobtrusively near the door on the sound stage of his production *Topper Takes a Trip,* starring Constance Bennett—if you remember, Cary Grant starred in the first *Topper*—he came over and invited me to meet his leading lady.

I had been writing some rather sharp comments about Miss Bennett in my column. And it's one thing to be brave in print and quite another when you are asked to meet the victim of your, shall we say nasty, paragraph. So I backed away and said, "No, no, I'm quite happy watching the action from here." But Milton would not take no for an answer.

"Well," I thought, "she can't kill me," so I followed him, slowly. "Connie," said the producer happily, "I want you to meet one of our good columnists, Sheilah Graham." She stared at me for a long few seconds, then loudly said (and this incident has become a Hollywood legend), "It's hard to believe that a girl as pretty as you is the biggest bitch in Hollywood!" For the first time, and not often since, I came back at once with a fast answer. Just as loudly I replied, "Not the biggest bitch, Connie, the *second* biggest bitch!" I cried all the way home, repeating over and over, "Not the biggest bitch, Connie, the second biggest bitch."

I was still crying when Scott Fitzgerald arrived for dinner. "Revenge," he declaimed. "We must have revenge." Dinner was forgotten while he wrote and discarded several murderous paragraphs. Then, for the only time that he wrote something for my column, he came up with: "Poor Connie, faded flapper of 1919, and now symbolically cast as a ghost in her last production!" Apparently Scott had seen her at the Princeton Proms during his time there. We will draw a curtain over what Miss Bennett said to Mr. Bren when she read that paragraph. But Claire and her husband remained my good friends.

THE GENTLEMEN

Humphrey Bogart was tested fifteen times before Jack Warner reluctantly agreed to Leslie Howard's request for him to join him as the gangster Duke Mantee in the film version of *The Petrified Forest*. I had enjoyed them both in the Broadway play. But I thought the film, released late in 1936, was even better because of Bette Davis as the girl who longed to escape with Leslie, the doomed poet, from the cheap restaurant somewhere in nowhere land.

For several years before my arrival in Hollywood, Bogart was number three on the credit sheet, or the lead in unimportant B films. He had worked at Fox and Universal before his final contract at Warners. In between jobs he would return in disgust to his acting career as a male ingenue in New York. He was known then mostly for having married Helen Mencken, the stage star, and for his line, "Tennis anyone?" while leaping through an open window onto the stage.

Between long waits while Leslie and Bette were in front of the camera, I chatted briefly with Bogey. He was hopeful that this role would lead to better parts than "some of the crud I've been getting in Hollywood." It did not. Every time I saw him, in the studio and out, he would complain bitterly against Jack Warner, whom he detested.

It was not until *High Sierra* and *The Maltese Falcon*, both released in 1941, that he was elevated to the stardom enjoyed at the studio by Paul Muni, Edward G. Robinson, Jimmy Cagney, George Raft, and Errol Flynn. And that was only because the first four had all refused *High Sierra*. Raft's added "No" to playing Dashiell Hammett's laconic detective in *The Maltese Falcon* was the real turning point in Bogart's career. And, remembering Ward Greene's advice to interview only the top people, I paid more attention to the man, who today is as much of a legend as Greta Garbo or any of the other great stars of the Golden Age in Hollywood.

He used to flirt with me behind the closed doors of his dressing room on the set. "Graham," he would growl unsmilingly, "when are we going to have that affair?" I never knew whether he was serious or not, but in any case, as I have mentioned, I was always rather wary of actors, and I thought he was too uncouth. He reminded me of some of the men I had seen as a child reeling out of the pubs in the East End of London. And yet, Bogey was one of the few actors in Hollywood who had come from a well-to-do family, and had been educated at Andover, a good private school in New England. So, I would always reply, coyly, "Let's wait until we are both in Heaven." "Aw, come on, Heaven's a long way away."

One time, when he was angry about something I had written in my column, he complained, "It isn't fair. You columnists can write anything you like about us, and we have no way of replying." I thought about this driving to my home, and came up with an idea. The next time I saw him I said, "Bogey, you're right, it isn't fair. I'm going to do one column a week called 'The Last Word,' for you and others who believe I have been wrong to give your side.' He shook his head. "Sure, and then you'll come back and slaughter us." I tried to reassure him that the last word would be what it said. I ran that column for several weeks, but gave it up, realizing that the press agents, not their high-powered clients, were replying for them.

Actually, I soon recognized that Bogart was brave mostly when he was drinking. This tiger was a pussycat, and the best way to handle him was to squash him when he got out of line, tell him off when he became rambunctious. I remember when he was starring in *Sabrina* with Audrey Hepburn at Paramount. He was in a bad mood from carousing the night before. Without provocation he swore at the scriptwriter, Ernest Lehman, who complained to Billy Wilder, the director of the film. "Apologize to him, or leave the set," said Billy. The chastened actor went to Lehman, put his arm around him, and muttered, "Sorry, pal."

Stanley Kramer, the producer of *The Caine Mutiny,* told me this story about Bogey, who was playing Queeg in the Herman Wouk story. They were on location in Hawaii and were all sitting around one evening when it was getting late. Stanley stood up, yawned, and said, "We have an early morning call. I'm going to bed." Bogey, in his cups, sneered, "What makes you think it's necessary for you to come to the set?" To which the angry producer replied, "To make sure that an ugly, no-good jerk like you is working." He expected a fist fight. Instead the actor roared with laughter. "After that," Stanley said, "I had no trouble with him."

Another producer, Hal Wallis, assured me recently, "I never had any trouble with Bogey. He had a rough exterior, but a very mellow interior. Some people have believed that because of his roles, beginning with Duke Mantee, he could not dissociate himself from the character."

I doubt whether the roles had anything to do with it. He was just a bad drinker who felt that his roots were still on the Eastern seaboard, but he had to live in Hollywood because that's where the work was. And the money. At one time he was receiving $750,000 a film. When a friend from New York visited him on the set, I heard him ask wistfully, "Do you ever go to Caswell and Massey" (a drug store) "on Lexington Avenue? My grandfather lived on 48th Street. I used to go there all the time for a soda."

It was *Casablanca,* produced by Hal Wallis and released in 1943, that changed Bogey from the tough guy character into a romantic hero. I remember hearing at the time that the stars did not know what the ending would be. Ingrid Bergman confirmed this in her autobiography. "But there *was* an ending," Mr. Wallis assured me.

"There was a discussion whether we'd use the ending we shot, or do another which would have her staying with Bogart. But we never shot that ending."

"Wasn't it rather daring in those days for Bogart, who was the star, not to end up with the girl?" "That didn't enter into it. The story dictated that as Paul Henreid was the freedom fighter, her place was with him, her husband. So we chose the bittersweet ending. And that's what made it a classic. If she had stayed with Bogart, the film would have been conventional and sticky. Paul Henreid liked to say that it was his understanding that he would get the girl. But that was not true."

Apparently the only trouble Mr. Wallis had with *Casablanca* was with David Selznick, who had Ingrid Bergman under contract and who, for a long time, refused to loan her for the film. They were a couple of tough bargainers. "I besieged him with telephone calls," Hal told me. "I followed him to New York, and registered at his hotel, and finally got to see him. David was always difficult when you tried to borrow any of his people. But after some hard negotiating I was able to borrow, over the years, Jennifer Jones, Joan Fontaine, Joseph Cotten, and Ingrid Bergman for two films."

It was all a question of cash. Ingrid had not yet attained the stature of a superstar and, according to Wallis, Selznick let her go for $60,000 for each of two pictures, with a working schedule of ten weeks. She made a weekly profit for her boss of $5,000. Ingrid's second film for Mr. Wallis was *Saratoga Trunk* with Gary Cooper. As with some of Ingrid's co-stars there was talk of a torrid romance behind the scenes. In fact, Gary winked broadly when I mentioned the rumors.

Gary Cooper! He was the second star I interviewed during my first year in Hollywood. I was so anxious to meet him that I crashed into a car while speeding to Paramount. Every woman was in love with him, and he was in love with every woman. So they said. Before Lupe Velez there had been Clara Bow, the wild "It" girl. Their affair had flourished during their 1927 *Children of Divorce*. After that rollicking time came the Countess di Frasso, who was credited with smoothing his rough edges, whatever that means. He had been educated in England, and in Montana his father had been a State

Supreme Court judge, so I doubt whether the Countess had much work to do in that area.

As far as the naked eye could see, Gary was the epitome of the gallant gentleman who would always rescue a damsel in distress. In fact he once rescued me from disgracing myself by throwing up my dinner when we were flying to Dallas in the autumn of 1940 with members of the cast and press for the Fort Worth premiere of *The Westerner*. In those days it was a long overnight flight from Los Angeles, and there were top and bottom berths for sleeping.

It was a bumpy ride in the non-pressurized plane and Gary, who was replying "Yep" and "Nope" in the pauses of my rather strained conversation, suddenly realized that my usual peaches-and-cream British complexion had turned a hideous green. Without so much as a by your leave, he scooped me up into his arms and laid me gently in the upper berth. He stood over me, his beautiful grey-blue eyes expressing concern. I thanked him weakly, but drew the line when he suggested rubbing my tummy. It could have been disastrous.

I had been told that if you wanted to have an affair with Gary, the woman had to make the first move. I found this to be true. The party after the premiere was held in a large suite at the Adolphus Hotel. Arriving early, I had gone into the bathroom to replenish my make-up. Emerging into the bedroom, I saw Gary coming in. Somehow we were inches from each other, him looking down at me, me looking up at him. The long pause was broken by a giggle, mine, and we went down together to the party. It might have been different if I had not been in love with Scott Fitzgerald, who was awaiting my return in Hollywood.

Gary was married only once, to a small-part actress, Sandra Shaw, formerly known as Veronica Balfe, a society lady from Long Island. I realized why she was nicknamed "Rocky" when Gary wanted a divorce to marry Pat Neal, with whom he fell overwhelmingly in love when they made *The Fountainhead*. Rocky was as hard as her nickname. She had convinced Gary to become a Catholic, as she was, for the sake of their daughter, Maria, who had been refused admittance to a Catholic school because her parents had not married in the Church. Gary took up deep-sea diving as a means of escape, but he could never marry the girl he loved above all the others.

In the course of his thirty-five-year career in Hollywood, Gary would win two Oscars, for *Sergeant York* in 1941 and for the courageous sheriff in *High Noon.* "He didn't want to *do Sergeant York,*" Hal Wallis told me last year. "I had to chase him to New York and threaten a lawsuit before he would sign."

Gary had started as an extra in the early twenties, and he was somewhat embarrassed by his chosen profession. "Silly way to make a living," he said to me one time after finishing a scene. He was accused of playing himself in every film. But those who knew, directors like Frank Capra (*Mr. Deeds Goes to Town*), Lewis Milestone (*The General Died at Dawn*), Cecil B. De Mille (*The Plainsman*), and William Wyler (*The Westerner*), regarded him as a fine, conscientious actor.

The last time I spoke to Gary was in 1960, on the London set of *The Wreck of the Mary Deare.* It was an action-packed picture, co-starring Charlton Heston. Gary did not look well, and I was worried about him. A year later, before the release of his final film, *The Naked Edge,* he was dead of cancer. It was Jimmy Stewart who alerted the world to this sad probability when his voice broke, naming the absent, dying "Coop" as the recipient of an honorary Oscar.

Erroll Flynn was the third star I interviewed in Hollywood. A 1934 film in London, *Murder in Monte Carlo,* had brought the ambitious adventurer to Hollywood, where he played a corpse for Warner Brothers in The *Case of the Curious Bride.* But even as a dead man, Errol was so handsome that the studio gave him the lead as the swashbuckling daredevil in *Captain Blood.* The film made him a star overnight. And that was why I was visiting the indoor set of *The Charge of the Light Brigade.*

That evening I was preparing to leave my Andalusia apartment when the doorbell rang. With keys in hand, hat and coat on, I opened the door. And there was Mr. Flynn, smiling like a man who was used to getting any woman he wanted. Or any man. But he wasn't getting me. How dared he come without an invitation! Besides, I was too old for him. Mostly Errol preferred very young girls, which got him into trouble with the law.

He had married Lilli Damita in 1935. She was a big star then. And when they divorced a few years later, it broke his heart and his pocketbook to have to pay her $300,000. He was even tighter with his money than Chaplin. Like some other stars who had been poor at the beginning of their careers, Errol could not forget that for his starring role in *Captain Blood* he had to make do on a salary that had started at $125 a week and ended at $150.

Before the filming of *The Sea Hawk* Errol had realized his potential as an important star, and managed to raise his contract to $750 a week. After that, with every film, he would not show up for wardrobe fittings or meetings until his contract was renegotiated. It was not long before he had brought his salary up to $150,000 a picture. He made two or three a year, several for Mr. Wallis.

It helped that Hal's sister, Minna Wallis, was Errol's agent in those years. $150,000 was then the going price for a one-picture deal with a top star. I remember the furor when Constance Bennett, a big star, was paid $150,000 by Warners for a five-week schedule. It was not until the early sixties that Elizabeth Taylor, reluctant to do the film, demanded, and received, more than $1 million for her time in *Cleopatra.* Today $3, $4, $5, and $6 million are paid to the superstars. The few we have.

Whenever I am asked, "Who was your favourite actor in Hollywood?" I always reply, "Bob Hope." I had met him in 1937. His press agent, Mack Millar, had arranged the luncheon at Lucey's Restaurant across the street from Paramount. They were worried. After Bob had completed *The Big Broadcast of 1938,* to be released the following year, he had received word that his option for further films would not be renewed. As I have already mentioned, I rarely interviewed the lesser players. Bob, as the juvenile lead, was not as important as W. C. Fields and the other Paramount stars in the picture.

But I had seen him on Broadway in *Red, Hot, and Blue,* a musical with Jimmy Durante and Ethel Merman. It had a silly plot about a search for a girl who could be recognized by the imprint of a waffle iron on her bottom. It had made me laugh and I thought Bob was good, dancing a little and introducing the song "It's De-Lovely" with Miss Merman. His agent thought that an interview with me, to appear in all my newspapers, might help his client to be renewed at the studio.

"It sure did," said Bob, when I visited him last year at his estate in North Hollywood. "I had signed a deal for three pictures at

$20,000 each. But they had the option of dropping me after the first or second. However, with your piece and the column Damon Runyon" (the Broadway columnist) "wrote—'Our boy did it with "Thanks for the Memory" '—Bill Le Baron, then in charge of production at Paramount, said, 'Hey, this guy must be pretty good,' and he picked me up for a year at $50,000 a picture." And that was really the beginning of Mr. Hope's important career in films.

In 1907, at the age of four, he had moved with his family from Eltham in Kent, England, to the United States. At that time Bob was called Leslie Townes Hope. But when he decided on a career in show business, he thought Leslie Townes did not sound right. "I changed it to Bob when I was starving in Chicago, but for a while I still starved as Bob."

That was in the late twenties. His fortunes improved with the new decade. In 1931, Bob was the Master of Ceremonies at the Capitol Theater in New York. In those days, between the four showings of the film, they used live performers, mostly monologues, singers, and dancers, and always an organ recital. I remember hearing Ethel Smith, the great organist, there.

The Capitol was a huge theatre with a fifty-piece orchestra in the pit. "When Bing Crosby was the singer," Bob told me, "he and I would kid around backstage to relieve the boredom while waiting for the movie to end." They had some funny routines: the President of Coca-Cola and the President of Pepsi-Cola meeting in the street and saying, "How are you?" then burping; two farmers meeting and joining fingers, pretending to milk a cow; two politicians, picking each other's pockets. And sometimes a little soft-shoe number.

Five years later they were at the Del Mar Turf Club (south of Los Angeles), performing for a charity event. You never knew who was in the audience, and that Saturday night there was a producer from Paramount. After the weekend he told the boss, "These guys work together like a charm." It took a couple of years to get the message across, but in 1940 we saw the first "Road" picture, *Road to Singapore*, with Bob, Bing, and Dorothy Lamour. It was originally titled *"Flight* from Singapore." The new name led to a whole series of "Road" films—the last was *Road to Hong Kong* in 1962.

Mr. Hope, without question, is the richest actor in Hollywood. Several years ago *Time* magazine mentioned that he was worth two hundred million dollars. I would double or triple that in view of his real estate investments and the deal he made with Paramount to own twelve of his films outright. "In 1945 I was making a vast amount of money," Bob reminisced happily. "Radio, pictures, and personal appearances. But after paying taxes I had very little left. My boss was then Y. Frank Freeman. I told him: 'I want an asset that I can keep for my kids.' When he refused I suspended Paramount for a year. The strike was over when he called me and said, 'Hello, darling, when shall we have lunch?' Result: a new contract."

It jumped to $100,000 when Sam Goldwyn told the audience at the premiere of *The Westerner*, which Bob emceed for Sam, "I want to make a picture with Bob Hope." Bob, who had an agent, Louis Shurr, did not need him to pin Sam down for the two films, *They Got Me Covered* and *The Princess and the Pirate*. $200,000 for the pair. In 1948 he was paid $150,000 for *one* movie, *Paleface* ("Buttons and Bows"), with Jane Russell. The same the following year for *Sorrowful Jones* with Lucille Ball. And on and upward, until he was making $500,000 for each of his films.

Bob would be even richer but for the bad deal for the payment of film residuals made in 1952 by the executives of the Screen Actors' Guild with the Producers' Association. Mickey Rooney has been suing them for the movies he made early in his career. He played supporting roles in hundreds of films, silent and talking, before the "Andy Hardy" series made Louis B. Mayer realize that he had a young star at the studio.

"They sold out the residuals from all those early productions at every studio for a ridiculous sum," said Bob, "when they should have received five or ten billion dollars for the films that have been shown on television, robbing, yeah, actors, musicians, writers, directors. You see, I made sixty pictures. So if I got a piece of those other forty-eight that I did for them, it would be a fortune, because they run them all the time. But they sold us out for nothing and they thought they were getting a lot of money for our retired workers" (in the Motion Picture and Television Lodge and Hospital in Woodland Hills).

When I asked Bob who was his favourite movie actress, he replied, "Madeleine Carroll," the ex-schoolteacher from England. "She was the most beautiful thing. On my radio monologue I used to say, 'I went to a football game and Madeleine Carroll was there and all the passes weren't made on the field.' Every week I did a joke about Madeleine and one day she called me and said, 'We've got to do a picture together.' I called the boss and gave him the title, *My Favorite Blonde,* and it was a smash."

Madeleine, who was so good in her two films for Hitchcock, *The Thirty-nine Steps* and *Secret Agent,* was married four times. Number one was Philip Astley (Eton and Oxford); Sterling Hayden, number two, was too square to last. They had made a film together (*Bahama Passage*) and that sort of closeness often leads to matrimony. I interviewed number three, Henri Lavorel, in Montreal when he was stationed there, flying American bombers to England during the war years.

The marriage to *Time and Life* magazine publisher Andrew Heiskell lasted for fifteen years. After the divorce, Madeleine lived in Spain for many years. Her home is now a farm near Paris.

The last time I saw her was at Elizabeth Arden's, then on downtown Wilshire Boulevard. I was having my hair fixed when Madeleine and Jock Whitney entered arm in arm. She proceeded to pick out most of the stock there, dresses, nightgowns, peignoirs, and make-up, for which Jock paid. I did not let them see me.

In my young time in England we made love to Bing Crosby crooning "Boo Boo, Boo Boo." He was almost as rich as Mr. Hope, give or take a million dollars. Like Bob he carefully invested his earnings —in property, oil wells, stocks, bonds, and a major interest in Minute Maid orange juice, all bought with what he earned from his films, personal appearances, radio shows, and records. No one ever sold more discs than Bing, 350 million at the last count. His "White Christmas" alone, first sung in *Holiday Inn* (1942), is still selling in the thirty-million-plus range.

I found Bing not as outgoing as Bob. Or perhaps he cared less about his relationship with the press. He always seemed to be in a hurry when I espied him on a Paramount street and tried to have a conversation with him. But if I could pin him down on the set, he would answer questions politely but briefly.

All I heard in those years was that Bing was having an affair with this and that leading lady in his films. I doubt that this included

Ingrid Bergman, the nun to his priest in *The Bells of St. Mary's*. Also, there was always talk that his wife, Dixie Lee, was drinking heavily. In actual fact she had taken to the bottle only after her marriage to Bing in 1930. To keep up with him. In that same year Bing had been arrested for drunken driving.

With his success in radio and films, he became somewhat more responsible, although he would still cause problems with his casual attitude about his work, being unwilling to rehearse and coming late to the set. But that casualness did not interfere with the finished result of those great musicals: Cole Porter's *Anything Goes* with Ethel Merman in 1936, *Pennies from Heaven* with Louis Armstrong, a year later, and much later, *White Christmas* with Danny Kaye. The "Road" pictures with Bob Hope were the icing on the cake, as also were *Going My Way*, for which both he and Barry Fitzgerald won Oscars, *The Country Girl* with Grace Kelly and William Holden, with Grace walking off with the Best Actress Award, and *High Society*, again with Miss Kelly, plus Frank Sinatra and Celeste Holm. And many more. I am omitting *Stagecoach*, a mediocre remake of the John Wayne classic. Everyone is allowed some clinkers. But most of Bing's films had kept him near the top of the popularity tree for many years. The young man who had been part of a trio, Paul Whiteman's Rhythm Boys, in the twenties, had come a long, long way.

Until he married Kathryn Grant, Bing's private life in Hollywood was subjected to much criticism, especially when he left for England to fulfil an engagement there while Dixie was seriously ill in a Los Angeles hospital. And while he gave each of his four sons with Dixie substantial trust funds, he seemed to pay them attention only when they did something that annoyed him and then, according to his oldest son, Gary, he punished them severely.

And yet he respected those he worked with. He was grateful to John Scott Trotter, his music mentor, whom he credited with shaping his style in singing. In his letters he often mentioned how much he owed him. I was once on the set when a friend said "Hello" to Bing, interrupting his conversation with Skitch Henderson (the bandleader) and then walking away. Bing called after him, "Why don't you get a broom?" Sarcasm for the man who had brushed off Skitch.

While Crosby was not a hypochondriac, he had reason to be concerned about his health. He suffered with gall stones and during attacks he would turn angrily on anyone who was close by, especially his sons. Everyone was relieved when he finally decided to have an operation. He was on the operating table and about to be anaesthetized, when he sat up, got off the table, dressed, and walked out of the hospital. Two years later, with the pain becoming unbearable, he finally had the surgery.

With all that pain in the past, he was a kinder and better father to the three children of his marriage to Kathryn Grant, the actress who was thirty years his junior. Kathryn wisely abandoned her career and devoted herself to the children and to Bing, who told me, in an expansive moment, that his only daughter, Mary, was named for his mother. Every year we could see them growing up as they appeared with Bing on his Christmas television show. And they were often on camera with him to advertise Minute Maid orange juice.

A few years ago, Bing brought them all to London to appear with him at the Palladium. A nice gesture. I made a point of being in the audience. Bing was in good form but the show would have been better without the others. In recent years Kathryn has had a television talk show in San Francisco. And Mary, as you know, has played Sue Ellen's sister in "Dallas." Nathaniel, the youngest, is a fine golfer and has continued the annual Bing Crosby Gold Tournament at Pebble Beach. The oldest boy is called Harry Lillis, which was his father's real name. He recently graduated with honours from Fordham University, with a business career in mind.

The two sets of children (like Ronald Reagan's two lots) are not usually in the same place, but they were together for Bing's funeral. He died as he would have wished, on a golf course in Spain, after completing the eighteenth hole, while walking to the club house.

Of all the macho movie men in my time (Gable, Bogart, Kirk, Robinson, Flynn, Burt), the most macho of them all was John Wayne, commonly known as Duke, and before that as Marion Michael Morrison. Most of them, as I have mentioned, were not such tough guys in real life. But even away from the camera Mr. Wayne projected a strong image. Although even he could not remain silent when Herbert Yates, his boss at the Republic studio in the San Fernando Valley, insisted on co-starring him with Vera Hruba Ralston, who would later become Mrs. Herbert Yates.

Can you imagine John Wayne almost weeping on my shoulder

every time the problem emerged? "She's an ice skater, not an actress," the big guy complained to me. (Miss Ralston had been the runner up to Sonja Henie in the 1936 Olympics.) He might have gone on permanent suspension but for the studio loaning him to John Ford to play the Ringo Kid in *Stagecoach*. Mr. Ford was always there to help him, in *The Long Voyage Home, She Wore a Yellow Ribbon*, and *The Quiet Man*, among others. In fact Mr. Ford was responsible for the Duke's career as an actor.

As Marion Michael Morrison, he had played football on a scholarship at the University of Southern California. To earn money in the summer holidays, he worked as a prop man at the Fox Studio, where Mr. Ford, who had also started in props, was then an important director. They became friends. And when Raoul Walsh was looking for a lead in *The Big Trail* (1930), the two directors agreed that the tall (six feet four) twenty-three-year-old ex-football champ could play the rugged cowboy. After that he would be more or less playing the same character in the two hundred and fifty movies before his death from cancer in his seventy-second year.

He once told me that his nickname was given him by the firemen on the engines he chased with his dog, Duke, during his boyhood in the Mid-West. He was lean and fit when I first knew him. I remember some of those early Westerns with him jumping on the horse from the balcony of a saloon, or taking a running jump to the saddle over the horse's rear end.

The Duke was always easy and ready to talk, sitting on the set, watching the other actors—Ward Bond, the Harry Careys, senior and junior—in so many of his films. "I was not always at Republic," he told me during our first chat on the set. "When sound came in, I signed a contract with Harry Cohn at Columbia, which then was also a minor studio. One day I was having a conversation with a starlet that Mr. Cohn fancied. Later he accused me of having an affair with her. 'When you are working for me,' he told me, 'you keep your pants buttoned!' " After that episode his roles diminished and before long he was fired.

Even though I disagreed politically with most of what the Duke stood for in his private life, I couldn't help liking him. He was open, friendly, and, strangely, rather shy. When his movie was finished, he would leave quietly without saying goodbye to anyone. He found it hard to part from the people he worked with; he was afraid he would choke up.

I did not need a warning never to discuss politics with him. We were at opposite ends of the spectrum. I was on the Hawaiian location of *In Harm's Way* the day his co-star, Kirk Douglas, a practicing Democrat, was quoted in the press as being on a certain committee. "You're a goddam liberal," Wayne shouted, then put his arm around Douglas' shoulder and said, "I'm not really mad." But neither the make-up man nor I could stand the conversation, and we both left the set.

Wayne was one of the founders of the Motion Picture Alliance for the Preservation of American Ideals, and just putting it on paper makes me nervous. It was as far to the right as you could get. He believed strongly in the Vietnam War, and urged President Lyndon Johnson to send in more Marines and let the Air Force go in and finish them all off. He was not only the star of *The Green Berets*, a film extolling the toughest fighters in Vietnam, but co-director as well. He wanted to be sure that the message of ruthless war got across.

This was the same man who gave a permanent job as his production assistant to Paul Fix, who had been his drama coach in 1929. When George Coleman, in charge of his company's transportation, was injured by a drunk in a Mexican bar room, he set him up in a car-rental business. And after Harry Carey, Sr., died his widow, "Ollie," always had an acting job with him. How could you not help liking this man?

Duke preferred Latin-type women, and I was always rather sorry that I was born blonde and green-eyed. The three women he married, Josephine, Esperanza, and Pilar, were all from south of the border. Josephine lost him when she nagged him about a woman she accused him of having an affair with. No woman, or man, could nag Mr. Wayne. The divorce from Esperanza was expensive— $50,000 a year for ten years, plus the home, *and* a car. He was still married to, though separated from, Pilar when he died. Recently one of his secretaries popped up with a book stating she had been his mistress for seven years.

Duke was making a movie in London, *Brannigan,* at the time of the Pilar divorce rumours. And when I saw him lunching at Les Ambassadeurs, I went to his table and asked, "Is there going to be a divorce?" "Now you know I don't answer questions like that," he replied. I smiled rather sheepishly, and went back to my friends.

Much earlier there was one other time when he was annoyed with me. It was when I printed in my column that Esperanza was planning an operation in order to become pregnant. The next time he saw me, at a party, he took me aside and said, "I don't like you going into my private life." But when it was a question of a divorce, a remarriage, or a new child, it was news and I had to.

There were four children with Josephine, three with Pilar, and none, in spite of an operation, with Esperanza, plus sixteen grandchildren. Michael, the oldest son, was in charge of Batjac, the family film company. A younger son, Patrick, is an actor. The youngest of the children, Aissa, was four years old when her father gave her a small role in *The Alamo*, in which he invested, and lost most of, $750,000 of his own money.

He was offered, but turned down, the fine role of the marshal in "Gunsmoke." The Duke didn't need the money. For twenty years, before winning the Oscar in 1969 for his craggy, one-eyed sheriff in *True Grit*, and for several years before, a John Wayne movie spelt success at the box office—with the exception of *The Alamo* (nonetheless, his favourite film).

When I had my daily television show for NBC in 1955, I filmed an interview with him on a tanker off the coast of Hawaii where he was making *Blood Alley*. The next time I saw Duke we were both patients at the Scripps Clinic in La Jolla, near San Diego. It was somewhat embarrassing as we had both taken purgatives for a barium X-ray. In the middle of a conversation one or the other had to dash to the john. It was at this clinic, after he had completed *In Harm's Way*, in the late summer of 1965, that cancer was discovered in one of his lungs.

After the operation he was warned, "No more cigarettes." So he returned to "chawing" tobacco, which Josephine had made him give up at the beginning of their marriage. He was sure that he had beaten what he called the Big C and he continued making movies. The night he won the Oscar for his performance in *True Grit* he became wildly drunk at a party for him at a bungalow at the Beverly Hills Hotel, emulating the hard-drinking Western marshal he had portrayed in the film. Perhaps he knew then that there would not be much more carousing for him.

I remember Duke's advice for his actor friends. "When you are with small people, sit down quickly so they can tower over you. It makes them feel good." Duke was six feet four. Most of the film tycoons were short men.

What a bonus for Hollywood when Vivien Leigh decided to leave London and join her lover, Laurence Olivier, in Hollywood, where he was filming *Wuthering Heights* with Merle Oberon. Otherwise Bette Davis, Lana Turner, Paulette Goddard, or even Tallulah Bankhead might have played Scarlett in David Selznick's production of *Gone with the Wind*.

The two-year search for the heroine of Margaret Mitchell's best-selling novel was still in progress, but George Cukor had started direction of the film with Clark Gable when Vivien visited the "burning of Atlanta" location on the arm of her agent, Myron Selznick, who introduced her to his brother, David. The rest, as they say, is history.

I had already met Vivien and Larry in London during June 1937, when I was getting my divorce from The Major. In the course of gathering news for my column I was taken to the set of *Fire over England,* where it was obvious to me that the two stars were in love. They were both married, Olivier to Jill Esmond and Miss Leigh to Duncan Holman. I wondered then if the romance would ever culminate in marriage. As you know, it did, in 1940, with a ceremony expertly manipulated by the press agent Russell Birdwell to coincide with the general release of *Gone with the Wind.*

For the rest of their marriage, Vivien would be trying and failing to compete with her husband, who became a bigger star than she was, indeed the greatest actor of our time, with such screen and stage epics as *Rebecca, Pride and Prejudice, The Entertainer,* his marvellous performance in *Richard III, Othello, Henry V,* for which he won a special Oscar in 1946, and another Oscar for *Hamlet* two years later.

Vivien also won a matching pair of Oscars—for Scarlett and later for the sad Blanche DuBois in the film version of *A Streetcar Named Desire.* Marlon Brando, who repeated his stage role of Stanley Kowalski, was merely nominated.

It was more in the area of theatre that Vivien lagged behind her husband. While he was always praised, she was nearly always criticized. She tried not to read the reviews, but she usually did and this caused her to retreat deep inside of herself and resulted in a series of breakdowns.

I did not know either of the Oliviers very well. They were not fond of talking to the press and attended only industry functions that concerned their films. They had a few close friends in Hollywood—Cary Grant, Katharine Hepburn, David Niven, the Selznicks, and George Cukor, who continued to coach Vivien privately even after he was fired from *Gone with the Wind*.

To digress for a few moments. When I talked in 1982 with Mr. Cukor I said to him, "Scott Fitzgerald was fired from the film because he had dared to change some of Miss Mitchell's prose. But why were *you* removed as director?" The story at the time was that he had been replaced by Victor Fleming because George had a reputation as a woman's director, while Fleming was known as a man's director, and Gable had complained that he was favouring Vivien.

"That's ridiculous, absolute nonsense," said George. "Some stupid press agent said I was a woman's director. It was bullshit. I used to say 'Thank you very much' when they brought this up. Now I just mention the men that I've worked with: Jack Barrymore, Spencer Tracy, Leslie Howard, everybody." He added: "When what's-his-name took over, he didn't go any place. He didn't even go to the premiere."

The one time I had a really good talk with the Oliviers was during the war, in their suite at the Connaught Hotel. I had returned to London in the summer of 1941 to write about the war for my syndicate. Larry had put in two hundred hours of flying in the United States in order to be accepted into the Fleet Air Arm of the Royal Navy, which found it more useful for him to make propaganda films. They were in London for a few days staying at their favourite hotel. The interview in the summer of 1941 had been arranged by the British Information people. My story with them would appear in all my NANA newspapers, and that was also good propaganda in America, which was not yet in the war.

Larry talked about the films he was making (although he said he would rather be doing the actual fighting). Vivien was nostalgic for her time in Hollywood and they both missed the friendships they

had made there. "When the war is over will you be coming back?"
I asked. They did not think so. "But that will depend on many
things," said Larry, who would always return to the theatre between
film making.

Most of their future stage and film productions would be in
England, after a disastrous *Romeo and Juliet* production on Broadway
in 1940. Olivier had wanted to make a film version of *Macbeth* in
England but could not raise the necessary cash. Hard to believe
today.

What stays most in my memory of their films is Larry's *Henry
V* in 1944—the wide screen opening for the Battle of Agincourt,
"For England, Harry, and Saint George!"—and Vivien, in addition
to her Scarlett role, as the fragile wartime girl in *Waterloo Bridge.*

My saddest memory of Vivien is the newspaper photograph of
Danny Kaye carrying the unconscious actress up the steps of the
plane returning her to England for the medical treatment she
needed. David Jacobs, the lawyer for the Oliviers, visited her on the
day she died in her London home. He told me afterwards that they
both knew she was dying and it was an agonizing meeting. She told
him how sorry she was for the misery she had caused her husband
with her tantrums, and especially her affair with Peter Finch. When
she died (in 1967) Sir Laurence, as he was then, had been married
to Joan Plowright for six years.

Later, in 1982, Lord Olivier was asked why, at the age of seventy-five, and after three operations for cancer, he was going through
a strenuous *King Lear* production for Granada Television. "Don't
worry," he said, "I don't intend to die," adding, "I want to make
as much money as I can for my children" (his children with Joan).

His illnesses and his long time with London's National Theatre
had apparently left him fairly broke. Which is why he had accepted
the awful remake of *The Jazz Singer.* "I always wanted to play a
rabbi," he joked. And *Dracula*—the great actor in a horror film. And
the role of General MacArthur in *Inchon,* an even worse $40 million
disaster, cut to nonsense by the Reverend Moon, who put up the
money, with Terence Young, the director, asking to have his name
taken off. And that bit in *Clash of the Titans* for which he was paid a
million dollars, and the same amount for *The Jigsaw Man,* which,
after a slight hiatus near the end, finally was completed.

Meanwhile, Lord Olivier has been receiving many honours—
from the Producers' Guild, and the Foreign Correspondents' Association in Hollywood, and from the Film Society of Lincoln Center
in New York. This annual benefit to honour a star who has made "an
extraordinary contribution to film" was hosted by Douglas Fairbanks and featured Maggie Smith, Kate Nelligan, Jean Simmons,
Trevor Howard, Glynis Johns, Richard Chamberlain, Christopher
Plummer, and George C. Scott, among many others.

There will, I am sure, be more honours for the greatest actor
of our time.

THE STAR MAKER

When I first came to Hollywood, Hal Wallis was head of production
at Warners, and producing his annual four films, editing four, with
four in production, his share of the studio's fifty films a year. Luckily
he had an understanding wife, the silent film star Louise Fazenda,
who would not complain when her exhausted husband came home
late, often at one in the morning.

"We lived in the valley then," Hal told me, "and Jack Warner
finally set up a projection room in our house for me to see the daily
'rushes' there. I would go home with ten or twelve reels of film and
a dictaphone and dictate notes." "And did they follow your instructions?" I asked him. "Oh yes," he replied, "They had to."

A funny thing happened to him one night when he was driving
home at about sixty miles an hour. It was close to midnight and he
was picked up by a police car. "The officer came up and took my
driver's license and all that, and he said, "You're in the picture
business, aren't you?" I said, "Yes," and he said, "I wonder if you
have ever come across my wife; she's in the picture business too."
I said, "What's her name?" He said, "Marilyn Monroe." She was
married then to this cop" (Jim Dougherty). "I met Marilyn, but
thank God I never worked with her. She was very difficult. She drove
everyone crazy."

I told Hal, who was known as the Star Maker, that during my
time in Hollywood I was often asked, "How can I be discovered for
a career in pictures?" He agreed with me that it helped to have had
some success outside of Hollywood; on Broadway, in a little theatre,

in a night club. One big exception of course was Lana Turner, discovered by Billy Wilkerson sipping an ice cream soda in a drug store opposite the Hollywood High School. After that young girls by the score descended on those stools hoping in vain for someone to say, "Little girl, here is my card. I will make you a star."

I asked Hal how he had discovered Kirk Douglas, Burt Lancaster, Shirley MacLaine, Dean Martin, and Jerry Lewis. "In 1946, I was going to New York on the Santa Fe Super Chief and on the train were Humphrey Bogart and Lauren Bacall. We were having drinks one night in the lounge and I said I was hoping to find some new talent in New York."

Up spoke Miss Bacall. "There's an actor there, Mr. Wallis; he's been in a couple of stock plays. He's good and you should look at him." Mr. Wallis looked and signed Kirk Douglas, with another small-part actor, Wendell Corey, for *The Strange Love of Martha Ivers*.

How did he find Burt Lancaster? "That was a little later. I heard about him in a play; I forget the name. He had a relatively small part; he came on in the last act. I liked what I saw, and the next day I got in touch with his manager, Harold Hecht, and put Burt under personal contract." Later Mr. Hecht would become Burt's partner in their independent films, and the victim of his sometimes foul language.

Shirley MacLaine was my neighbour at the beach one summer. I remember that she had a good-looking husband and a big dog, and was very pregnant with Sachi (now all grown up and pretty; she was with her mother when she won the Oscar last April for *Terms of Endearment*). But in 1956 Shirley had made one movie, *The Trouble with Harry*, on a loan-out from Mr. Wallis. It was one of the few failures directed by Alfred Hitchcock. But her producer did not lose his belief that she could be a star. How did he find her?

"I happened to be in the theatre to see Carol Haney in *Pajama Game*. That night there was a note in the programme that Haney had hurt her ankle and her understudy would go on. I was disappointed, but I thought, now that I'm here I might as well stay and see it. And Shirley stopped the show. She had that 'Steam Heat' number and a couple of other numbers and the audience went wild.

"I went backstage and saw Shirley going upstairs to her dressing room with the other bit players. I beckoned to her and shouted,

'Shirley!' She said, 'Me?' I said, 'Yes.' She came down and I met her manager-lover, Steve Parker. I took them to the Oak Room at the Plaza Hotel, and not long after that I signed her." On the strength of which she and Steve married. That year at the beach was almost the only time that they continued to live together. Steve prefers Japan, which is why, Shirley explains, their marriage was successful.

I sometimes know the answer before I ask the question, and at the time of the Martin and Lewis break-up, I knew that it was caused by antagonism between their wives. But that was not the only reason. There was some jealousy. Dean had begun to feel that Jerry was taking all the bows. "And he was," said Mr. Wallis. "Dean was very easy-going and he used to say to me, 'Do whatever my buddy wants,' and Jerry did what he wanted. But after a while it made Dean angry.

"We were in Phoenix doing *Three Ring Circus*. We were at the Arizona Biltmore one night, and Jerry and his wife came in. Dean and his wife were sitting there and Jerry and Patti walked right by them. There was no recognition. We had all the Clyde Beatty performers, the circus trains, and the whole circus set-up on the fairground with the big tent and all. Dean and Jerry would play the scene and after the director said 'Cut' they turned and walked away from each other. After a few days of seeing the dailies, I saw what was happening. It was bad. There was no humour.

"I called the boys in and told them, 'You fellers are up there on the screen. I'm not, and if you intend to go on this way I'm going to cancel the picture. Now, if you'll get down to business and forget your personal problems, I'll reshoot these first few days of work.' They saw the light and pitched in and gave the performances that were expected from them." It was the last picture they made together.

Zsa Zsa Gabor was also in the film, playing a ballerina. She was staying at a guest ranch near Scottsdale. One day Rubirosa, her lover, arrived in his private plane (his parting gift from Barbara Hutton). The press swarmed after him asking, "Where is Zsa Zsa?" Unable to shake them off, he finally returned to the airport. There they asked him, "What are you doing in Phoenix?' and he replied, "I was headed for Nicaragua, but I was blown off course."

Dean and Jerry were already successful when Mr. Wallis had caught their act at the Copacabana night club in New York. "I tried to sign them up there and then, but they said they were coming to Hollywood and we could talk there. So I went to Slapsy Maxie's" (owned by the boxer Maxie Rosenbloom) "and Louis B. Mayer was there. He said, 'Well, the guinea looks good but what will I do with the monkey?' " The "guinea" was Dean, the Italian. Jerry was the "monkey."

No one expected Dean to be a success without Jerry, but he made a fortune when he took off with his own television show. Jerry's show was not as successful, but he continued to make money with his movies, which are more popular in Europe than America. He was in Palm Beach not long ago, making *Hardly Working.* His entire family, including his wife, Patti, was there to help him celebrate his birthday. She told me the secret of their happy marriage. "We never allow Jerry Lewis" (that is, his acting persona) "into the house." I had not long left the set when they announced their separation. I guess she had let him in. After the divorce, Jerry married a much younger woman.

CHAPTER 3

SOME MEN IN MY Hollywood Life

CHRISTMAS 1936 was rather bleak for me. I had expected to spend it with King Vidor, whose direction of the great tear-jerker *Stella Dallas*, starring Barbara Stanwyck, would soon be acclaimed. I had met him during the spring racing season at Santa Anita. Roaming around from the paddock to the stands to gather news for my column I had chatted with Paulette Goddard, who told me that her neighbour, Mr. Vidor, on Summit Hill Drive, in Beverly Hills, had mentioned that he wanted to meet me. "I can take you there after the last race," she said. My escort to the races in those early months was Carl Laemmle, Jr., that same junior who had found Bette Davis so unsexy. He didn't like my leaving him, but I reminded him that we would be seeing each other the next day for a game of tennis.

Paulette dropped me off at Mr. Vidor's house. I found him attractive, and even more so when he plied me with delicious fried shrimps, cooked by his Filipino man, washed down with sweet rum drinks. And while the servant played the guitar in the next room, King sang "Summertime" from *Porgy and Bess* in a soft, seductive voice, and before I knew it, I thought I was in love with him.

Several visits later, King showed me the blueprints for a house he was planning to have built higher up on the hill. "As you will be living in it," he said, "I want you to approve of them." I had never seen plans for a house and I approved of everything. But when he talked of marriage, aware of the Hollywood gossip, I asked, "What about that girl, Betty Hill? I've seen your name linked with hers in the columns." "Oh no," he replied, "that's over. In fact she's been staying for some time with her family in Philadelphia."

I was living in a happy dream. The Major, impotent in essential areas, had always said he would allow me to divorce him if I wanted to marry someone else. I would give up my column, and as the rich Mrs. Vidor, the wife of an important director, I would give lots of parties and play tennis and swim every day in the big pool I had okayed on the plans. We were seen around town, dining here and there, but the other columnists assumed that I was interviewing the director for a book and did not mention this new twosome. So I did. Something about the new, blonde columnist that King Vidor was mad about. The item was read by Betty in Philadelphia, where my column appeared in the *Bulletin*.

A few days before Christmas, my lover told me, "Betty is coming back to Hollywood. I must meet her at the train to tell her about us." Seeing that I was rather worried, he added, "If it will make you feel better we can go now to get the engagement ring." "Oh no, you don't have to do that now," I said. A mistake. King was careful with his money, an understatement, and if I'd had the ring, the man would have followed the expenditure.

To cut a miserable Christmas short—which I actually spent at a party with the Ritz Brothers, the Ritz Brothers!—I did not see Mr. Vidor again until the middle of January 1937, when he asked me to lunch with him at the Hollywood Brown Derby. To inform me that he and Betty had spent their honeymoon at Garmisch in Bavaria, the place I had chosen for *our* honeymoon!

As for the junior Laemmle, the time came, as it did with several of the men I knew in my younger days, and sometimes even now— a single woman is always a target—that he wanted to have an affair with me. Until then I had regarded him as an escort to Santa Anita, and an occasional tennis opponent. The big moment came after a dinner at Perino's when his chauffeur drove us to my home where he followed me inside. I can see him now, sitting on the lowest step of the staircase leading to my bedroom, and saying, "How about it?" I knew what "It" meant. I also knew that Carl was a confirmed bachelor.

"Alright," I said brightly, "but let me tell you what it will involve. I will probably get pregnant, and then I will insist on us getting married." He tried to talk me out of this awful threat. I was firm. He left, hurriedly. Carl, who never married, was an invalid for a long time, but we were friends during my Hollywood years. Platonic friends. He died in 1949.

Jock Whitney called me. It was the 1937 spring racing season at Santa Anita. Jock had some horses running, and how would I like to be a guest in his box? I would like it very much. It was exciting sitting there, surrounded by the crème de la crème of the horse-racing world. Louis B. Mayer always had horses running and Clark Gable would be at the track to bet on them. Also Harry Cohn, the president of Columbia Pictures.

It was good professionally for me to be seen with Mr. Whitney. Pretty soon I was known as his girl and we would be invited together to various homes, most frequently to the David Selznicks'. Jock and his cousin Cornelius Vanderbilt Whitney were, together with MGM, putting up the money for David's production of *Gone with the Wind,* which he had recently bought from Margaret Mitchell for the comparatively low price of $50,000. They stopped counting after the first $100 million of profit, although by that time the usually astute Mr. Whitney had sold his percentage to MGM. The film is still being re-released every seven years.

One afternoon I was playing tennis with Jock, his tennis pro, and Fred Astaire, at the house he had rented from the star Johnny Mack Brown. We stopped when a servant hurried to the court with the news that Fred's wife, his beloved Phyllis, had unexpectedly given birth to their son. Fred did a dancing leap over the net and was gone before the sentence was finished. I rushed to the house to telephone the story to my newspaper syndicate.

When Jock decided to honour Marlene Dietrich with a dinner dance at his home, I was hurt that he did not invite me. His estranged wife, Liz, a great horsewoman, was coming in from Philadelphia for the party and perhaps that is why I was not invited. "But I want to come," I insisted. "There will be no press, not even Louella," said Jock which made me more eager to be there. "You see, darling, knowing you, if you came you would write about it in your column." "Of course I would, that's the only reason I want to come." He finally yielded. "Okay, but don't let anyone see you making notes." I promised.

My time at the party was spent dashing into the cloakroom writing down what I had gleaned eavesdropping on the stars, directors, producers, and all the most important people in Hollywood. I was more in the toilet than in the reception rooms. When the pages of my notebook were filled, I decided to leave. I was happy with the night's work but it was late and I was tired. Jock saw me to the front door and into my car. "I'll call you later," he whispered.

I waited half an hour for the call, but I knew the party would continue until dawn. I was half asleep when I put the phone off the hook. I have never been able to sleep again when awakened by the telephone, and with all those guests to look after I was sure Jock would not have time to call me.

At about eight in the morning I heard some insistent clicks coming from the phone. I had forgotten it was off. As soon as I put it together, there was a shrill ring. Jock. Furious. "I've been trying to get through to you all night," he yelled. Like all the rich men I have met, he was used to getting what he wanted when he wanted it.

Probably for the first time, he now decided to make our relationship more permanent. He asked me to be his mistress. I liked Jock but I was not in love with him. He was too rich. I have tried, God knows, but I have never been able to fall in love with a very rich man. So I declined his proposition. If he had said, "Will you marry me when I am free?" that might have been different. But it was just as well. For not long after, on 14 July 1937, to be exact, I would find Scott Fitzgerald in Robert Benchley's bungalow at the Garden of Allah, and after that, until his death on 21 December 1940, there was no room in my life for any other man.

Meanwhile, after a brief visit to London in 1937 to divorce The Major, I had moved into a house on North King's Road, about a half a mile straight up from Benchley's bungalow, which I visited almost daily at cocktail time. Bob would often take me to dinner at The Players restaurant at the bottom of my street, and across the road from where he lived. I would walk down there to meet him. But Bob, who was terrified of the traffic, always took a taxi, gave an irrelevant address to the driver, then told him to bring him to The Players, which was owned by Preston Sturges, the director of such master-pieces as *Palm Beach Story* and *Sullivan's Travels.*

I would sometimes see Howard Hughes come into The Players with his latest girl. They would walk in, not looking to the left or right, and go upstairs to Preston's more private dining room. Some-times the girl was Katharine Hepburn. He was in love with her and she must have liked him because she flew with him in his plane to visit her family in Connecticut. He wanted to marry her, but, in view of his later strange phobias, she was wise to refuse him.

Ginger Rogers, among many others, was also dated by Mr. Hughes. *Roberta* and *Top Hat* with Mr. Astaire had made her an important star. During my time in New York, we had thought she would marry George Gershwin. They had met when Ginger ap-peared in his musical *Girl Crazy* on Broadway in 1930. In the sum-mer of 1937 I would see her in the congregation at a downtown synagogue for the memorial service for George. My escort was the Marquess of Donegall, who had come to Hollywood to write about the funeral for the *Sunday Dispatch* and to ask me to marry him.

Everyone had considered the brilliant composer to be a hypo-chondriac because he was always complaining of this and that ail-ment. In 1934 I had been one of the guests with him at a country house near New York. We had been a tennis foursome in the after-noon but not for long, because he had a bad headache, he said. Later, after dinner, he sat at the piano and played his music. It was lovely hearing him play "Rhapsody in Blue," to which I had danced during my time with "The Midnight Follies" at the Metropole Hotel in London. After his death, they discovered a large tumour in his brain. It was a miracle that he had lived with it for so long. He died a few months before his thirty-ninth birthday.

CHAPTER 4

THE WITCHES' CAULDRON

HEDDA HOPPER, the erstwhile starlet (née Elda Furry), had evolved into an elegant woman as famous for her weird hats as for her arrogance and biased opinions. She had been married to the Broadway actor DeWolf Hopper, chiefly remembered for his recitation of "Casey at the Bat." Until Hedda became a Hollywood gossip columnist in 1938, she usually played small roles in pictures as a society lady. She supplemented that uncertain income as a real estate saleswoman.

Louella Parsons, then a reporter in the East, had come to California in the twenties hoping to cure her tuberculosis in the desert, where fashionable Palm Springs was already flourishing. Louella would soon become Hollywood's Boswell, writing a daily column for Hearst's King Features syndicate. One of her main jobs was to praise the film performances of Marion Davies, the pretty blonde mistress of her boss. In those early years, Louella had the gossip field all to herself. Later there would be more than four hundred correspondents sending stories from Hollywood to all parts of the world.

Hedda was lucky in her manager, Dema Harshberger, who masterminded every facet of her career, making her as great a celebrity as those she praised or murdered in her column. It was Dema who advised her to feud with the illiterate Louella, who hid her shrewdness with a vagueness that took in everything that was going on. She could never understand why Hedda was trying to hurt her so much. "I always praised her," she told me, "when she was a nothing actress." Her eyes filled with tears at such ingratitude.

There was a time when Hedda tried to get her rival fired. While it was common knowledge that Citizen Kane, the Orson Welles classic, was about the infatuation of a ruthless newspaper baron (modelled on Mr. Hearst) for a pretty young, blonde actress (Marion Davies), there was no action taken during its production, not by Mr. Hearst. And not by Louella Parsons, who, before the preview for the press in 1941, had seen the film privately and had reported its contents to her employer.

Perhaps they thought it would go away if they remained silent. Even Hopper waited until after the preview before going into action. With well-simulated wrath, she telephoned Mr. Hearst and demanded, "Where was your columnist when the movie was being made? Surely she could have stopped the production and saved you and Marion from great embarrassment. Why didn't she? If this exposure had been about *my* boss, the movie would never have been finished." Stirred by Hedda's blast, Mr. Hearst *did* go into action. His sole aim now would be to damage the film and everyone connected with it.

Citizen Kane was edited by Robert Wise, who would go on to win two Academy Awards as the director of *West Side Story* and *The Sound of Music.* The film editor has to work closely with the director. And in this case Orson Welles was not only the director but the writer and the star, and even at the age of twenty-six, he was used to doing things his way.

"Were you aware that you might have trouble with Mr. Hearst?" I asked Mr. Wise when I saw him two years ago in London. "Oh yes. We believed he would be upset. But it was Hedda's telephone call that sparked the fire." *Citizen Kane* was finished and ready for release when Mr. Wise's boss called him. "You've got to get on the plane tonight and fly to New York with a print of *Citizen Kane.*" It was mid-winter and several of the airlines had cancelled their flights because of bad weather, but Mr. Wise said, "The hell with it, let's go."

The purpose of the trip was to show the film to the presidents of all the film companies and their lawyers to see whether the industry as a whole would say to RKO, "Never mind about Hearst, go ahead and release the film." Or, "In the interests of our industry, put this on the shelf." The film was shown at Radio City Music Hall for the Schencks, the Warners, the Atwater Kents, etc., and their lawyers, with Orson as the host. I have known him since the late thirties, when he was young and slender, and he can be very nice when he wants to be. How he charmed all those studio presidents and lawyers!

They decided that with a few trims and changes they could release the film. John Houseman and Herman Mankiewicz rewrote some of the dialogue. Actors were brought back. It was redubbed and recut, and after several weeks there was another showing, this time for the lawyers only, who okayed the film for release. *Citizen Kane* has been listed as among the best films ever made.

In cinematic terms *Citizen Kane* had an immensely effective and novel style. It was unusual in its camera treatment, its story continuity, its storytelling. It was all just so right in that film. It explored this man (Kane-Hearst) through his different ages, all through the years, what made him tick, not revealing until the last shot the mystery of Rosebud, which is referred to throughout the film, and turns out to be a child's sled.

Nonetheless, Mr. Welles was taking enormous chances, especially as most of the cast were new to films. Until *Citizen Kane* we had not seen Joseph Cotten or Everett Sloane or George Coulouris or Agnes Moorehead or Paul Stewart, who played the butler. All of them, including Orson, were banned for many years from the Hearst newspapers.

Except when Miss Parsons had something nasty to write about them. How she gloated when Orson ran into financial trouble while making *It's All True* in South America, a semi-documentary aimed at improving Pan-American relations and countering Nazi influence, very strong there during the war.

While I appeared in more newspapers than either Hedda or Louella, I was never as powerful in Hollywood as they were. Perhaps because I did not use power the way they did, although at times I could be just as nasty. For instance, during the fifties, when I heard that a British newcomer was throwing his weight around at the studio, I put this morsel into my column: "The messenger girls at MGM have a new pin-up boy, Stewart Granger. They have pinned him to the board with a dagger through his heart." I wonder if this is why he has never been too friendly with me!

But at least he never swore at me as he did at Hedda when she told Elizabeth Taylor not to marry Michael Wilding, who was sharing a house with Granger. In her book *The Truth, the Whole Truth, and Nothing But,* Hedda had implied strongly that Michael and Stewart were lovers. The MGM publicity director was worried. If they really were gay it would have diminished their box office appeal—I'm not sure it would today.

The London office was contacted and the head man, Paul Mills, was asked to make discreet enquiries. "Are you able to prove that they are *not* homosexuals?" To which Paul replied, "As far as we know, they are both sleeping with ladies." A sigh of relief from coast to coast.

Mr. Wilding sued Hedda for $100,000, and won. I remember how anguished she was, going all over town asking known homosexuals to back her up. A gay producer friend of mine gleefully told her to go to hell.

One of Hedda's many problems was that she thought she was superior to the people she wrote about. And she believed in her holy mission to keep Hollywood pure, which made her more disliked than Louella. To Marlon Brando she was "The Hat." He called Louella "The Fat One." I never knew what he called me and I did not ask.

Hedda was always telling people what to do and, when they had done it, to give her the exclusive story. Louella waited until they were *going* to do it, then demanded the story. But while she would be angry if it went to her rival, to my knowledge she would not threaten them with *total* ruin, as Hedda did.

I remember when Claire Trevor neglected to tell Miss Hopper that she was about to marry Mr. Bren. Hedda called her and threatened, "I will ruin you." The same threat was given to Joan Crawford when Hedda read of Joan's impending marriage to Phillip Terry in Louella's column. Claire merely shrugged. Joan was upset. At a party when Joan was alone in the ladies' room with Hedda, she came towards her with outstretched hand. The columnist walked past her as though she were invisible.

The clients of Henry Rogers, who included Paul Newman,

Danny Kaye, and Doris Day, were barred for a long time from Hedda's column. For the usual reason—he had given some exclusives to Louella. He always explained this when anyone signed with him. I talked with Henry Rogers last year, asking him what he now thought of the long-gone pair.

"Hedda was imperious," he said. "She was a dynamic, aggressive, humourless, essential bitch, with a knife in each hand. She was truly an impossible woman. In contrast, Louella was essentially a bumbling person who had been placed in this powerful position by Mr. Hearst and was always struggling to keep this position. She could be mean and bitchy, but she was fundamentally a nice person. Although during all the time I knew her, I always felt she was half drunk.

"Warren" (his partner) "and I took Louella and 'Docky,' her doctor husband, to a play one night. They'd been drinking and they kept falling asleep. Two days later she wrote a rave review of the play, which she hadn't really seen. She did it because she liked Warren so much."

Celeste Holm remembers them differently: "Hedda was venal. Louella was stupid. But I think Louella did more harm to people in Hollywood than Hedda did." I don't agree. Hedda not only tried to ruin people if they gave their stories to Louella, but also if their politics or religion were different from hers. She was the epitome of the now hackneyed phrase (Lord Acton, 1834–1902) "Power tends to corrupt, and absolute power corrupts absolutely."

When I first came to Hollywood, I was invited to dinner at "Pickfair." Mary was then married to the actor Buddy Rogers. Ginger Rogers, no relation, was among the guests. Both Ginger and Mary were in disgrace with Louella for refusing to appear on her radio show. Why should they do it for nothing, they told me, when they could command enormous fees? Mary was beyond Louella's scalpel. Not so Ginger. So while Louella praised Fred Astaire in those marvellous musicals, she reserved the knife for his co-star: What a pity that she did not quite come up to scratch! And those awful gowns! . . . Or worse still, she ignored her completely.

I remember when Nelson Eddy was never going to be in Louella's column because he would not do her radio show. And Charlton Heston was never going to be in Hedda's column, because he would not give his free services for her early television pilot. But no matter how hard Louella and Hedda tried to ruin talented people, they did not succeed. Ultimately both columnists had to forgive the stars who were brave enough to say "No" to those free appearances. A star is a star. And their readers wanted to know about them.

Louella was furious when her "great" friend Clark Gable eloped to San Francisco with Lady Sylvia Ashley, while she was attending a film premiere in Hollywood. She received the news from the wire services. But she did not raise a whimper. In a rushed-out edition of the *Los Angeles Examiner,* she gushed about how she had known about it all along, but had promised to keep the secret. Secret my eye. Unlike Hopper, Louella was a good newspaper woman and, friendship or no friendship, she would have come out with the story.

Of the two, I much preferred Louella. We were neighbours in Beverly Hills. I was at 607 North Maple Drive, and she was four doors away at 615. We would meet walking around the block, she with her small dog. On Halloween "trick or treat" night my children would call first at her house and she always had candy and apples ready for them. One time she asked them to call her "Aunt Lolly." "But we already have an Aunt Lolly," they told her. Our housekeeper was called Lolly.

Louella was more loyal than Hedda. And more grateful. If you gave her a story she was your friend for ever—as long as you didn't give the next one to Hedda. They both fought for production scoops—the title, when it would start, who would be in it. But unless it was something rare, such as the casting for *Gone with the Wind,* I was less interested in future films than in what happened on the sets and what they were doing away from the camera.

Sometimes on a Sunday afternoon I would know the title of the production that was leading Hedda's column on Monday morning. I would phone this to Louella, who could use it for her first edition on Sunday night. My reward was to get two consecutive headlines in Louella's column when Jerry Wald at Twentieth Century–Fox bought the movie rights to my autobiography, *Beloved Infidel.* Hedda never mentioned it.

The rivalry between them was a problem for the studios. If you gave Louella the scoop, Hopper would be angry. And vice versa. I never had that problem because neither Harry Brand at Fox, nor Perry Lieber at RKO, nor Howard Strickling at Metro would ever call me with a scoop. I had to get them myself.

The number one and two gossip columnists had fairly large staffs. I had me, and a secretary who took messages and worked in the office at my home. But because I visited the sets more than they did, I made friends of the producers, the directors, the writers, the stars, and even members of the crew, who would give me their news as it was happening. So I was sometimes able to scoop them. Then they would *both* call the Publicity Office and scream bloody murder.

There was one time—I forget now what my story was except that it concerned MGM—when Hedda phoned Andy Hervey in the Publicity Department and called him everything horrible you can imagine. And yet she owed her column to Andy. He had recommended her to the *Esquire* syndicate in 1938 when they were looking for a columnist.

Today, it is hard to understand the power of these two women in Hollywood. At one time Louella invited me for lunch at Romanoff's, and before we left every star, producer, director, and agent there had come to our table and verbally kissed her rear end.

It amazed me that the famous, highly paid people of Hollywood, some revered all over the world, were so afraid of these two old women. And while I was considered dangerous by the publicity heads because of the sharp comments in my column, I don't think anyone was afraid of me. And I was glad of that. But those two old girls revelled in the fear they created. Hedda, for example, was showing a visitor the piled-up presents from the stars and studios under her towering Christmas tree: "Fear put them there," she gloated.

Louella, apart from her number one gossip position, had another edge over Hopper. Her husband, Dr. Martin, a urologist, was the doctor for Twentieth Century–Fox, so he knew who had this or that social disease. And you know how husbands and wives talk things over in bed. Both of them were heavy drinkers; Docky, as his loving wife called him, drank even more than Louella. It was late, about three A.M. at a party, and the doctor had passed out on the floor. When the host started to shake him, Louella grabbed his arm and pleaded, "Please, oh please, don't disturb Docky. He has to operate at eight in the morning!"

I had wondered why Hedda was at first unable to get jobs for her actor son, Bill Hopper. I believe there was a drinking problem. When he finally did land a small role in a live television show with Claire Trevor, she ran "interference" for him and helped him over the rough spots. On the night the show was televised, Claire received a huge basket of flowers with the note, "Thank you for being so kind to my son." Which proves that even Miss Hopper had a heart, or something.

Hedda detested Rex Harrison. And vice versa. When Kay Kendall married Rex, she told her, "I'm devoted to you, Kay, but I loathe your husband." During the first run of *My Fair Lady* on Broadway, Hedda went backstage and tried to see him. He slammed the door in her face. She also had the nerve to fly to Rome after Ingrid Bergman went to Rossellini. At first he would not allow Ingrid to see her. But she knew how vicious Hedda could be. So they saw her. Roberto was angry at some of her questions and stalked out. Result: a horrible piece about them in her column.

Louella was happy when Lana Turner, soon after her marriage to millionaire Bob Topping, agreed to appear on her radio show. But Radie Harris, the Broadway columnist for the *Hollywood Reporter*, had already booked Lana for *her* radio show on CBS. She was naturally angry when the day before the broadcast she was informed that Lana had cancelled. No reason was given.

Radie did some sleuthing and learned that Louella had told Louis B. Mayer that Lana had to appear first on *her* show. Or else. So Radie, not a girl who gives in easily, went to Mr. Mayer's boss in New York, Nick Schenck. Lana appeared first for Miss Harris, making an enemy of Miss Parsons. But not for too long, as Lana's star was in the ascendant.

When King George VI and Queen Elizabeth came to the United States, Miss Harris was asked to invite the British stars in Hollywood and Broadway for a radio broadcast in their honour at the Hyde Park home of President Franklin D. Roosevelt. Among those enlisted were Leslie Howard, David Niven, Merle Oberon, Laurence Olivier, Vivien Leigh, Gertrude Lawrence, and Freddie Bartholomew. Hedda demanded to be on the show and was furious when refused. Of course she vented her anger in her column. I doubt that the Royals read it.

James Mason had never heard of any of us Hollywood gossip columnists, and he demanded, "Who is she?" when Louella asked him to appear on her radio show. He was speedily informed of her power to make or mar a performer. So he listened to her on Sunday evening. "Absolutely not," he said after hearing all that fumbling and mumbling, and shuddering at "My verst eggsglusive."

Mrs. James Mason, Pamela, had met Hedda Hopper in England and had admired her for being so successful, a woman who had made it on her own. They had become friends. And she was surprised when Hedda called her one day and demanded, "What's going on between Jean Simmons and Richard Burton?" Jean at the time was married to Stewart Granger, and Richard was in Hollywood with his then wife, Sybil. Jean and Richard had co-starred in *The Robe*, and there had been some rumours of a romance.

The Masons, the Burtons, and the Grangers were a close-knit group. In fact Richard and his wife had stayed with the Masons and were now staying with the Grangers. But when Pamela told Hedda, "I haven't the faintest idea," the columnist retorted, "Don't be ridiculous, you are great friends with them all and you are together all the time. You must know that they're having a hot romance."

"Well, as it happened, they were," Pamela told me. "And I *did* know, but naturally I was not going to say so. But when I said, 'Hedda my dear, I know nothing about it,' she called me a liar. 'You *do* know because they are your best friends!' 'In that case,' said Pamela, 'I would be the last person to tell you, even if I knew, which I don't.' 'You're going to regret this,' Hedda screamed. 'You're going to learn which side your bread is buttered.' And there for many years I had thought I was a friend of hers. I had invited her to my parties, and many people had said, 'If you're going to have Hopper, I'm not coming.' They were so afraid of her."

At film premieres Miss Hopper was often escorted by a young man, usually an actor. I thought then, "Ah, he's hoping for a mention in her column," and that was probably true. But the reason Hedda used him, I learned, was that a doctor had told her that if she had sex with a young man, it would keep her young for ever.

Louella's "Marion never looked lovelier" became part of the Hollywood joke language, but I think Miss Davies actually preferred Hedda Hopper. She even did a television show for Hedda, with both ageing ladies using what they called "lifts" on their faces, the skin pulled up and taped behind their ears, which made them both look younger, but somewhat mummified.

One time Marion, who was fun-loving, teased Hedda saying, "Why don't you get that Quaker ice water out of your veins, and toss your petticoat out of the window?" A year before his assassination, Hedda told Marion that she knew for a fact that John Kennedy could have an affair with a woman only when they were both in a bath tub! Marion was amazed and demanded, "Who told you that?" "Confidentially," said Hedda, 'it was Perle Mesta." Mrs. Mesta was the Washington Hostess with the Mostess satirized in the Ethel Merman play and movie *Call Me Madam.*

I met Marion four times only. At that first party in her home at Santa Monica; on the set at Warners, where her private dressing room had been moved from MGM because Hearst had accused Mayer of neglecting her; and, the third time, at the testimonial dinner in the Ambassador ballroom, given by Mr. Hearst in honour of his columnist, Louella Parsons.

Marion had not wanted to appear but her powerful lover had insisted. She had always resented the fact that Hearst had found it necessary to use Louella to promote her career. She had already proved she was a good comedienne who could stand or fall on her own feet.

On the day of the testimonial dinner she had started drinking in the morning. When Louella was at the microphone thanking all those who had made praising speeches, the tanked-up lady staggered to her feet and screamed, "Fuck you. Fuck you." At Mr. Hearst's nod, Marion was carried to the exit, still shouting, "Fuck you. Fuck you."

The last time I saw Marion she was the wife of Captain Horace Brown, who resembled her late lover. The party at her house in Beverly Hills was in honour of Johnny Ray, the "crying" singer. Marion had been drinking heavily and was absent until near midnight, when she appeared teetering at the top of the staircase, glass in hand, and would have fallen to the bottom if some male guests had not raced up to grab her.

Hedda Hopper died of emphysema at the age of seventy-five. Louella, then nearing her nineties, was in a vegetable state in a nursing home. Her sole occupations were watching television and eating ice cream. When she was told that her rival was dead, she smiled for the first time since she had been there.

Chapter 5
Off Duty

WHEN YOU ARE a columnist, especially a gossip columnist, you are never quite relaxed, even when you are supposed to be enjoying yourself. You are always alert to what is happening around you. To fill seven columns a week most of what you see and hear is grist to the column: an interesting overheard remark, a couple holding hands, a wife at a party without her husband, or vice versa. But for me it wasn't all work and no play. I managed to have a good time, especially during my early years in Hollywood.

I drove frequently to the Santa Monica beach for a swim and I played tennis an average of four times a week. When *Life* magazine, in their first issue in 1936, did a layout of a day in the life of Robert Taylor, I was asked to be on the other side of the court lobbing balls across the net, while the camera focused on him. It was a new experience for me to be the back of a head in a photograph. I was a regular at the West Side Tennis Club, and later at the Beverly Hills Tennis Club, sometimes playing in mixed doubles with Gilbert Roland. And there, for two glorious weeks, I was the number one woman player.

On Sundays there was tennis on the Jack Warner court. Or, with pretty starlets watching, at Arthur Lyons', a top agent in those days. And if I wanted to see some cricket, it was being played on a nearby suburban green. With so many British and other Europeans under contract in the studios (it was one of those periodical invasions from abroad), C. Aubrey Smith—later Sir C. Aubrey—who had played cricket for England, was able to put two elevens together on most Saturday afternoons and Sundays.

Laurence Olivier could sometimes be seen looking on or swinging a bat, also Leslie Howard, David Niven, Basil Rathbone (Sherlock Holmes), his Doctor Watson, Nigel Bruce, Ronald Colman, Errol Flynn, the author C. S. Forester (*Captain Horatio Hornblower*), and assorted free-lancing writers and actors who were hoping to make it in Hollywood, plus a few Americans who were trying to master the game.

C. Aubrey Smith was considered the epitome of the European aristocrat. He was the forbidding Earl in *Little Lord Fauntleroy*, the Duke of Wellington in *House of Rothschild*, and Lord Capulet in *Romeo and Juliet*. I had met him in London during my stage days when I applied for a role in one of his plays. He had turned me down with such kindness that I had gone away as happy as though I had been successful.

I was often at the old Trocadero on Sunset Boulevard. Later Dean Martin would buy it and lose his investment, but in the late thirties it was a popular place for dining and dancing. You could reckon on seeing at least a half-dozen stars on any given night, and Louis B. Mayer. The food was expensive and not very good, a fact noted in my column: "Not even the doubtful pleasure of bumping into Louis B. Mayer on the dance floor can compensate for the high-priced, inferior food." What I did not know then, but was soon made aware of, was that the Trocadero was owned by Mr. William Wilkerson, who also owned the *Hollywood Reporter*.

It was open season on this difficult new columnist. An ex-Mrs. Wilkerson had been given the cushy job of writing the page two gossip column. About once a week there was something derogatory about me. Once she confused me with the night-club mimic Sheila Barrett, and that was the only time I laughed. Later, in 1940, Scott Fitzgerald, with whom I had fallen in love during the summer of 1937, would challenge Wilkerson to a duel because of an editorial demanding that I be kicked out of Hollywood.

There were better dancers at a little Spanish dive to which I was taken by Anthony Quinn. The rhumba had just reached Hollywood, and I remember seeing Errol Flynn wriggling his hips there, as well as Ann Sheridan, who had recommended the place to Tony, then a struggling actor. He attended drama lessons in that same building when Lee Strasberg opened the Actors' Studio West. This was long after his marriage to Katherine De Mille, the adopted daughter of Cecil B. De Mille. I am sure he had assumed that he would then be on easy street for the rest of his acting career. But De Mille made his life such hell with the small parts he played in his pictures that he was glad to work for other directors. *La Strada* for Fellini in Italy made him an important star.

All the Brown Derbys—Beverly, Hollywood, and Downtown—served good food at reasonable prices. Writers, agents, and reporters frequented them. In the winter of 1937, when Scott and I were in the Beverly Derby on a Saturday evening, we saw Hedy Lamarr dining there alone. "How typical of Hollywood," said Scott; "the most beautiful girl in the world alone on a Saturday night." I was sorry to see on my recent visit that the Beverly Brown Derby was boarded up and for sale.

There was also Ciro's on the Strip for dancing and gambling, although I never visited the room where they gambled. The first time I went there with Scott, Humphrey Bogart was sitting with his second wife, Mary Phillips, just inside the entrance and looking disconsolate. Miss Phillips was visiting briefly. Like his first wife, her career was on the New York stage. Mayo Methot, wife number three, was also an actress, as was wife number four, Lauren Bacall, but not until she was spotted modelling an outfit in a magazine by the then Mrs. Howard "Slim" Hawks.

Mayo had been a pleasant, sensitive person when Bogart married her. Soon after she changed into the virago who threw the table hard- and soft-ware at him in restaurants, and whacked him on the head with her handbag in the street. Early in the war they had been sent by the State Department to North Africa to entertain the GIs. But their fights were as dangerous as the actual battles and they were hastily recalled to America.

Of the good restaurants in those early years, only Perino's is still in existence. Voisin, where Scott and I often lunched on Saturdays, has long since been gone. So has La Rue's, owned by that same Mr. Wilkerson. When Helen Hayes refused to take an ad in his paper for her performance in *Farewell to Arms,* having previously won the Oscar in 1931 for *The Sin of Madelon Claudet,* her name was actually omitted from the review!

Romanoff's, then on North Rodeo Drive, also had excellent food. It was financed by several of the Garden of Allah writers— Benchley, Dorothy Parker, John O'Hara. I was there with Scott on the opening night, and at the end of the evening there was not enough money to pay the waiters, so there was a hasty whip round for cash.

Mike's place was so popular that he had to move to something larger. "One of my problems," he told me, "was that all the big shots wanted those tables at the front with the banquettes. At the new place on South Rodeo every table had a banquette." But the bigger restaurant was never quite as good, even though Frank Sinatra and Humphrey Bogart could be viewed at lunchtime when they were not working on a film, eating at the table near the door. For some time now it has been a magnificent Chinese restaurant. When the premier of China was in town he dined there with his entourage. But few people go there now, although the food is good.

"Prince" Mike Romanoff, born Harry Geguzonoff in Lithuania, changed his name to Gerguson when he came to America. He had worked as a tailor in New York before deciding to be a Russian aristocrat, and had been imprisoned for fraud. But his effrontery amused the intelligentsia and the film stars in Hollywood, who, by their patronage, made his restaurant *the* place for lunch and dinner.

When Dave Chasen, an ex-vaudevillian, opened his restaurant on the fashionable Beverly Boulevard, the regulars on Thursday, cook's night out, included W. C. Fields, Cary Grant, Clark Gable, Bogart, Sinatra, Errol Flynn, and any top star of the Golden Age you can think of.

Everyone loved Dave, including Howard Hughes, who, when Dave was recuperating from a bout of the illness that would eventually kill him, sent his own plane to bring him to Las Vegas, where Dave was ensconced in a large suite at his hotel, with all expenses paid by Howard. I remember asking Dave whether he had seen Howard, who was then becoming somewhat of a recluse. "No, and I didn't try."

And after Dave's death his wife, Maude, continued the fine cuisine. In 1982, when I was there with Shelley Winters, the service and the steaks were great, but most of the stars had gone to wherever stars go when they die. Another popular restaurant today is Ma Maison, which is so exclusive that its telephone number is unlisted.

One block below South Rodeo is Spago's, owned by the former chef at Ma Maison, and also Morton's, where a table is always ready if you are a celebrity. Then, too, there is the Bistro on North Canyon Drive and the Bistro Garden just up the street. On one of my recent visits, I saw Warren Beatty and Jack Nicholson dining there together: two of the most eligible girl-loving actors in Hollywood, without a woman!

For breakfast these days, if you want to make a business deal, the Polo Lounge in the Beverly Hills Hotel is the place to go.

The three favourite clubs of my time are still going strong. Hillcrest was, and still is, more or less the Jewish club. Sunday evening at Hillcrest was the best and probably still is the best eating place in Hollywood. I was taken there not long after I arrived. What a feast! On the long table, you helped yourself to chopped chicken liver, marinated herring, lox, gefilte fish, boiled beef, etc. The membership now includes Frank Sinatra. Lakeside was mostly for gentiles. The other was the Los Angeles Country Club, which bars blacks, Orientals, Jews, and actors. Many years ago, when Jack Warner tried to join Lakeside, he was blackballed. Ronald Reagan, who was a member, resigned in protest, which did not hurt him with his boss. But it wasn't altogether anti-Semitism, I was told at that time. Lakeside is near the Warner Brothers studio. The members didn't want Jack coming over unexpectedly and seeing which of his people were playing instead of working.

Bob Hope is sometimes at Lakeside. "I thought you had your own course," I said to him recently. "Well, I have six holes, now I don't play so much because of the operation on my eye. But when I do play I go to Lakeside." When I mentioned the Jack Warner incident, he laughed and said, "I think it was something else—they didn't want to hear those awful jokes."

CHAPTER 6

YES, MR. DE MILLE

IF CECIL B. DE MILLE had not been jealous of his older brother, William, he might not have journeyed to Hollywood in 1913 and almost singlehandedly founded the film capital of the world. William was well known as a playwright on Broadway, while his kid brother was still uncertain about his future. Desperate to make a name for himself, young Cecil enrolled at the New York Academy of Dramatic Art. And in 1900, at the age of nineteen, made his acting debut on Broadway.

But acting, managing his mother's theatrical company, and sometimes working with William on his moderately successful plays did not satisfy him. He was still accepted only as William De Mille's good-looking kid brother. It was when he went to California and directed his first film, *The Squaw Man,* in 1914, that he felt equal to William, who in fact soon followed him to Hollywood to write and direct for the infant film company.

As a movie director, William was not as successful as his brother, and in 1934 he returned to his career in New York. He was now jealous of Cecil. In that same year C.B., as he would be known, was praised for another success, *Cleopatra,* starring Claudette Colbert, made for under one million dollars (and reviewed more favourably than the $44 million production would be in 1961).

Mr. De Mille, a big man physically, made big films. He was to make *The Ten Commandments* twice, a silent version in 1923, and with Charlton Heston as Moses in 1956. Some other mammoth productions included *The King of Kings* in 1927, with Jesus portrayed by

81

H. B. Warner, who was commanded to lead a Christ-like life in private and public. No drinking, no smoking, no anything unpious. (There were no such restrictions for Jeffrey Hunter in the 1961 remake.)

C.B. was so in love with *The Squaw Man* that he made it three times, the second version in 1918, and as a talkie in 1931. *The Crusades,* released in 1935, was the only film he made that year, a pattern he would follow to the end of his life. *Samson and Delilah* was made in 1949 with Victor Mature as the shorn Israelite bringing down the papier-mâché pillars in the Temple, and was followed by *The Greatest Show on Earth* in 1952. After *The Ten Commandments,* there were none at all during the three years before his death in 1959 at the age of seventy-eight.

I missed him with his megaphone and riding boots. His sets had always been interesting to visit and write about. He had a group of retainers whose main job was to agree with everything he said—it was always, "Yes, Mr. De Mille," "Yes, Mr. De Mille"—and to follow him with his director's chair, his name writ large on the back, into which he would descend without looking. I never dared to think of what would happen if the chair by some mischance had not been there.

He was a stern taskmaster. If an extra or bit player made an unexpected sound, C.B.'s wrath was shattering, and depending on the extent of his anger, he or she would be fired on the spot, accompanied by a stream of sarcasm. De Mille, like some other directors, Otto Preminger for example, would usually pick on the most vulnerable people on the picture and reduce them to emotional rubble.

Preminger's *Saint Joan* was Jean Seberg's first film. She was weeping more than she was trying to act. In Otto's *Exodus,* filmed in Israel, Michael Wager was his chief target. I was there during the shooting and couldn't understand why Michael didn't take a swing at him, but perhaps he needed the job. Otto's reason was always that he was trying to extract a good performance.

Mr. De Mille's training as an actor was useful when in 1936 he agreed to be the Host in Hollywood for the CBS Lux Radio Theatre. He would announce in deep, confident tones, "This is Cecil B. De

1. 1936: "One of my early publicity shots—glamour girl"

2. *Opposite above:* Merle Oberon surrounded by members of the Hollywood Cricket Club— David Niven on far left, Sir Aubrey Smith on Merle Oberon's right.
3. *Below:* Sheilah with George Brent at Warners, on the set of Submarine DI (1937): "Working, or flirting?"

4. *Above:* Louella Parsons, as Mae West, with Randolph Hearst, the boss's son: "Party Time." 5. *Right:* Hedda "The Hat" Hopper.

9. Ernest Hemingway: "Macho man" on a hunting expedition with Gary Cooper, 1943

. *Opposite far left:* Dorothy Parker: "A
red Renoir." 7. *Left above:* Robert
Benchley: "I always thought of him as The
Happy Walrus." 8. *Left below:* John
O'Hara: "Was he sober?"

0. *Right:* Howard Hughes and Jean
Harlow at a Hollywood party in the early
hirties: "When we were young,
earie." 11. *Below:* The incomparable
Fred Astaire: "Off Duty"

12. Joan Crawford with her second husband, Franchot Tone: "Love in the thirties"

13. *Right:* Douglas Fairbanks, Mary Pickford and Charlie Chaplin, who together founded United Artists.

14. *Below:* Errol Flynn, getting into shape with his trainer, the popular Mushy Callahan.

15. *Right:* Marlene Dietrich with Melvyn Douglas in *Angel:* "The glamorous hausfrau"

16. *Left:* Cecil B.
DeMille signing
Evelyn Keyes to a
personal contract.
17. *Below:* Gary
Cooper, Barbara
Stanwyck and Robert
Taylor at the
Mocombo nightclub

18. *Top:* Bob Hope, Dorothy Lamour and Bing Crosby in *The Road to Morocco,* 1942: "Hot stuff."
19. *Above:* Charlie Chaplin, King Vidor, Pat O'Brien and Pat's daughter: "An evening out"

Mille bringing you the Lux Radio Theatre from *Hollywood,*" with great emphasis on the last word. He knew with his flair for showmanship that it was Hollywood that would attract the listeners as much as the top stars and the important film plays that he presented.

A J. Walter Thompson executive, Savington Crampton, had persuaded Lever Brothers, for whom they did the advertising, to broadcast the show from Hollywood rather than continuing in New York. "You already have the movie stars endorsing your product in newspapers and magazines," said Mr. Crampton. "They will be only too happy" (for $5,000 per show) "to appear for you on a radio programme that advertises Lux."

On Monday evening, 1 June 1936, I was backstage at the Music Box Theater on Hollywood Boulevard for the first show. Clark Gable and Marlene Dietrich were starred in *The Legionnaire and the Lady* (the radio version of *Morocco*) and were delighted to be reading from a script, instead of having to memorize their lines. The following Monday, William Powell and Myrna Loy were repeating their roles in a condensed version of *The Thin Man.* Asta was also at hand, or rather heel, to bark at the right moments. It was a turning point for Hollywood stars to appear in plays on radio and was accepted by the studio heads as a means of advertising their films, although later they would put up strong resistance against the threatening intrusion of television.

Monday, at six P.M. Hollywood time, nine P.M. in the East, had been chosen deliberately as the best day and time to attract the largest audience. After a going-out weekend, listeners, 35 million of them, mostly stayed home on Monday evening, and were in the mood to settle down and hear the voices of Cecil B. De Mille and his great Hollywood stars.

He might have gone on indefinitely as the host, but he left the show in November 1945. As were all performers on radio, he was a union member of the American Federation of Radio, AFRA, and had always paid his dues. But when he learned that some of the money deducted from his paycheck was going to the rather leftist Political Action Committee, he threatened to resign. It was the beginning of the McCarthy harassment of left-wingers in Hollywood and De Mille was a staunch right-winger. Arguments were useless.

He stated that he would not help to support what he considered was a Communist-tinged organization. The Lux Radio Theatre continued, but not with C.B.

I had been a guest on the De Mille show, giving out the latest gossip, and perhaps that gave him the idea of inviting me to his ranch in the country for a weekend. I was warned about the peacocks that screamed through the night sounding like a woman being murdered. But I was not prepared for the Big Production that was a regular feature of the weekends.

On arrival, the male guests were given a choice: they could hunt for tame mountain lions in the hills, or they could clean out the swimming pool. The ladies were supposed to rest in their rooms. I don't know what C.B. was doing, but there wasn't a man in sight until the late afternoon, when we would all change for the evening festivities.

No drinks were allowed until eight o'clock, when Mr. De Mille would appear in a sort of white cowboy regalia, with large white leather gloves, flourishing a cocktail shaker adorned with bells that chimed melodiously as he shook the contents. Until eight o'clock the ladies had to wait on the men, carrying non-alcoholic drinks to them, lighting their cigarettes, bringing chairs for them to sit on. But when dinner was announced the situation was reversed. The men would wait on the ladies. They led us to our seats at the table, where there was a present for each of us. I was glad when the weekend, which had begun on Saturday afternoon—there was filming in the morning at the studios then—had ended on Sunday after a buffet lunch and we were all driven back to Hollywood.

One of my last meetings with C.B. was in the early summer of 1955, when I filmed, at the Paramount entrance gate, the award I gave him as "The Greatest Showman of the Year." We screened the presentation on the television programme I had then, to coincide with the release of his film *The Greatest Show on Earth.* In actual fact, since the retirement of D. W. Griffith, Cecil B. (for Blount) De Mille had been the greatest showman of every year in Hollywood.

CHAPTER 7

WRITING FOR THE MOVIES

THE WRITERS' BUILDING at MGM overlooked a cemetery, and on a clear day you might see Dorothy Parker leaning out of a window and talking to the headstones. "Hello down there," she was heard to say. "It might interest you to know that up here we are just as dead as you are." Dorothy and her husband, Alan Campbell, were among the hundreds of writers who were brought to Hollywood with the advent of the talkies. The lure of finding gold had brought the prospectors to California in the 1840's and it was the same golden opportunity that brought the writers from the East to the West Coast during the thirties and forties. In 1932, for instance, there were one hundred and fifty-five writers under contract at MGM, and almost as many at the other major studios, all churning out their allotment of so many pages a day.

I had met Miss Parker and her husband in New York several months before I left for Hollywood. There had been an item in a gossip column that they had visited a tattoo parlour, where something had been engraved on her anatomy. My job was to find out where.

I was aware of her sharp wit, usually at another's expense, and I was not prepared for her overwhelming graciousness when I arrived at the suite in the Lowell Hotel on East 63rd Street. John O'Hara was literally at her feet, glass in hand. Her husband was also there, in an armchair, and I was somewhat embarrassed asking my question. But she soon put me at my ease.

"I'm so sorry," she said, "but it was only on my arm" (we had hoped for a more erotic area), and she pulled up the sleeve of her dress to show me. The tattoo was blue but very small and I couldn't make out what it was. I've always been shortsighted and I did not like to peer too closely. Before I left, she begged me to visit her again but when I tried, several times, the message came down that she was not at home.

As a friend of "Mr." Benchley and the girlfriend of Scott Fitzgerald, she said she was delighted to see me again, although I did not know what she would say about me when we left the room. People sometimes stayed longer than they wanted to because they knew that she would murder them verbally as soon as they left.

Because my education in England was aborted at the age of fourteen, I was always very much in awe of famous writers. And after my arrival in Hollywood, when I heard that H. G. Wells was visiting Charlie Chaplin, I wanted to interview him for my column. "Don't bother," I was told; "writers don't count." I soon learned that even though they were paid thousands of dollars a week by the uncultured studio heads who hired them, they were treated as those chiefs wouldn't dare treat their servants. They were frequently ordered to rush to Hollywood and then kept waiting for weeks and sometimes months before the producer or executive who had wanted them so urgently found the time to see them.

Only the most important writers were allowed to work at home. Otherwise they had to report to the studio by nine-thirty in the morning—at Warners they actually had to clock in and out—and supposedly put in a full day's work, but there was a lot of visiting each other in their rooms. At MGM there was a little man whose chief job was to tiptoe down the corridor to hear which typewriters were clacking and which were not. There was also a certain amount of drinking, soft or hard. When Scott was on the wagon, he stocked up with several cases of Coca-Cola for thirst quenching and work stimulation. He was a night writer and found it hard to be creative in what was, for him, the dawn. He would have asked to work at home, but in the eighteen months of his contract at Metro he was so anxious to please and be part of the scene there that he dragged himself to the studio every day.

There is the classic story of William Faulkner, who worked mostly with the director Howard Hawks at Warners. But when he was at a different studio and was given permission to write at home, he went all the way back to Oxford, Mississippi.

Frances and Albert Hackett had been brought from New York by the producer Hunt Stromberg to write the "Thin Man" movies for William Powell and Myrna Loy. Their director was Woody "One Take" Van Dyke. They preferred to work at the studio, because if anything went wrong with the shooting on the set, the whole scene had to be rewritten, since Mr. Van Dyke was incapable of correcting the one mistake.

"We would get to the studio at nine-thirty every morning," the Vassar-educated Frances told me before her death last year in New York, "and as soon as we had something to show, we would take it to Stromberg. We were lucky that he liked us and we got on well with him. Unfortunately, Scott was not as lucky, and there was some friction between them."

After Scott's death I took them a verse he had written for them. We were about to have dinner at their home in Beverly Hills when he was called to the telephone. Stromberg. "He wants to see me right away," he told us and left. It was common practice for producers to send for their writers in the evening. In putting Scott's papers together I found this: "Stromberg sent for Poppa, Though Poppa hadn't et, To do what Jesus couldn't, Save Marie Antoinette."

I remember when Eddie Mayer's planned seduction of Hedy Lamarr was foiled because his producer sent for him on the evening he hoped to have her. I don't know whether Hedy was aware of this but she was looking on him favourably after receiving an impassioned ode from him. I was somewhat jealous. He had been in love with me before getting me together with Scott. I liked Eddie but was not in love with him. In fact Dorothy Parker had told people that I had treated him badly.

Poor Eddie. He was supporting a whole bunch of relatives. He told me one time that he had to earn $26,000 for them, before he could have money for himself. He was quite broke and very ill during his last years, and when he died in 1960 he was being looked after by one of the sisters he had supported. I was happy to see his name in the credits of the 1984 Mel Brooks version of *To Be or Not to Be*, as the author of the script for the original Ernst Lubitsch film (1942).

"Any messages?" was the first thing a writer would demand on arrival at the studio. The dreaded reply: "Yes, your producer wants to see you right away." It could mean dissatisfaction with what had been turned in the previous day, and a consequent energy-sapping long story conference.

Some of the producers fancied themselves good writers. During his years as a producer, Joe Mankiewicz rewrote a great deal of what his writers turned in. Joe happened to be a good writer, but that did not assuage the pain for the author who had been signed for the job.

The producer Walter Wanger had signed Willie K. Howard to write the script for Vincent Sheehan's *Personal History*. At the interminable story conferences, Wanger took the script apart, bit by bit. Finally the exasperated writer said, "If you want it to be *The Desert Song*, for God's sake call it *The Desert Song*." Wanger, as you may remember, had even more trouble with Scott Fitzgerald when he hired him to write the script of *Winter Carnival*. He not only fired him, but let all of Hollywood know the reason why—drinking on the job.

Writing for the movies could be fun and very rewarding financially ($5,000 a week for Donald Ogden Stewart) if you were not too sensitive to criticism or being rewritten by someone else. It was Irving Thalberg, the boy genius, who had started the policy of writers working in tandem, then another couple, riding piggy back, then another couple, all working towards the final script. The one, or the couple, whose writing survived the best received the vital screen credit. It was a discouraging process. Perhaps that's why they drank so much.

On my dates with John O'Hara, for instance, I never knew whether he would be sober. Usually not. I don't remember Marc Connelly ever being drunk, which perhaps is why he lived to be ninety years old, while Scott was dead at forty-four, O'Hara at sixty-five, Dashiell Hammett, who vied with Scott in the alcohol department, at sixty-six, Faulkner at sixty-five, and Robert Benchley, who in his later years had started drinking martinis well before lunch, at the age of fifty-six.

Writers such as Charlie MacArthur and Ben Hecht, who had written *The Front Page* for Broadway, were often called in (with a six-figure fee) to give the final polish to a script that could have been written by any number up to eight writers. It was assumed that it was Mr. Hecht who had written *Woman of the Year* when it was submitted anonymously to MGM in 1941. The agent had hinted strongly that it was the work of a famous writer, which is why they paid $100,000 for the original script. They would discover after the deal was signed that the writers were two then unknowns, Ring Lardner, Jr., and Michael Kanin. Garson Kanin has said that *he* actually wrote it but could not use his name for contractual reasons. *Woman of the Year* was the first film together, and meeting for, Katharine Hepburn and Spencer Tracy. They would make many more and have a close relationship until Tracy's death in 1967.

Playwrights, visiting or brought to Hollywood for a one-picture deal, were treated with respect. I was told of the fuss made over George Bernard Shaw when he visited William Randolph Hearst in the early thirties. And American playwrights such as Sidney Howard and Robert Sherwood were given the full treatment when they came for a one-time assignment. But if a playwright remained to become a contract writer, such as Eddie Mayer, he was treated with the same contempt as those who had been signed on the strength of one successful book. No wonder the writers huddled together in their closed society like sheep trying to keep out of the cold.

One way of keeping some self-respect was to make fun of the people who paid them. And why give of your best when most of your work, if not all, would be rewritten, or put on the shelf? There are hundreds and hundreds of scripts written by famous writers still gathering dust on the shelves of the major studios in Hollywood. Scott's script for *Babylon Revisited,* one of his best stories, has never been made. Neither has the script written by Ogden Nash and S. J. Perelman on Norman Vincent Peale's famous book *The Power of Positive Thinking* (I doubt whether Shakespeare could have done anything with that!) nor, even more recently, Joe Mankiewicz's script based on Dee Wells's best-selling novel *Jane.* "It was the best script I ever wrote," says Joe, 'but because of the costs piled against it, it was shelved."

To add to the problems of the writer, there was the ridiculous censorship imposed by the producers as a result of the nasty Fatty Arbuckle scandal, when Hollywood was castigated as a city of evil.

In my early years there the Hays Office took care of morals, in and out of films. There was a clause in every contract stating that the agreement could be cancelled if a performer made scandalous head-lines.

If a man and a woman were in bed in the same room, even in separate beds and even if they were married, they had to have one leg on the floor! A hand would grope into Lana Turner's cleavage, and insert a cover-up of lace. And I remember Scott's amusement when the Hays Office insisted on changing the title *Infidelity*, on which he was working, to *Fidelity*, which changed the whole idea. The star, Joan Crawford, added her own silliness, telling Scott to "write hard!"

I have deliberately not written too much here about Mr. Fitz-gerald because I have already written a great deal about him. But my time in Hollywood would be incomplete without more than a casual mention of him.

If you have read *Beloved Infidel* you know that we met in Robert Benchley's bungalow on the evening of 14 July 1937, to celebrate my engagement to the Marquess of Donegall. We did not speak then but were aware of each other. My only thought then was that he would have made an interesting paragraph for my column—the roaring twenties, the jazz age, and that sort of thing. It was only when Eddie Mayer brought us together a week later, and we danced at Ciro's, that we fell in love.

Those few years before he died in my home on 21 December 1940 would change my life. For a start he gave me a two-year course in the humanities—history, poetry, music, painting, politics; what I called my "College of One." He taught me Left from Right. Like some of the ignorant poor of England in my time there, I had been a staunch Conservative, for we expected them to take care of us, like the nobles in the Middle Ages and their serfs. Because of the books Scott had me read, I became such a liberal that later, at the height of the Joe McCarthy investigations and the House Un-American Activities Committee, I would be accused of being a Communist!

Scott and I rarely gossiped. In the evenings we discussed what I had studied that day. And if he sometimes dropped a studio tidbit, he would warn me sternly, "Don't you dare print that in your col-umn!" In the beginning, before he started drinking again, and in between bouts, we saw a lot of his writer friends. Not too much of Robert Benchley, who didn't like Scott for some long-past reason; but we had many dinners with Dorothy Parker, John O'Hara, the Nathanael Wests, the Hacketts, and Herman Mankiewicz, the brilliant writer brother of Joe.

I remember Margaret Sullavan dropping by with her three small blonde children, two girls in dainty dresses and a boy, at a cocktail party at the hillside Mankiewicz house. I am glad we could not foresee the future, when the attractive actress would end her life, and one of those little girls, Brooke, would write an unkind biography of her mother.

But mostly we would be dining at the homes of Scott's writer friends. After dinner there would always be a brain game of some sort, like character charades.

In the last two years of Scott's life, during the time he lived in Encino, and then at his apartment in Hollywood on the street next to mine, when he was freelancing and no longer under contract to any studio, he worked on *The Last Tycoon,* his unfinished novel. In the evenings he read to me what he had written that day. It promised to be his best book. What a pity the producer, Sam Spiegel, made such a mess of it in his film.

Chapter 8

The Tycoons

FOR THE THEATRE, the written words are the most important ingredient in the play, perhaps even more important than the actors who say them, or the directors who tell them how to say them. However, in films it is the director who is most important. He can take a bad script and improve it, or spoil a good script. But in my time in Hollywood even the director, with few exceptions, had to take orders from the boss, the Mr. Big who was responsible for all the product at the studio.

There were a few tycoons, such as Sam Goldwyn, who rarely interfered with the director. But even he would sometimes stray on to the set to see how his money was being spent—Goldwyn's press agent had put out the story that he used his own millions. The one time he visited the sound stage where Willie Wyler was shooting *Dodsworth* the director at once stopped the filming and waited patiently until Mr. Goldwyn left. Goldwyn never did that again—not to Mr. Wyler, who had been careful to insert as a condition into his contract that Mr. Goldwyn was not allowed on to his set.

Other tycoons were not as tactful. Darryl Zanuck at Twentieth Century–Fox kept a firm rein on every aspect of production. You never knew when he would appear on the set, in the café, or on a studio street. He worked closely with writers, directors, and casting. And with the young female extras. It would be hard to add up the number of his affairs. I think one of the few he missed among the beginners was Marilyn Monroe. In the first place he disliked her.

And in the second she was having an affair with his boss, Joe Schenck.

Darryl could be vicious. Celeste Holm, who won an Academy Award as Best Supporting Actress in *Gentleman's Agreement,* refused to remain at the same salary, since her option called for a raise. "He broke our contract and I left," Celeste told me. "Then he called the head of every other studio and said he had fired me because I was too difficult to work with."

Luckily, Joe Mankiewicz insisted on having Celeste for *All About Eve,* at three times the salary, or she would not have worked for a long time. She says that Darryl's revenge was to have her dressing room put in the alley outside the sound stage. The others were inside. Celeste and I agreed over a recent lunch that while he was always swinging his polo mallet, to strengthen his wrists, he said, it was also a menacing gesture to the person he was talking to.

Another unhappy actress, Alice Faye, who had been brought to Hollywood by Rudy Vallee, was often in collision with Mr. Zanuck, and would later accuse him of ruining her career. She would refer to the studio as "Penitentiary-Fox." "I had few friends there, only Tyrone Power and Annabella" (his then wife) "and Henry King," who directed Alice in several movies. Among them were *Alexander's Ragtime Band* and *In Old New York.*

I remember the big campaign when Mr. Zanuck brought Simone Simon to Hollywood from Paris—"Seemoan Seemoan," insisted the ads. He bought her a town house in New York City, which she later gave to her mother, who converted the house into apartments. I am now living in one of them. Zanuck also tried and failed to make an international star of Juliet Greco (with whom he had perhaps his stormiest love affair), and Bella Darvi, whom he paid off with a large sum of money which she lost gambling in European casinos. Also Genevieve Gilles, the young actress he teamed with Michael Crawford in a dreadful film, *Hello, Goodbye.* Amazing that this experienced producer would consistently foist such untalented women on to the public. All this, with the cost of *Cleopatra,* contributed to his downfall.

When there were rumours of a divorce from his long-suffering wife, Virginia (a former Mack Sennett bathing beauty), my editor at the *New York Daily Mirror* asked me to check the story. "Before I leave my wife," he assured me, "they will have to carry me out feet first." A prophetic statement. They were reconciled and Virginia was at his bedside when he died in 1967.

Louis B. Mayer was even more of a womanizer than Zanuck. Or should I say, starlet-izer. He had that infamous automatic lock on the door of his office: the spider trapping the unsuspecting fly. Gertrude Astor, a young actress of the early days, blonde, beautiful, was more than a match for him. At his first advance she lisped, "Oh, my mother says I shouldn't." The same plea for his second, third, and fourth, always eluding his grasp.

As Gertrude told it, the frustrated tycoon finally screamed, "Fuck your mother!" and dragged her down on the couch. Using all her strength, she pushed him away and he fell to the carpet. "Okay," he said, rising and dusting himself off, "you're fired!" You will never guess who L.B. signed to replace Miss Astor—the young starlet Hedda Hopper, who proceeded to become such a stern guardian of Hollywood morals.

While Mr. Mayer rarely interfered with the film production, this man, who was once described as "crude, inarticulate, and profane," was vitally interested in everything that concerned his people, their politics, their lovers, whom they should or should not romance, how they walked, their habits, their life styles, and even the colour of their hair. He was a rabid Republican, and made political shorts to be shown in the Loew's theatres. He advised the audiences to vote for whoever was running for President on the Republican ticket, starting in the late twenties with Herbert Hoover, who appointed him treasurer of the Republican Party in California.

He could be as vicious as some of the other tycoons. The famous story goes that he ruined the career of John Gilbert, romantic idol of the silent screen—and all because of a fist-fight in the men's room. John said to Mr. Mayer, "I want to marry Garbo." Mayer replied, "Make her your mistress—sleep with her, don't marry her." John knocked him down and Mayer swore to ruin him. They say that Mayer tinkered with the sound recording, distorting the superstar's voice in his first starring talkie, ironically called *Redemption*. Whatever the reason, Gilbert was dropped from MGM. He took to drink and died at forty-one.

Mr. Mayer did not believe in his contract ladies having affairs with married men, himself excepted, of course. When he brought Natalie Schafer, a well-known stage actress, from New York to play Lana Turner's mother in a film, he wanted her to sign a seven-year contract. She told him, "I'm not going to start a movie career by playing Lana Turner's mother. Next I'll be playing Clifton Webb's mother" (he was in his fifties). And she returned to New York. A few months later he brought her back to Hollywood to play Lana's best friend, a girl who went to school with her.

"Now will you sign a seven-year contract?" he asked, adding, "You could have a big career in Hollywood, because there are no ladies here and you are a lady." To which she replied, "I can't sign, Mr. Mayer." "Why not?" "Because I'm in love." "What has that got to do with it?" "Well, he lives in New York." "We'll bring him out here." "I don't think it's possible." "Why not?" "I don't think his wife will let him." "What, a married man! And I thought you were a lady! Get out of my office!" Incidentally, the married man was the playwright George Kaufman, that busy lover. "Was he that good?" I once asked her. "He was wonderful, and I was very much in love with him."

MGM's first *Ben Hur,* starring Ramon Novarro, in many ways resembled the chaos and extravagance of the 1961 *Cleopatra.* After months of filming in Italy, Mr. Mayer brought the production to Hollywood under the supervision of Irving Thalberg, who suffered his first heart attack while watching the famous chariot race.

As I have mentioned, it did not matter where the locale was supposed to be: most of the movies were shot around Los Angeles —"A tree is a tree, shoot it in Griffith Park." When Thalberg put an ocean in the background of his film *Paris,* a brave employee told him that Paris was far from any ocean. To which he replied angrily that he would not cater to the few people who knew where Paris was! Nonetheless, the ocean was left on the cutting room floor.

At Warner Brothers, the Hollywood studio was ruled by the younger brother, Jack. He sometimes did this by telephone at ten A.M., sitting on the toilet in his bathroom at home. After a batch of orders, he would dress leisurely and be driven to the studio at noon, where he would have lunch in his private dining room with his top producers and directors. He was a great punster and he loved to make speeches, heavily laced with doubtful jokes, dutifully appreciated by the slaves.

To call Mr. Warner a tyrant is understatement. A star had only to whisper, "I don't want to make the picture," for him or her to be put on suspension without pay. Even Jimmy Cagney and Gary Cooper were threatened. Jimmy's brother was his manager and it was he who informed the Boss that *Yankee Doodle Dandy* was not to Jimmy's liking. The film had already been started, with costs accumulating, and there is nothing like a lawsuit to bring an actor to work.

When Gary Cooper refused *Sergeant York,* for which Sam Goldwyn had loaned him to Warners, he took off for New York. But everywhere he went there was a man from Warners carrying a legal document. As you know, Jimmy and Gary each won an Oscar for the film they didn't want to make.

Greer Garson, incidentally, was hysterical when asked to play the mother in *Mrs. Miniver.* "I'm too young for it," she stormed. She and Mr. Mayer were both on their knees, yelling at each other, "You will," "I won't," "You will," "I won't," "You *will!*" And she too won the Oscar. She also won the young man, Richard Ney, who had played her son. Not long after their divorce he retired as an actor and became a successful stockbroker. His books on the subject are bestsellers.

I remember how disappointed Julie Andrews was when Jack Warner insisted that Audrey Hepburn should star in the film version of *My Fair Lady.* Julie had made a huge hit on Broadway in the musical and it was assumed that she would repeat her role in the film. Warners had paid $5,500,000 for the film rights, the highest price at that time paid for any property. Audrey was chosen because she was an established film star. Julie would not make her debut in films until *Mary Poppins* in 1964. Julie would have made a better Liza Doolittle. In addition to which she could have done her own singing; Marni Nixon sang for Audrey.

When Audrey was starring at Warners in *Wait Until Dark,* the British director Terence Young stopped filming every afternoon at four-thirty for the cast and crew to have tea. Recently, when I was dining with Mr. Young at his posh Belgravia flat, he told me of the telegram he received from Mr. Warner:

"I understand you stop work at four-thirty every day and you all have a cup of tea. This must stop immediately." Terence telegrammed back: "I am nine days ahead of schedule, aided and helped by our break for tea at four-thirty." On receipt of which, said Terence, "Mr. Warner charged on to the set and bellowed, 'Where's the fucking tea?' And had a cuppa."

On the last day of shooting, at four-thirty, Jack ordered tea for everyone, but instead of the familiar brew, the cups were filled with whiskey or gin. Even a movie mogul can have a sense of humour.

And even a tyrant tycoon could sometimes be manipulated. Mr. Warner had a firm rule: independent press agents were not allowed into the studio. One day, while Joan Crawford was making a film there, she called Jack and told him, "I'm taking three hours off for lunch." "What do you mean?" he said. "Well, as you don't allow my publicist on the lot, I'm going to Beverly Hills" (a long ride from Burbank) "to have lunch with him." Presto, Henry Rogers was allowed on the lot.

His partner, Warren Cowan, gave me the sequel: "One night I called my exchange and there was a message from Jack Warner. I thought it was a gag, but I called the number to see which of my friends was having me on. His secretary said, 'Wait a minute, Mr. Warner wants to speak to you.' 'Cowan,' he said, 'As you may know, I've sold the studio; I'm going into independent production and I want to hire you. I understand your office has all the clout in this town.' He paid us a lot of money. The only bad part was that we had to listen to his awful jokes."

The price Warner received for the studio was $34 million. Jules Stein, the brilliant head of MCA, told him, "You could have had $40 to $50 million if you had played your cards right." Warner lived for another eleven years and it wasn't satisfying enough to make a film now and then. He missed his lovely studio and the power that went with it. He was a sad and lonely old man with no one to bully at ten in the morning from the seat of his toilet. All the fun was gone.

Jack was still playing tennis at eighty-two, but one day on the court he suffered a stroke. He hung on for another four years, but it was a living death for the man who had been so powerful and active. At the beginning he could talk and recognize people, but he was more or less a vegetable in the last three years. He had really started dying when he sold his studio. He had nothing to live for. He had wanted to disinherit his only son but left him $100,000, provided he did not sue for more. He never forgave the boy for siding with his own mother against Ann, Jack's second wife.

Robert Benchley once described the Columbia lot as "The Pine Tree Studio"—"because it has so many Cohns." Ouch. It was true. At one time there were twenty-nine Cohns and assorted relatives on the corporation payroll. Harry Cohn, the Boss, was the most foul-mouthed of all the tycoons. It was the only way he could talk. In fact Glenn Ford tried, unsuccessfully, to break his contract at Columbia because, he said, he could not stand the language of his boss any longer. He was the most hated of all the tycoons, especially by the writers who needed the work. He had a system for reducing a new writer to jelly. After a few weeks on a script he would call the writer in, and tell him that it was the worst piece of shit he had ever read. If the writer apologized he didn't last long. Like all bullies, he respected only those who stood up to him.

As with most of the tycoons of old, Cohn had a huge appetite for sex. There was a secret passageway from his office to a certain dressing room that was occupied by a succession of actresses. When Bette Davis was the occupant, Cohn once came charging in—then he ran for his life.

He was ruthless, vulgar, and his ethics were of the dirty street fighter of his childhood in the Lower East Side of New York. After he died in 1958, a wag explained why so many people had come to the funeral. "It was to make sure that he was really dead." It would have made him laugh. He enjoyed being hated and feared. "I don't get ulcers," he boasted. "I give them." His employees were afraid to talk about him even in his absence. It was known that he had a microphone on the set hooked up to his office, and by pressing a button he could listen to the conversation, not always complimentary, about him.

Mr. Cohn was shrewd enough to hire good people. Columbia had been a minor studio until he brought in Frank Capra, one of the best directors in Hollywood. He tried to use him to bargain with Louis B. Mayer, Capra in exchange for Robert Montgomery for *It Happened One Night*. Robert refused. Nothing, he said, could induce him to work for that loud-mouthed vulgarian. A similar turndown came from Myrna Loy.

Surprisingly, Clark Gable said, "Yes" (but only after Mayer insisted), although grumbling at having to work at a second-rate studio. But Claudette Colbert agreed at once, wanting the chance to work with Mr. Capra. The film was a critical and financial success and yielded an Oscar apiece for the two stars.

There were only two really good restaurants in the studios, at Warners and at Mr. Cohn's Columbia. I remember interviewing Jennifer Jones in the latter and exchanging a few words with the Boss. That's all I ever did with him. I was too inhibited by his reputation to risk more than that. But the food was good. He hoped it would lure people from the nearby Hollywood Brown Derby. He had been insulted there, he said, which was why he built his own lunch place.

Bob Thomas, the AP correspondent in Hollywood, wrote a fine biography of Mr. Cohn. In it he mentions Cohn holding forth at lunch about how he always knew when he had a good movie. Even when he was alone in his private projection room, he said he had a foolproof device for judging whether a picture was good or bad. "If my fanny squirms, it's bad. If it doesn't, it's good. It's as simple as that." There was a short silence, then Herman Mankiewicz jeered, "Imagine, the whole world wired to Harry Cohn's ass!" He was fired there and then.

A feature of the dining room was an electrified chair that Mr. Cohn could activate by pressing a button at his foot. It was always reserved for a newcomer. But during one lunch Mr. Capra entered and sat on the chair by mistake. And when his employer pressed the button—he had been deep in conversation with his neighbour—the infuriated director picked up the chair and smashed it. Mr. Cohn had another one built.

Isn't it strange that a man like Harry Cohn, with little education and all the rough edges you can think of, had such a sure instinct for choosing films that the public would like, and finding people, diamonds in the rough, who would become superstars, such as Rita Hayworth and Glenn Ford. And that his once puny studio could produce winners like *The Jolson Story, The Caine Mutiny, On the Waterfront, The Bridge on the River Kwai,* and after his death, *Lawrence of Arabia* and *Doctor Strangelove.*

And for all the crudeness of some of the other bosses, they protected their stars, nursed them through failures, and carried them forward with a success. When Bette Davis was in a hit, Jack Warner sent word to his whole organization, "Get another story for Bette Davis." When Gable made a hit in *It Happened One Night,* Mayer sent word, "Get a good story for Gable." So while the stars often complained about slavery with their long contracts, they were also protected and promoted.

THE LAST TYCOON
(With apologies to FSF)

In my early years, Universal was a B studio that would not become important until Lew Wasserman's MCA Agency swallowed it in 1962. But RKO, a major studio in the thirties and forties (then called RKO–Radio Pictures), actually declined in importance soon after it was bought by Howard Hughes in 1948. Mr. Wasserman was to bring a new concept to making deals with the superstars. The deal with Jimmy Stewart for *Winchester 73,* for instance. Jimmy would do it for nothing, and instead receive ten percent of the gross; that's ten percent of the first dollar taken at the box office. This changed the entire way of making deals in Hollywood. Mr. Stewart came away with millions; others have not been as lucky. But until then, no one, not Gable, not Garbo, not Cooper, had received a percentage of their films. Just a salary, diminished by spiralling income tax.

Mr. Hughes also changed the method of making film deals in Hollywood, stretching the payments for as long as twenty years, at the rate of $50,000 a year for Jane Russell. She received this payment long after completing *The Outlaw,* one of her few films for Mr. Hughes—she was mostly loaned to various studios. *The Outlaw* was first shown in 1941, then taken back and not officially released until 1950, after nine years of changes and more changes. Actually, Jane's contract cost her employer very little. He received much more than he paid her from the other companies.

Howard's first contact with Hollywood started in 1926, when he was twenty years old. Two years before, at the age of eighteen, he had inherited on the death of his father the prosperous Hughes Tool Company in Houston, Texas. He invested some of his millions in silent films, *Two Arabian Knights, The Mating Call,* and *The Racket.* When talkies came in, he redid from scratch *Hell's Angels,* which had starred Greta Nissen in the almost-completed silent film. The sound version made a star of Jean Harlow, and established Howard as a respected tycoon.

He was the one I grew to know best in Hollywood. As with Mr. Mayer, I had met him before I went there. He was twenty-nine years old when I was introduced to him in 1935 at a cocktail party on Park Avenue in New York. The liquor was flowing and with glass in hand, I found myself next to a tall, slender young man who turned to me and said, "My name is Hughes, *Howard* Hughes." His clipped, dark brown hair was well groomed. His clothes bore the stamp of a good tailor. His expensive brown leather shoes reflected the glass in his hand. His nails were short and clean.

We made polite conversation. How long had I been in New York? Did I like it? But his mind was obviously elsewhere. He was looking past me at the pretty models in the elegant living room of our bachelor host. In every city I have visited or lived in, there has always been a man about town who knows all the pretty models and the rich men who want to meet them. The party was packed with samples of both.

Striving for his attention, I asked him about his film activities in Hollywood, and said, "I'll be going there soon, and I'd like to write about you and your movies." "Ah," he said, looking at me closely for the first time, "when you go to Hollywood, write about my work, not about me." He left me abruptly for one of the models, who was giving him the come-hither sign.

In Hollywood I did not contact Mr. Hughes for some time, and then only because I had missed a car ride to Palm Springs and I knew that most weekends he piloted his own plane there. At the cocktail party in New York I had been aware that I was not his type. But I was not prepared for his crisp brush-off. "Sorry, I never take women in my plane." He was not only flying his girls all over the place but he was teaching some of them to fly!

He was good copy for my column. His fights with what was now the Johnston Office, over Jane Russell's décolletage, her suggestive positions on the bales of hay, in fact everything to do with *The Outlaw,* was a running story for years. To get his own way, he finally left the Producers' Association.

I also wrote about his girls. He had a good line with them. While not overly generous, he would shower them with flowers and small trinkets; each girl—Yvonne de Carlo, Terry Moore, Mitzi Gaynor, Janet Leigh, etc.—would assure me, "Howard wants to marry me, but he says we must wait to be sure." I could see that the girls were sure. Especially Terry, who recently claimed she had married Howard on a boat and repeated the marriage vows on top of a Hollywood hill. Rather than hold up the millions by an investigation, Hughes' relatives paid off Terry with an undisclosed sum. At one time Howard also drove Joan Fontaine to the top of Laurel Canyon and said, "I, Howard, take thee, Joan, to be my wife in the sight of God." She still laughs about that.

It really wasn't my business, but I took him to task in my column and on my Sunday radio show, which I knew he always listened to. One time a friend of his called me at the station and said, "Howard and I have a bet. He says you're English, I say Boston." Of course Howard knew I was English. He never bet on anything unless he was sure.

Another call to the radio station was not as friendly. It was from Howard's lawyer. I had a feature on my programme: "What are the stars really like," I would ask sweetly, "with their make-up off and their hair down?" When the show was too long, something had to be snipped. Usually the good bits, which were not as interesting as the bad bits. At the end of the feature I announced who would be analyzed next week. When the name was Howard Hughes he rushed into legal action.

A switch in content was necessary. "But I'm going to say only the nicest things about him," I protested to the station lawyer. Really! And without being saccharine, I did. I talked about his flying achievements, his record flight around the top of the world, the two hundred and fifty hours he had spent learning to be a commercial flyer to prepare him for when he bought Trans World Airlines.

But the column was something else. As long as I printed the truth there was no censorship. I confirmed a story that he brought a girl from Europe on a pretext of a film contract, then kept her locked up in a house with iron bars on all the windows to prevent her from getting out.

I received a call from Johnny Meyers, an ex–Warner Brothers press agent whose job now was to take care of Mr. Hughes with the media. Years later he would be doing the same for Aristotle Onassis and Jackie Kennedy. I agreed to have a drink with Johnny in the Polo Lounge of the Beverly Hills Hotel. After some casual chatter, he came to the point. "Howard is upset." "Really, why?" "He doesn't like what you are writing about the girls. You can have anything you like, but lay off the girls."

I did not let him see that I was insulted. How dared he try to buy me off! I soon had good fodder for the column. Howard's passion for Elizabeth Taylor was an open secret in Hollywood. I had known and liked Elizabeth ever since she had arrived in Hollywood just after the start of World War Two. When she was twelve she had presented me with the book she had written about her pet chipmunk, *Nibbles and Me.* At the age of fifteen she was the most beautiful girl in the world. I can still see the visiting Orson Welles, fork suspended in air, as, wearing a tight red sweater and a black brief circular skirt, she entered the MGM commissary. And now Howard had flown the teenage Elizabeth and her mother to Lake Tahoe for the weekend. Clever of him to try to get the mother on his side. In vain, however. To Elizabeth he was an old man, the same age as her father.

A message arrived from the Hughes office. Mr. Hughes wants to see Miss Graham in his office at three o'clock on Tuesday afternoon. I was a bit nervous but decided to go. It was my first meeting with him since the party in New York. He was somewhat less well dressed, the suit more casual, sneakers instead of leather shoes, and his nails were not quite as well manicured.

I was surprised that all the window shades were down. Later I would learn that the windows in his Las Vegas hotel suites were covered with blankets because he believed that sunlight brought the dreaded germs. But something else had changed: his hearing, the hereditary deafness that would alter his personality. He watched my lips closely as we sat down, facing each other, knee to knee.

"Well," he said jovially, "you have done well for yourself since we last met." Unprepared for this, I gulped, "So have you!" Then he said, throwing me completely off-balance, "Why do you hate me?" What, me hate Howard Hughes, the multi-millionaire, the owner of a movie studio, the powerful business man with interests in oil, machine tools, commercial airplanes? It would be professional suicide to hate him. "I don't hate you," I said weakly, "I'm just trying to do an accurate, interesting column and radio show."

"I'll make a deal with you," he said, getting up and walking a few paces, then sitting down again. "If you stay away from the girls —all that stuff hurts me in my business—I will be available to you, day and night when you have a question you think I can answer. Also," and he smiled, "I can give you some scoops for your column and radio show."

"But what if you were to marry one of those girls?" I asked. "It would be a front page story. I would have to write about it." Howard put his hand on his heart. "I promise you will be the first to know." "Okay," I said. "It's a deal." We shook hands on it and he escorted me to my car.

For Mr. Hughes to be available to me was a tremendous coup for my column. Not even his contract players could reach him at this time. When Robert Mitchum was arrested on drug charges, even he could not get through to the boss who supported him financially, but from a distance. Whereas I could pick up the phone, ask for his man, Bill Gaye, and say, "I want to speak to Howard." Bill always asked, "Are you alone?" And whether I was or not, I always answered, "Yes." A few minutes later, Howard would say, "Hi, Sheilah, how can I help you?" He had an amplifier on the phone and with it could hear quite well.

But it wasn't always I who initiated the calls. Sometimes it was Howard with a scoop that made the front page of my hundred and sixty-five newspapers. Louella was furious when I had the scoop of the elopement of Cary Grant and Betsy Drake. Howard had flown them to the secret ceremony in his plane.

Another scoop Howard gave me by accident, and accident is the key word. Two seconds before my Sunday evening radio show, a news flash came in: Howard Hughes had crashed his plane in Beverly Hills! His injuries included a lacerated skull, a crushed chest, and nine broken ribs. I was the first to put it on the air. Doctor Verne Mason, the best physician in Los Angeles, saved his life. The grateful tycoon took Doctor Mason from us and put him in charge of his new Medical Research Center in Florida.

Howard's deafness was increasing. He was becoming more reclusive. He was wearing gloves, indoors and out, afraid of picking up other people's germs. He was no longer visible, although his latest girl, Jean Peters, was seeing him privately. He was not sure about marriage with her until, after waiting vainly for his proposal, she married his best friend, Stuart Cramer III. Now, for the first time since his first marriage in his early twenties, Mr. Hughes was sure. He married Jean after her quickie divorce. And he gave the story to Louella Parsons, on condition that she use it in her column instead of on the front page where it belonged and where he knew I would have put it.

The last time I saw Mr. Hughes was outside the Ritz Carlton Hotel in Boston. He was on a stretcher being carried to the waiting ambulance. Not many years after, one of the richest men in the world would die of malnutrition in the plane carrying him to a hospital in Houston, Texas, a desperate flight to return to the city where he was born.

They seem to have given up searching for his will. But I am sure it will surface one day from where it was hidden by the suspicious billionaire. It was unlike him to leave his vast fortune without directions for its disposal.

One day I remember I had been waiting to see Russell Birdwell when Howard drove up in his old battered car. He was there to discuss the premiere of *The Outlaw*. He repeated his instructions over and over. I noticed that he kept scratching his face with his nails. The sun in Russell's office was irritating his skin. But the point I'm making is that a man who went into every minute detail of his business was surely the kind of person to make a will.

* * *

Note: I was sure all along that Clifford Irving's "authorized biography" of Mr. Hughes was a fake. Because in it Howard is quoted at length talking about all his girls. I knew from experience that he never did. And what a fool Irving was to believe that the book would pass unnoticed by the man most concerned. Howard would have fought God for what he believed were his rights.

CHAPTER 9

THE WAR YEARS

IN THE BEGINNING, the war in Europe made no difference to what was going on in Hollywood. For more than a year before Hitler's *blitzkrieg* into Poland, we had listened on our big radio to his screaming exhortations to the German people, and the booming "Heil Hitler" that followed. He was obviously mad. We never expected he would plunge us all into World War Two, especially after Neville Chamberlain's "peace in our time" visit to Munich in 1938.

At the time Errol Flynn was playing a dashing Earl of Essex at Warners, to Bette Davis' Queen Elizabeth; the thirty-five-year-old Cary Grant was concluding at RKO his British officer role in *Gunga Din* with Douglas Fairbanks, Jr.; Richard Greene, aged twenty-one, was completing *Here I Am a Stranger* at Twentieth Century–Fox; Anna Neagle and George Sanders were being praised for their performances in *Nurse Edith Cavell,* about the executed heroine of World War One. Anna and I had been "Cochran Young Ladies" together at the London Pavilion in 1928, and when she came to Hollywood in the late thirties we often lunched at Romanoff's with her husband, Herbert Wilcox.

Seventy-six-year-old C. Aubrey Smith was playing a Russian aristocrat in *Balalaika* at MGM with Nelson Eddy; David Niven, aged thirty, had three more weeks in *Raffles,* his first starring role for Sam Goldwyn; forty-seven-year-old Basil Rathbone was tracking his enemy, Professor Moriarty, in *The Adventures of Sherlock Holmes,* with Nigel Bruce his forty-four-year-old Doctor Watson. And Laurence

107

Olivier, then aged thirty-two, was being acclaimed for his Healthcliff in *Wuthering Heights.*

Of all the leading British actors in Hollywood, only three returned to England—David Niven, Laurence Olivier, and Richard Greene, although the last, after dilly-dallying, was more or less pushed into returning by some of the others who were staying behind.

With Britain at war with Germany in September 1939, Niven, who had served with the Highland Light Infantry, begged Mr. Goldwyn to allow him to return there at once. "Oh no, you must finish the movie first," he was told sternly. "Then please rush me through my scenes," he pleaded. To make sure of leaving, he had a friend in England—the famous Trubshawe, whose name was used in every Niven film—send him a cable ordering him to return to his regiment. This hurried things up and he was off before the final wrapup. On arrival in England he joined the British Army as a commando. I learned most of this from Scott Fitzgerald, who was employed on the set to change some of the *Raffles* dialogue.

The older Britishers in Hollywood were anxious to help the homeland. They were active in the Bundles for Britain project and contributed to all the British causes. Cary Grant, who had lived on and off in the United States since 1920, and seemed more American than British, donated $300,000, his price then for one film. He had taken out American citizenship papers in 1937. The final papers came through in 1942.

After the war, Mr. Greene returned to Hollywood to finish his contract at Fox. He had married the British actress Patricia Medina in 1941—they were divorced in 1952. Eight years later she became Mrs. Joseph Cotten, and still is. I see both of them now and then, and it's a good marriage. Richard did not become an important actor until he starred on British television in the *Robin Hood* series. It was as popular in America as in England.

In 1938, Scott had advised me to become an American citizen. "You are doing well here," he had said, "and you never know, England and America might one day be at war, and I would lose you." So I had taken out my first papers, naming him as my sponsor. But after his death all I wanted to do was to go back to England. My boss, John Wheeler, said, "You mustn't go, you could get killed." That did not seem to matter much then. He compromised: "You can go providing you get an exit permit. As you are still a British citizen you might not be able to come back."

I cabled Lord Beaverbrook asking for help: "My only object in coming to England at this time is to serve our country," adding as an after-thought: "and my newspaper syndicate, of course." It took six months, but I received the exit visa.

Before leaving New York I spent several days with Edmund Wilson and his wife, Mary McCarthy, at their home in Wellfleet, Massachusetts. The Scribners publishing house had asked him to put together Scott's unfinished novel, *The Last Tycoon*. I told him everything I knew of what Scott was going to cut, and how he had planned to finish the book.

Within days of Scott's death I had sent the unfinished manuscript to Max Perkins, his editor at Scribners, with a letter explaining all the changes Scott had planned. "He worked so hard and so hopefully on the book and if it could be published his dying would not be so awful and so sad." The letter might have had something to do with the decision to publish it.

Travelling to Europe in wartime was not easy. I had wanted to fly over on a bomber: it would have made a good story. Lord Beaverbrook told me later why that was not possible. "There was only one toilet—a bucket—for the men." Pan-American's seaplane would drop me off in Lisbon. From there a British plane would take me to England.

My first assignment for NANA in England was to interview George Bernard Shaw on the occasion of his eighty-fifth birthday. I've always been a lucky reporter, and I was delighted to find that Gabriel Pascal, who had the film rights to all of his plays, was also on the plane. I asked the stewardess to introduce us, and he came over and sat in the vacant seat next to me. He promised to help me see Mr. Shaw, then slept on my shoulder most of the way over.

The plane for England was not leaving until the next evening, and Mr. Pascal invited me to accompany him to the casino at the nearby resort of Estoril. The place was crawling with spies, German, British, Italian, French, Russian. While I was playing roulette, a man I had been told was the chief Italian spy approached me and said that before the war he had worked as an extra in Hollywood films! He had seen me on the sets. Before driving back to Lisbon, my escort tried to put his hand up my dress. I decided I would get to Mr. Shaw without his assistance.

Pascal was probably remaining in Lisbon, as I did not see him at the secret rendezvous to board the seaplane for England. It was cloak-and-dagger stuff. I had been warned by the British consul to tell no one of the plans for leaving, not the place, not the time. German spies were always on the lookout. Two years later they shot down the plane in which Leslie Howard was flying, believing Winston Churchill was a passenger. I would be flying with a contingent of British servicemen from the war in North Africa, some of whom were wounded, all of them exhausted.

The windows of the plane had been covered with black cloth. Warned in a whisper to make no sounds, we boarded in complete darkness. Packed tightly together in the flying boat, and quietly chugging towards the open ocean, we took off for England. For the first time I realized that there was a war on.

Ensconced at the International Sportsmen's Club in Upper Grosvenor Street, I telephoned the Shaw residence in Hertfordshire. It was answered by Miss Patch, Mr. Shaw's secretary. "When can I see him?" "Oh no. Mr. Shaw does not see reporters. But if you will post your questions to him, I am sure he will answer them." I never take chances with important letters. I delivered them to Miss Patch in person.

Several days later, Miss Patch telephoned. "Mr. Shaw has answered your questions. I will put them in the post this afternoon." "No, I will come and get them." Again I rented a car and drove to the Shaw home. Miss Patch and I were making polite conversation when the Great Man entered the room. He apologized for not seeing me when I had come before. I was not prepared for him and could only stutter that it was perfectly alright. He sat down and waited for further questions.

I was so intimidated by the man, with his piercing blue eyes, shaggy white hair and beard, rampant white eyebrows, and translu-

cent pink skin, that I could only think of the questions he had
already answered. "No, no," he said irritably. "Don't change them.
You'll only spoil them."

He took pity on me. "Let me show you my garden and where
I grow my vegetables." I was more relaxed as he pointed out the
carrots, celery, and tomatoes that comprised his vegetarian diet. But
I was relieved when it was over and I was driving back to London
with the questions and answers safely in my briefcase.

They seem quaintly old-fashioned now, mostly about what
would happen to the class system after the war. He did not think
there would be any change—"The daughter of a duke can seek a
husband at a ball given by a millionaire shopkeeper, and her brother
can seek a rich wife there." I had asked what he thought should be
done with Hitler after we had won the war. "The Germans may have
settled that before the defeat is consummated."

One of my questions was how long he thought it would be
before England and Russia were *actually* friendly with each other.
His answer: "I suppose you mean how long it will be before the
capitalist newspapers stop lying about Russia. I don't know. There
is no other obstacle to reciprocal kindness."

For me, trying to forget Scott Fitzgerald, it was a wonderful
summer. I had some good interviews. One with Margot Asquith,
now Lady Oxford and Asquith. The Asquiths had been living at
10 Downing Street when I as a child had been living in an orphanage. It gave me some satisfaction to pay for the lunch at
the Savoy.

I interviewed Lady Astor at her house in St. James's Square. I
did a broadcast to NBC in New York from the BBC basement in
Cavendish Square. I wrote stories about women working in war
factories all over England and Scotland, and after watching the
bombing from the roof of the Dorchester Hotel with Lord Donegall,
I also had an air raid to write about.

Quentin Reynolds, like most of the American reporters in London, including Eddie Gilmore for United Press and George Lait for
the International News Service, was trying to get to the Russian
front. I wanted to join them and was about to get my visa when Mr.
Wheeler ordered me back to America. The Duke and Duchess of
Windsor were planning their first visit to Washington since their

marriage and he wanted me to attend their press conference in early October. I was sorry to leave London.

Mr. Wheeler agreed that I would now work for NANA from New York, where my base was the Shoreham Hotel on West 55th Street and from where I was sent on assignments all over the country. By the time I returned to Hollywood in late October 1942, I was carrying some extra luggage, my baby daughter, Wendy Westbrook.

I had met her father, Trevor Cresswell Lawrence Westbrook, during my six weeks in London at a cocktail party at Claridges given by Rear Admiral John Bergen, then in charge of Grumman Aircraft. Trevor was Lord Beaverbrook's right-hand man during his time at the Air Ministry. It was close to the first anniversary of Scott's death, and to obliterate the anguish I married Trevor.

Six weeks after Wendy was born, I was on the plane to California with her and with Miss Haines, the nanny, a tough old lady. "Just for the winter," I cabled Trevor. It was impossible for him to get money out of England so I took my column back and remained there for a year.

Then, as now, it was a different Hollywood to which I returned. For the first time in American history, I believe, there was rationing. Not as much as in England, however, but because gasoline was rationed you could buy a house at the beach in Malibu for a few thousand dollars. Eggs, butter, bacon, and meats were in short supply, as were paper products. But the sun was shining and smog was still an eye irritant of the future.

During the few days it took me to find a house—on South Palm Drive in Beverly Hills—the three of us stayed at the Garden of Allah. All the writers I had known were still in Hollywood, with some impressive additions from Europe, including Thomas Mann, Christopher Isherwood, and Aldous Huxley. Igor Stravinsky had managed to get out of Europe. Also Franz Werfel and his wife, Alma, the widow of Mahler. Errol Flynn, between marriages, was staying in the bungalow next to ours, which caused Miss Haines some apprehension. I didn't know whether it was for herself or the baby!

Some of the important stars were missing. Clark Gable, shattered by the death of his wife, Carole Lombard, in a plane crash, was among the first to join up. He was sent to the Air Force Training Camp at Pensacola, Florida. He would emerge as a flight officer and later chalk up many daylight missions over Germany.

When a Hollywood star went into the service during World War Two, many of the enlisted men would be laying for them, to show they were not impressed, that "We are all equal now." I heard Clark's flying instructor had said, "I'd like to say he's an egotistical bastard, but I can't. He's marvellous."

Jimmy Stewart had joined the infantry as a GI. "The only thing I minded," he told me after the war, "was having to sleep in a roomful of men." His discomfort did not last long. He was soon promoted and he finished the war with the rank of brigadier general.

William Holden, Glenn Ford, Van Heflin, Robert Stack, and Dan Dailey were among many young actors who had volunteered for war service. As they had only recently started their careers in Hollywood, they were not sure if they would have a job when they returned. Fortunately their contracts were merely postponed.

Freddie Bartholomew, now all of eighteen years old, was in the U.S. Air Corps. Victor Mature was in the Coast Guard. He had been having a romance with Rita Hayworth and she had tried to join up with him! Captain Ronald Reagan was in the Army making propaganda films at the Hal Roach Studio in nearby Culver City. Douglas Fairbanks, Jr., and Robert Montgomery were in the U.S. Navy, and later Robert would be driving an ambulance in France, while some leading directors—John Ford, George Stevens, Frank Capra, Willie Wyler, and several others—were either making propaganda films for the government or filming the actual fighting.

There were some new faces in Hollywood, among them Van Johnson, Robert Mitchum, and Ava Gardner. Van was winning *The War Against Mrs. Hadley.* Mitchum was playing the heavy in some *Hopalong Cassidy* Westerns. As for Ava, the barefoot beauty winner from North Carolina, she had just married, at the age of twenty, the smallest, but one of the biggest stars in Hollywood, Mickey Rooney, who was two years older. At the time I thought she had married him to advance her career. She was a Miss Nobody then. But I have come to know her better and have learned that, like several other young actresses in Hollywood who would be fascinated by Mickey—Elizabeth Taylor and Judy Garland, to name two—Ava was in love with him. I had a dream about him soon after I arrived in Hollywood and I remember I woke up saying, "Oh Mickey, I could teach you so much!"

Arrivals from England, in addition to Elizabeth Taylor and her family, included Angela Lansbury, whose grandfather, George Lansbury, was a powerful Labour leader. With *Gaslight,* her first film in Hollywood, she received an Oscar nomination for Best Supporting Actress. I can still hear her singing that song with the dreadful line, "I'm just a bird in a gilded cage!" Roddy McDowall was only thirteen when he landed *his* first Hollywood role in Fritz Lang's *Man Hunt* and then a bigger part in *How Green Was My Valley.* Roddy was a friendly soul and popular with the stars. Many years later he would be involved with Elizabeth Taylor and Richard Burton during the *Cleopatra* caper.

Hollywood was facing the war with a stiff upper lip. Gold and marble bath tubs were out for the duration. Gloria Swanson's famous tubs from her C. B. De Mille films went on to the scrap heap. Sam Goldwyn exhorted his stars, "Don't think of the money, think of your country," which gave him the best excuse for cutting salaries. Louis B. Mayer shed crocodile tears while doing the same. In fact, *all* salaries were reduced.

Every studio was awash with patriotic pictures. Pat O'Brien starred in *The Navy Comes Through.* Errol Flynn was in *Desperate Journey.* Robert Preston and Brian Donlevy slugged the Japs in *Wake Island.* There would be *The Last Train from Berlin, From Here to Victory, Bataan, The Commandos Strike at Dawn, Mission to Moscow, Song of Russia* (then our ally), and Irving Berlin's *This Is the Army.*

A bit later there would also be "The Hollywood Canteen," founded by Bette Davis, where she and other stars served sandwiches and coffee to the inductees. And Betty Grable, posing in that famous swimsuit, would be the new pin-up for the GIs.

In October 1943 I returned to England and Trevor, leaving our one-year-old daughter, Wendy, with my friend Valerie Bell, then married to the son of the General Mills chairman. I knew that Wendy would not starve in spite of rationing; Valerie had a son a few months older than Wendy, and, thinking ahead, I thought it would be nice to have all that food with a rich son-in-law.

My visit to England was to get to know my husband, to find a house for us near London, and, if everything was right, to come back and get Wendy; then, in spite of the war, the three of us would live happily ever after. It was not to be.

First of all, the house we wanted was requisitioned by Holland's refugee Queen Wilhelmina, for her ladies in waiting. It was demolished several months later by a buzz bomb. Trevor and I were nearly killed during an air raid—fortunately we were on the safe side of Putney Bridge, which was the German target. In the winter of 1943 there were several raids every night. Trevor was overworked and irritable. We quarrelled a lot and we both realized that the marriage was a mistake. And, above all, I missed my daughter and had to get back to her.

Yet, my time spent in London had not all been quarrelling with my husband and moping for my daughter. Clark Gable, on leave, was staying at Claridges. He was getting some rest and a change from the gruelling missions over Germany. I had tried for an interview but he turned me down. Being in the service, he could not talk to the press, and, in any case, he disliked me.

Bob Hope had also been in England, visiting U.S. air bases. "I was in the north of England," Bob told me recently, "and we were playing two or three shows a day. When I pulled into the Air Force base the guard said, 'You know who's here? Clark Gable! He's just coming in from a mission.'

"So I went over to the line and waited for him. He got out of the plane and he was shaking. He said, 'Bob, this is a lot of crap.' He was scared to death. He had come back through that flak and seeing those planes with his friends knocked down. Boy, oh boy, he was just shaking. But he stayed the course."

They met many times after that. "We went to the Embassy Club in London a couple of times and had a lot of fun. The last time I saw him I was in a golf cart with him down in the Bermuda Dunes" (near Palm Springs), "where he had a house, and he said to me, 'I wish they'd stop running my old pictures on television.' I said, 'Hey, let me tell you something, Moose, those pictures you were in—*Gone with the Wind, Boomtown*—let 'em run them all the time. It ain't going to hurt you.' " I suppose Clark did not like to see them on the small screen. Of course now everyone has their old films on television.

Another friend I had seen in England was Jock Whitney, now Major John H. Whitney. He was a top military aide to General Eisenhower. I called on him at the U.S. Army headquarters in Grosvenor Square. "Would it be possible," I asked him, "for me to interview General Eisenhower?" He smiled. "I don't think so. You see, he is very busy trying to win the war." I settled for an interview with General Eaker.

When it was over, Jock took me to a pub and we had a drink. We talked of the old, more or less peaceful, days in Hollywood. Before we parted, he asked me, "How's your love life?" (Today it would be "How's your sex life?" Same thing.) "Well," I replied (I had shown him the latest photograph of my baby daughter), "it's very discriminating. When you realize what can emerge, you have to be very careful about what goes in." I became somewhat embarrassed. "I didn't mean to say that." "No, it's alright. I like what you said." In his last years, living on his estate in Long Island, Jock was very ill. When he died I had lost a good friend.

After I had returned to Hollywood, I found it wasn't easy getting my column back. Mr. Wheeler had thought I would remain in England and had hired Ingar Arvad, a reporter in Washington, to take my place. Ingar had known Mr. Schicklgruber in Germany. He had designated the blonde, blue-eyed girl as his idea of the typical Aryan beauty, a fact that was to cause her some trouble. Mr. Wheeler, famous for the low salaries he paid his people, had originally wanted to pay her $100 a week. "She can't live on that in Hollywood," I had told him and he added another $50, still a bit cheaper than what he had to pay me. So he wanted to keep her on. Thank God most of my editors wanted me back.

To be on the safe side I asked around to see if another syndicate was in need of a Hollywood columnist. Johnny Campbell, my Hollywood contact at Twentieth Century–Fox, informed me that an executive of the McClure syndicate was in town for that purpose. I contacted him and I was offered a contract. I called Mr. Wheeler and said, "Now that I am not working for you, it's alright for me to sign with them, isn't it?" "No, it isn't," he replied. "You are working for us." I was, and he raised my weekly guarantee from the $200 he had been paying me to $300, *and* a car. I had sold my own when I had gone to England. How sweet it is to negotiate from strength.

THE BEST YEARS OF OUR LIVES?

The war was over. The fighting men had come back. Every sound stage in every studio had a film in production, sometimes two films, and space was extremely scarce. It was still the Golden Age of Hollywood. Sam Goldwyn was so optimistic that it would continue forever that he invested some of his own money in what would be his finest film, *The Best Years of Our Lives,* for which Fredric March, as a returning war veteran, would receive his second Oscar. (The first, in 1932, was for *Dr. Jekyll and Mr. Hyde.*) In 1946 Mr. Goldwyn would collect the prestigious Irving Thalberg Award.

That same year, two macho stars appeared in the Hollywood heavens, Kirk Douglas in *The Strange Love of Martha Ivers* with Barbara Stanwyck, and Burt Lancaster in *The Killers* with Ava Gardner, who was at that time Mrs. Artie Shaw, having divorced Mickey the year after their marriage. A six-pound future star, Liza Minnelli, was born on March 12, a few months after my son, Robert Trevor Westbrook.

In 1946, Cary Grant was nibbling on Ingrid Bergman's ear in Alfred Hitchcock's *Notorious,* William Powell was making his second appearance, in *The Ziegfeld Follies,* as the great Florenz Ziegfeld, Katharine Hepburn and Robert Taylor had almost drowned their careers in *Undercurrent,* and Spencer Tracy finished *Without Love* with the aforementioned Hepburn. Jimmy Stewart was proving *It's a Wonderful Life* for Frank Capra. The fourteen-year-old Elizabeth Taylor was playing second fiddle to a dog in *Courage of Lassie.* Greer Garson had supplanted Norma Shearer as Queen of Metro and was starring in *Adventure,* a forgettable film with Clark Gable. Clark would also make *The Hucksters* with a new British arrival, Deborah Kerr. And all was merry as a marriage bell.

All except for a menacing red glow on the horizon: the House Committee on Un-American Activities. In the following years they would threaten the livelihoods of many important stars, writers, directors, and producers in Hollywood. Before the end of the decade there would be another threat that promised to make a ghost town of the film capital of the world. Television. But even more devastating to the industry was the United States government's anti-trust lawsuit in 1948, ordering the film companies to divest themselves of the cinemas in which their films were more or less forcibly shown. All this caused the combined net studio profits to drop from the peaks of ninety million dollars in 1946, and more than a hundred million in 1947, to fifty-five million in 1948.

Book Two

Chapter 10

Misfits

Ben Lyon was the new casting director at Twentieth Century–Fox. From the early thirties until the fifties, Ben and his wife, Bebe Daniels, a star of silent films and early talkies had lived in England, often performing at the Palladium and during the war bringing cheer to the American GIs stationed there. But now they had returned to live in Hollywood.

Ben, unbeknownst to Bebe, was having an affair with a girl who was hanging around the studio hoping for a screen test that would lead to a contract. She would never make it, of course. Bad complexion, dirty-looking hair, and an atrocious dresser. She was becoming a nuisance, always asking Ben, "When can I have the screen test you promised?" It was the bait he had used to lure her to bed. It was time to get rid of her.

Mr. Lyon had an idea. The casting director for Sol Wurtzel, a producer of B films, was a friend. He called her. "You could do me a favour by giving this girl a small role in one of your movies. It would get her off my back." He used that part to get her a contract at his studio.

Her most important role was to serve drinks, cigarettes, and cigars to Darryl Zanuck, Joe Schenck, and their friends while they played gin rummy in a private room at the studio. There were other starlets besides her waiting on their masters. They were known as The Gin Rummy Girls, and most of them were let go after six months or a year for a new batch of starlets who would perform the same duties. This one, because of her protector, Joe Schenck, re-

121

mained for eighteen months. Near the end of her term, she was given a small role in *Scudda Hoo, Scudda Hay*, most of which was left on the cutting room floor.

Marilyn Monroe was next seen at Columbia, where, according to report, she had an affair with Freddie Karger, a piano player, who would later become a producer and marry Jane Wyman after her divorce from Ronald Reagan. Marilyn was one of the *Ladies of the Chorus*, a B musical. Then she was dropped. And that is when she agreed to pose in the nude for the photographer Tom Kelly. For fifty dollars. The calendar, for the company that sold it, made around $750,000.

Marilyn, after re-signing with Fox, was loaned to John Huston at MGM for a small role in *The Asphalt Jungle*. Her new lover, Johnny Hyde, the agent, had begged the director to give her the part, which brought a flood of fan letters for the pretty starlet. When the calendar story surfaced, that she was the naked girl reclining on all that red plush, she had become a potentially important star. I won't go into the story of her piteous plea when cornered, "I did it because I was hungry," because it was a lie. She was not hungry, as her ample curves testified. She was getting three meals a day at the Studio Club, and they were also not in the habit of throwing anyone out, as she claimed, when she could not pay the small rent.

She was warned to deny everything, or it would ruin her career —this was in 1952, when such things as public nudity mattered. But she was smarter than the advisers. She herself gave the story to United Press. She knew that she looked so beautiful on that calendar that every man would dream of possessing her and every woman would envy her figure. But while Marilyn went to bed with half of Hollywood, including Brando, Sinatra, and two members of the Kennedy family—JFK and Bobby—strangely she was a sex symbol who didn't care too much for sex.

Having been raped as a young teenager in a foster home, all she wanted from men was to be protected and treated with tenderness. I think she would have leaned on a lamp-post if it looked masculine. Or even female, although she was not a lesbian. But sometimes she was the leaned-upon. She had an affair with a young homosexual during *There's No Business Like Show Business*. "To make him feel like a man," she explained, without revealing how she managed it.

Marilyn unwittingly spoiled two of my vacations. I was at Elizabeth Arden's Maine Chance in Arizona, shedding some pounds, when the news was flashed that she had eloped with Joe DiMaggio. I left at once for Hollywood. And I was drinking coffee at Florian's in St. Mark's Square in Venice when I was told that she had died of an overdose of sleeping pills.

Before leaving Hollywood I had seen her at Trader Vic's in Beverly Hills, quite drunk, with Frank Sinatra. They were celebrating her thirty-sixth birthday. I cabled my story of what I knew about her (I had known her at the beginning, the middle, and almost the end) from the desk at the Danieli Hotel in Venice.

There was a rumour at the time of her death that she was pregnant by Bobby Kennedy. I did not believe that. She wanted a child so badly that she surely would have given up the liquor and the pills. Also, she had suffered several miscarriages because of a malfunction in the vital area, and it was probable that she could never have a baby. Marilyn loved children, and long after her divorce from Arthur Miller she was very friendly with his children.

I never met her first husband, Jim Dougherty, but some of her lovers—Yves Montand, DiMaggio, and Arthur Miller—had the same kind of facial structure, long and lean. Sort of hawky, with long noses. She had been introduced to Joe DiMaggio when he had wandered on to the set of one of her films. I was among the reporters outside the rented house in Beverly Hills when Marilyn tottered out on the arm of her lawyer, Jerry Geisler, on the way to the court to divorce him.

It was the mismatch of the century. In America, they were equal in fame but not in habits. Joe, the baseball hero, was obsessively neat. Everything on his dressing table was arranged in alphabetical order: A, aspirin; B, brush; C, comb; etc. The maid would go in to make up his bed and it was already done. You could find Marilyn by following the trail of her stockings, her bra, her handkerchief, and her handbag, all dropped as she went.

Joe was always picking up after her. He was always trying to train her. And he could not. So, as she saw it, she was always being nagged. And he was going crazy acting as her maid. "Marilyn, what's this? I just sat down on your panties." And she saying, "Oh, for God's sake! Leave me alone." They reached a point where they could not speak without screaming. They had loved each other, but because Joe was so mortally neat and Marilyn was so mortally unneat, they could not live together.

Her dressing room at Twentieth Century–Fox was just as awful. Every time I went there, I saw open pots of hair dye all over the place, fan magazines on every chair, underwear and dresses scattered on the floor. But the owner of the rented house on North Palm Drive, Barbara MacLean, found the house, as she described it to me, "Neat as a pin." Mr. DiMaggio had rolled up his sleeves and made sure that it was.

Marilyn had left a note for Barbara, "If anything is broken, please let me know and I will pay for it." She also left behind a small rug. Her security blanket. As for Joe, he still hasn't forgotten his love and the pain of Marilyn. As you may know, until recently he remembered the anniversary of her death with flowers. And after more than twenty years he has not remarried.

Marilyn's marriage to the playwright Arthur Miller was a surprise, but it could have been foreseen. While she was still a child emotionally, she wanted to be a grown-up, educated intellectual. But she had no idea of what that was. Also, she didn't know that an intellectual can be boring. She believed that Mr. Miller, as Johnny Hyde had been before his death, was someone who wanted to take care of her, who understood her, who worshipped her.

It was more difficult to understand why Mr. Miller had married Marilyn. A psychiatrist friend of mine in London believes that the reason some Jewish men marry blonde gentile women is to punish their mothers. Pamela, the ex–Mrs. James Mason, whose father was Jewish and mother a blonde blue-eyed Irish Catholic, has a different theory. She thinks it's the guilty dream of every Jewish boy to marry a shiksa because of the idea that they look better. In Marilyn, Mr. Miller had the shiksa of all shiksas. The movie moguls also preferred gentile blondes, and although they would sign Jewish actors, they rarely gave a contract to a Jewish actress.

Marilyn's mother, as you may know, had not been married to her father, Edward Mortenson, and she had also been in several mental institutions. This always worried Marilyn, who sometimes startled her associates with raging tantrums. And, fearful of insanity, she frequently underwent therapy. She had loved her mother and helped her financially in the days of her stardom.

Marilyn had told one of her psychiatrists that every time her mother was nice to her it was followed by her turning angrily on her. He thought this was why Marilyn was so mistrustful of people, even of him. One time when she called him in desperation, he was busy and told her to take a drive. She construed this as cruelty because she said that everyone knew that she hated to drive, although she often drove Sidney Skolsky, the columnist, who had never learned to drive.

Sidney was one of her father confessors. Tom Ewell was another. She was always calling him at home during the filming of their film *The Seven Year Itch*, asking, "Should I do this? Should I do that?" I was on the New York set of that film when there was a call for her from the White House. JFK making an assignation with her at the Carlyle Hotel.

But none of the men really knew her. She was so vague about her emotions, up and down, with no landmarks, like most growing-up girls have—the day they first went to school, the first time they were in love, a mother, a father, sisters, brothers. There were no pegs on which to hang her life. And how she longed to be admired as an intellectual. All those heavy books she always carried, picked at random in the book stores because of their weight. Once when Frank Lloyd Wright was driving with her and some others, he was talking about architecture. Marilyn interrupted him with, "And Lincoln said—" "My God," said one of the passengers, "she's met everyone!"

Another time she was with Johnny Hyde and a group at the La Rue Restaurant on the Strip. The talk was about acting and whether acting lessons were valuable. Marilyn sat through dinner without saying a word. Johnny, trying to bring her into the conversation, said, "Marilyn, what do *you* think?" She looked startled and said, "Well, I . . . I . . . I think Stanislavsky . . ." Everyone was waiting for the rest of the sentence, but that was it.

I had always thought that it was Mr. Hyde who had transformed Marilyn from the badly dressed, mousey, kinky-haired, plump, bad hairline, less-than-ordinary-looking girl into the beauty of the screen. He had a lot to do with the amazing change. But I learned recently that Marilyn had tried to model herself on Betty Grable— her talk, her walk. As with bad copies, it was exaggerated. At the beginning of Marilyn's career, she walked and talked like anyone else. She had heard Cary Grant's remark that if you want to make it, as a producer, director, or actor, you have to create an image for yourself, a special difference that will make you stand out from the crowd.

For a time Marilyn had her drama coach, Natasha Lytess, on the set when she was working. And no matter whether the director was pleased with the take and said "Cut," she would look at Natasha, and if she shook her head, Marilyn asked to do the scene again. After which she would apologize to everyone.

In the last years of her life, she arrived at the studio or at social functions even later than she had before. She had promised to come to the reception for my third wedding (I had divorced Trevor in 1947 and married again in 1953). Most of the guests had left by the time she arrived, all little-girl and breathless, saying she was sorry. Then she kissed my then seven-year-old son. She wanted all males, no matter what their age, to believe that she loved them, and in return they would love her. Even my old, craggy boss, John Wheeler. He had that smug look on his face when I told him that Marilyn had asked about him, which she did every time she saw me.

Some years ago George Cukor told me about his Uncle Morris. "He was an old gentleman and he wanted to meet Marilyn. We arranged the meeting at the home of Constance Collier" (the veteran British actress who gave drama lessons in Hollywood) "and Marilyn didn't show. I couldn't wait any longer and I said, 'Tell Marilyn we'll be at my uncle's hotel.' She appeared after an hour, while Uncle Morris and I were having lunch. She was wearing a mink coat, with no hat on, and looked lovely. My uncle, who was seventy-six at the time, was absolutely taken. He told me the next day that he had slept very badly that night!"

At one time, Marilyn tried to explain to me why she was always late getting to the studio. "I simply can't face them all. So I drive around and around, for hours sometimes, before I have enough courage to go in." Billy Wilder, a patient director, was almost driven mad by Marilyn's lateness and her wanting to rehearse over and over the dialogue for their successful film, *Some Like It Hot*. He told me resignedly, "My Aunt Minnie would always be punctual and never hold up production, but who would pay to see my Aunt Minnie?"

I attended the press conference at the Savoy in London, with the reporters asking Marilyn and Laurence Olivier about their forthcoming film, *The Prince and the Showgirl*. She was always fast with repartee and she had them eating out of her hand. But a pro like Olivier was to suffer during the actual filming, from her lateness and her inability to memorize more than a few words at a time. He grew to detest her, as he reveals in his autobiography, but he was never as cruel in print as Tony Curtis during and after their movie for Mr. Wilder.

Marilyn's last completed film was *The Misfits*, written by Arthur Miller, whom she was in the process of divorcing. Clark Gable was to die of a heart attack soon after it was completed. Marilyn received some blame. Clark, bored with the long waits before her appearance on the set, insisted on doing his own stunts, being dragged by those powerful horses. He would have been pleased with the edited film, and with Marilyn's performance. Starting with *Bus Stop* for Josh Logan, she had learned to be a good actress. I always thought it was a pity that she was not allowed to play Grushenka in *The Brothers Karamazov*.

Something's Got to Give would have been Marilyn's last film. But it was finished a year after shutting down, with Doris Day in her role. Marilyn's fear of coming to the studio had become paranoid. In the seventeen days of shooting, she had actually worked for only five. Not even her then drama coach, Paula Strasberg, could help her. She had also taken off without leave to sing "Happy Birthday, dear President" to John F. Kennedy, at the celebration in Madison Square Garden in New York. I can still hear her lisping the song, and see her wearing the tight see-through flesh-coloured dress. I wasn't under the beds, but rumour had it that she slept with both brothers after the party that night.

Something had to give and it would be Marilyn. An executive on the film telephoned me with the news that Marilyn had been fired. My story was in time for the first edition of the *New York Daily Mirror*, with the banner in big black letters on the front page. But

I was sorry for her. It would be the end for the girl who might still be alive today if she had been less vulnerable and more able to cope with the fame she had sought so eagerly and the publicity that had been thrust upon her.

Judy Garland will be next, I thought, after hearing of Marilyn's death. Liquor and pills. Unlike Marilyn, Judy was born to be a star. But the pattern of their adult lives was somewhat similar. They were both unable to cope with the pressures of stardom. They both tried several times to commit suicide. And of course, if you keep trying, one day you will succeed.

Judy was tougher than Marilyn. She had children, who would sometimes keep her more stable, but even they could not save her at the end. She was fifteen when she invited me for tea to her mother's house in Hollywood. The tea was an excuse. She wanted my opinion on a poem she had written to Oscar Levant, the witty concert pianist, famous for his playing of the Gershwin songs and symphonies. What could I say? I said it was fine.

The last time I saw Judy was a year or so before the forty-seven-year-old star was discovered dead by her sixth and last husband, the thirty-five-year-old Mickey Deans, of natural causes they said, but the pills and booze were responsible. She had been appearing at the Talk of the Town in London. As usual she was late, this time later than usual. It was embarrassing sitting there while the people at the tables kept up a steady clapping, then booing and hissing when she finally appeared. But, as always, she was marvellous and at the end of her performance they were applauding and shouting "Bravo."

Most of the blame for Judy's breakdowns has been charged to Louis B. Mayer, who, we were told, suggested the pills for her when her sleeplessness made it hard for her to report to the studio in the morning. But surely her mother was to blame, pushing her, nagging her. She should have removed her from Hollywood when she saw that the work and the publicity were too much for the adolescent girl.

She *was* difficult. But James Mason, a dour personality, had adored her in spite of the problems during their musical *A Star Is Born* (the second of three versions under that title—Fredric March and Janet Gaynor were first in 1937). It was a miracle that this particular *A Star Is Born* was ever finished. In the first place, no one wanted to hire Judy because of her reputation for being late, and for her drinking and arriving on the set half asleep from the pills. But because of her sensational personal appearance engagement at the Palace in New York, Jack Warner decided to take a chance on her.

Even drunk and half conscious, she was still better than most of the sober, industrious stars in Hollywood. Jack's idea was to team her with Cary Grant, her girlhood idol. But there was a problem with Cary. They were three weeks into rehearsals when he decided he could not go on with it, either because he did not like playing a weak anti-hero, or because of Judy's reputation.

The story at the time was that Cary's then wife, Betsy Drake, crashed through the window of Judy's bedroom on Mapleton Drive and begged her, "You've got to let Cary go. You've got to release him. He can't stand it. He doesn't want to make the picture." It was the first Judy, or anyone else, had heard of that. He had been rehearsing all day but had not said a word about wanting to leave when he had taken off for dinner. Then at ten o'clock his wife arrived at Judy's home saying, "You've got to let him go." And then Cary disappeared and no one could find him. James Mason, who could sometimes be forgetful, stated in his autobiography that Cary only took part in story conferences, and when he backed out the role was first offered to and declined by Brando and Montgomery Clift.

Three weeks went by and Jack Warner was frantic. He needed another leading man at once. The William Morris Agency, which represented Cary, also had James as a client and a script was rushed to his home. "I'm not right for the part," he told them, "and I don't want to do a remake." At that time he also read that Judy had fallen through the glass in her shower and was bleeding all over. Besides, James usually disliked a script the first time he read it. He always thought someone else could do it better. He was finally persuaded that he was the actor for the part.

On the Monday morning that he was due at the studio for the run-through, he fell out of bed to the floor, which gave him vertigo —so he said. It was obviously psychosomatic. After three weeks of being treated, he still could not get out of bed without falling down.

"The room is going round and round," he complained. They shot around him for another two weeks; then, seeing there was no way out, he finally reported to the studio.

Judy was pretty good during the first months of filming. But she relapsed into the bad Judy during the song-and-dance numbers. The "Born in a Trunk" routine was added after the director, George Cukor, left the project. It was twenty minutes long but took weeks to complete.

Judy's husband, Sid Luft, had insisted on the title of producer. His chief job was to make sure his wife reported to the set. This was difficult sometimes, especially when in despondence she would slash her wrists. During one absence, it was said, Sid came up with an idea. "Let's have dinner," he said one evening to Mr. Warner. He knew how anxious he was to get Judy back to work. "Well, the best way to get Judy back to the set is to make her happy."

"That's obviously true with anyone," said Jack. "But how do we make her happy?" According to an aide to Mr. Warner, Mr. Luft then said he knew the way to make her happy—to buy her a certain racehorse. She had seen it run at Santa Anita, and if she owned that horse, it would make her very happy and she would be back to work the next day.

So Jack said, "Well, why don't you buy her the horse?" And Luft reportedly said, "Well, I have no money. But if you will loan me $10,000 I'll buy her the horse." Jack gave him the $10,000 and charged it against the film. Two years later, when Mr. Warner no longer needed Judy, he wanted to sue Mr. Luft for the money. He was dealing with a clever man. Sid reportedly convinced Jack to settle for ten cents on the dollar.

A year after finishing *A Star Is Born,* Judy was at the Cedars of Lebanon Hospital in Hollywood, waiting to give birth to baby Joey Luft. It was Academy Award night, and everyone was sure that Judy, who had been nominated for Best Actress, would win the Oscar. Television cameras were set up around her bed—it was a question of which would come first, the Award or the baby, and the network was taking no chances. But if you remember, Grace Kelly won it for her role in *The Country Girl.*

In her last years Judy accelerated her liquor intake. At parties I used to see her carrying her own special brand, King James Irish whiskey. She would take large gulps from the bottle while greeting friends, quite tipsy, but very jolly.

Near the end of her life she rented an apartment at 40 Central Park South in New York. She had become fearful of what she imagined she saw in the dark. There was always a lighted candle by the window when she tried to sleep. It sometimes set the curtains on fire, and at the first sign of smoke, the next-door neighbour would rush in and rescue the intoxicated actress.

Hollywood had been wooing the late James Mason ever since his 1945 success in *The Seventh Veil*. Not only Hollywood, but matrons and maidens of all ages. My son's nanny, not usually given to aberrations of this sort, once said to me, "If I have to be beaten, let it be by James Mason!" You may remember that in *The Seventh Veil* he used a walking stick to rap the knuckles of his ward, Ann Todd, at the piano.

Soon after his arrival, and with my female readers clamouring for news of the British import, an interview was set up for me. He was most forbidding, answering yes or no to the questions, except when he did not answer at all but looked somewhere over my head. Pamela, who was his wife then and for many years after, and with whom he had two children, Portland and Morgan, has always been much more talkative. James had become a little mellower in recent years, but to understand the man you need to hear Pamela.

"He should have been a professor," she told me. "He was much too over-educated to be an actor. His excellence in Latin gave him a scholarship at Cambridge, where he MAed as an architect; that's what he wanted to be. But at that time, during the depression of the thirties, there was little building going on in England. It was impossible for an architect to get going. So he fell into doing something on the stage in a repertory company because he couldn't do anything else."

Born in Huddersfield, he was one of three brothers. One is a schoolmaster, the other in textiles, his father's business. They came from a long line of army officers and schoolmasters, and that is really what he was cut out to be, a schoolmaster. When I mentioned to Pamela that I had found him almost unapproachable, she agreed. "Completely. He has no small talk at all. He has no interest in anything outside of working. He will work on anything. When he decided to learn Spanish, that's all he did, day and night. When he decided to study the guitar, ping, ping, ping, all day long. If you want him to talk," Pamela continued, "you have to ask him something at the right moment. If there is something on his mind, he will usually say it. If you asked him, as he came off the set, let's say, 'How did you like working with Racquel Welch?' he'd say, 'I hated it. She has no talent. She's an idiot.' But if you asked him the same question a week later he would have forgotten it."

A few years ago, for the first time since I had known him, I had a good conversation with James while he was making *Inside Out* in Berlin with Telly Savalas. He was steamed up about the injustice of an article in a London newspaper accusing Telly of carousing all night and coming in late for work in the morning. "It's not true, and I will testify to that," he said angrily. "Telly is a pro, and whether he was carousing or not—I wouldn't dream of asking him—he would always be on time for work." As you probably read, Mr. Savalas sued the newspaper and won a whopping £34,000.

I doubt whether Roberto Rossellini was ever really in love with Ingrid Bergman. He was flattered when she wrote to him one day out of the blue praising him extravagantly for his direction of *Open City,* and ending with the much-misinterpreted *"t'amo."* It was the only Italian phrase she knew, and I love you has always been in common usage in Hollywood and does not mean more than friendship. The lasting love of Rossellini's life was the Italian actress Anna Magnani. He was at her bedside when she died long after his marriage with Ingrid was over.

Also, I doubt whether Ingrid was ever in love with Rossellini, although the fact that by her standards he was poor, with patches on his sleeves, had some charm for her. She was in love with what she thought he could do for her then unsatisfactory Hollywood career. She was always honest about her priorities, and number one was her acting career. Her daughter Pia was next on the list. Her husband, Dr. Peter Lindstrom, was a distant third. She said once that the reason she had married the doctor was because she loved his mother, Anna (Pia's name was constructed from A for Anna, P for Peter, I for Ingrid).

When Ingrid arrived in Rome in 1949, she told a reporter, "Nobody understood me in Hollywood. They didn't know how to treat a sophisticated European. They thought I was a good, ordinary person." She also said that she disliked having so many people around her there, that like Garbo she often wanted to be alone. Yes, she missed her daughter, and hoped that as she grew older Pia would understand and forgive her.

I heard that when she left him, Dr. Lindstrom had told their daughter, "The reason your mother left us is because she doesn't love us anymore." It was not true. He was angry and made her wait for the divorce she wanted so badly, to be Signora Rossellini before the baby was born.

Ingrid had always been a disciplined actress. At the Royal Academy in Stockholm, it took three years before you could get to the stage where you were allowed to say, "Dinner is served." And she was disturbed by Rossellini's methods in *Stromboli,* her first film for him. "Where is the dialogue?" she would ask him. It was either on the back of an envelope or, he said, "In my head.'

Rossellini was a mystic, another irritant for Ingrid. He was a Catholic who didn't go to church. One night, driving his Cadillac over a high mountain road, he stopped suddenly and exclaimed, "Look what God has given us!" Another night, on a high pass, he stopped the car and looked down and shouted, "God is so good, he has given me eyes to see!"

Then he saw that a car below had overturned and the body of a woman was lying on the ground. He drove down and took her to a hospital in Rome and paid her bills. When Rossellini came to see her there, an American friend who was also visiting said, "This is the man who saved your life—Mr. Rossellini." "Mussolini?" "No, *Ross*ellini." Shock. "Not the man who lived with Ingrid Bergman!"

Some years ago, when her twins, Isabel and Ingrid, were small children, I had a date with them all in the bar of the Raphael Hotel in Paris. While my daughter talked with the girls, I asked Ingrid whether she would ever return to Hollywood, which had blacklisted her after the flight to Rossellini. Her answer was an emphatic no, but she hoped that her former husband would allow Pia to visit her in Rome. As you know, all was forgotten and forgiven when Ingrid won the Oscar for her performance in the title role of *Anastasia.* But while she would visit Hollywood, she would never again live there.

Intermezzo and Casablanca had made Ingrid a star, but the adjective "important" was added only after she played Maria in the movie version of Ernest Hemingway's For Whom the Bell Tolls, with Gary Cooper as the American freedom fighter. She owed the role to Hemingway's then wife, Martha Gellhorn, who had been on the same ship in 1939 when Ingrid was bringing Pia to the United States. Martha introduced Ingrid to Hemingway a few years later in San Francisco, and he insisted, over Paramount's objections, that Ingrid, and no one else, would play Maria.

Ingrid outlived Rossellini by five years. And it was typical that she ignored the cancer that was killing her by working almost to the end. She was happy with the praise given her performance in the televised documentary on Golda Meir, the Israeli Prime Minister. And who but Ingrid would ignore the pain and have a champagne birthday party on the afternoon of the day that she died?

Chapter 11

Loverboys

SEVERAL YEARS AGO, when Frank Sinatra was sitting at a table in the Cub Room at the Ambassadors Hotel in Chicago, David Susskind, the producer and television talk show host, was alone at a table across the room. Suddenly Sinatra stood up and hurried over to David. "I see your show all the time and I love it," he said enthusiastically. "I'm a great fan of yours."

A week later, Susskind was at a table in the same place, this time with his then fiancée, Joyce Davidson. "Ah, there's Frank Sinatra," he said to her, "he's a great friend of mine. Come on, I want you to meet him." They went to his table. "Frank," said David, "please say hello to my fiancée." The singer just stared at him. The pause became embarrassing. "Don't you remember me? I'm David Susskind; you said you liked my show." Frankie's hands had been under the table. Now he slid them very slowly across his lap, "Well," he said to Miss Davidson, "I'll shake your hand, but I won't kiss it." Was he trying to be funny? Mr. Susskind did not think so.

But this is why many people are afraid of Frank Sinatra. He is the chameleon of all time. You never know what form he is going to take. He can be friendly one day and hostile the next. The only time you know for sure that he will cut you dead or be rude is if you have said, or written, something about him that he does not like.

Sammy Davis, Jr., a gentle, pleasant person, once made an amusing remark about Frank in his night club act. It was not intended to upset him, but it did. Sammy, who had been a member in good standing of the famous Rat Pack—Sinatra, Judy Garland,

Dean Martin, Peter Lawford, etc.—was ostracized for several years by the man who seems to believe that he is some sort of god, who will dole out favours or disfavours according to his mood.

He can be generous, giving cars and other expensive gifts to people who work for him, taking care of hospital bills for friends who are short of cash. As he did for Lee J. Cobb when the actor was hospitalized, and he did it in a way that would not seem like charity. He called Mr. Cobb's agent and said, "I want to make a deal for three films with your client. I will pay $150,000 in advance for each one." Lee, who was having a lean time in his career at that time, protested that it was too much. But Sinatra insisted. (Mr. Cobb, now dead for some years, is best known for playing the Willie Loman role onstage in Arthur Miller's *Death of a Salesman.*)

There was a story in a British newspaper that a woman was about to be evicted from her home because of non-payment of rent. It was she who revealed that the cheque that saved her home bore the signature of Frank Sinatra. But this is the same man who publicly called a prominent Washington columnist a prostitute and other choice epithets. He ridiculed the late Dorothy Kilgallen about her receding chin in his night club act. And later he chewed out Rex Reed, the film critic, who had not gone overboard for one of his films.

Another columnist, Earl Wilson, was a favourite of Frankie's until he printed something that was not entirely laudatory. Soon after he found himself barred from a night club in Miami, where the famed singer was starring. I expect you are wondering where *I* stand in Mr. Sinatra's "Drop Dead" list. Somewhere near the top, I imagine.

And yet we were good friends when he first came to Hollywood in the early forties. As I remember, I had reported that the bobby soxers were screaming for him and fainting in the aisles when he appeared at the Paramount Theater in New York. He even flirted a bit with me when I interviewed him in his dressing room at RKO.

The first time I realized his dislike for me was during the intermission of a concert at Carnegie Hall. Walking in the corridor I almost bumped into him. "Hi, Frankie," I said with outstretched hand. He did the same thing that Hedda Hopper had done to Joan Crawford: he walked past me as if I were invisible.

Ah, I remembered, I had written in my column that he was treating Ava Gardner badly in their divorce suit. Ava has never spoken harshly about any of her husbands, which is why they are all still friends. Far from demanding the usual million-dollar alimony, Ava paid for the ticket that enabled Frank to return to Hollywood to fight for the role of Angelo Maggio in *From Here to Eternity*. Some nodules on his throat had made his singing career non-existent.

Frank had been visiting Ava in Africa, where she was starring in *Mogambo* with Clark Gable and Grace Kelly. He was so desperate for the small part of Maggio that he accepted a total salary of $8,000. It was a good investment, winning him the Oscar for the Best Supporting performance of the year. After that there was only one way for him to go. Up.

Frankie was to marry twice after the divorce from Ava. But, like Nancy, his first wife, Ava has remained single. I think, again like Nancy, that she is still in love with him. Some years ago, when she was in Europe making *Mayerling* for Terence Young, she received a cable from Sinatra in Puerto Vallata, Mexico: "I need you. Come at once. You will know why when you read the headlines in the morning papers." Frankie and Mia Farrow were getting a divorce.

Mr. Young took her to the airport. She was happy and excited, thinking perhaps this would mean a reconciliation and remarriage. But when she arrived at his hotel in Puerto Vallata she was informed that he had already left. You can see why he has the reputation for treating his women badly.

Mia Farrow didn't have a chance. He was flattered that she had reacted to his attentions by falling headlong in love with him. And she was amazed that a worldly man like Sinatra, who could have any woman he wanted, was paying her so much attention.

The Sinatra children were shocked. Mia was younger than Nancy, Jr. And to be fair to Frank, he hesitated over continuing the relationship. This angered Mia, who, in a sudden fit of anger, cut off most of her long blonde hair. The marriage was doomed from the start, even on the honeymoon in the south of France, where they stayed at the home of Terence Young. He had put them in a separate wing of the house so they could be more or less alone. "But they joined us all the time." Sinatra referred to her as "my child bride," and he would always treat her like a child. One time there,

he sat her on a stool and sang "September Song" to her, while the
other guests smiled behind their drinks.

While he regarded Ava as a good chap, one of the boys, drinking with them, swearing with them, never fussing, Mia was a piece
of porcelain, guarded, but not particularly cherished. A woman
friend saw her sitting alone and miserable in a corner of a gambling
room in Las Vegas, while Frankie was having a good time with the
boys at the tables. She sat with her and tried to cheer her up. "He
doesn't see me at all," Mia said sadly. It was getting late and it
seemed that he had forgotten about her. But at three A.M. he left his
chums to give his wife three words of command: "Go to bed."

I thought Mia's marriage to André Previn would last. How can
you break up when you have six children? André was a sensitive
change from the roughness of Mr. Sinatra. But I guessed it was over
when Mia made plans to return to her career. If Mia marries her
constant lover, Woody Allen, as his wife and the co-star in his films
she can have the best, or the difficulties, of both worlds. Marriage
and a career.

Frankie seems happy enough in his last marriage, to Barbara
Marx. She is everything he likes to display on his arm—chic, slender,
and beautiful. And she did not fall too eagerly into his lap. The one
way *not* to marry Mr. Sinatra is to tell the press, "We are engaged."
This spelt "End" to his romances with Juliet Prowse and Lauren
Bacall. The latter denies that she said it, but says that her agent did.
She still refers to her ex-lover as a "shit."

Not long ago on television, I watched Marlon Brando as Fletcher
Christian and Trevor Howard as Captain Bligh in their 1962 version
of *Mutiny on the Bounty.* It was terrible, especially when compared to
the Clark Gable/Charles Laughton success of 1935. Why did Marlon choose to speak in a prissy, tight-lipped British accent that came
out as a caricature of English upper class? He should have known
better after the fiasco of his Napoleon in *Desirée,* when as the French
hero he also spoke in a nancy British accent.

If I seem to be "knocking" Mr. Brando, I am. But, as we prefer
to say, it is more in sorrow than anger. He was so great as Stanley
Kowalski in 1947 when I saw him on Broadway in *A Streetcar Named
Desire,* the Tennessee Williams play. I knew Jessica Tandy, his

Blanche DuBois, from her time in Hollywood, and after the show I went backstage and asked her to introduce me to her co-star. "He's so virile, so exciting with that torn shirt," I gurgled.

Marlon's dressing room seemed to be as narrow and as long as eternity, as, guided by Jessica, I stumbled towards the stationary figure at the other end. "Oh Marlon," said Jessica, who was also flustered by his stern visage, "I want you to meet—" He interrupted: "Your mother?" My complete deflation. He was probably joking, but I didn't stay long enough to find out. In fact this was the only close encounter I ever had with him.

Practical jokes, Paul Newman was saying recently, can sometimes be malicious, to make the victim look stupid. Which is why, he said, he had stopped doing them. I don't imagine that Marlon will ever stop. Josh Logan, the director, can laugh about it now, but he nearly had a heart attack, he told me, when he was filming *Sayonara* with Marlon in Japan. "There were just a few days left when he came to work with his right arm in a heavy sling. Broken, Marlon told me. We would have had to close down." It was Marlon's idea of a joke. He laughed and laughed. Mr. Logan did not laugh with him.

In *The Men*, Marlon's first film in Hollywood, he played a paraplegic in a wheelchair, injured during World War Two. To bring authenticity to the role, he spent several hours a day in a hospital that cared for paraplegics, living as they did. One day he startled some visitors by jumping out of the wheelchair and running across the lawn. It made him laugh every time he remembered the look on their faces. Why don't I find this funny?

Some years ago, Marlon's love of practical jokes almost got him arrested when he asked the stewardess on a National Airlines plane in New York, "Are we going to Cuba?" This was during a spate of hijackings to Cuba. He had grown a beard and she did not recognize the actor. The airport police were called and Marlon had to do some fast talking before they let him go.

The joke he played on me was just as unfunny. I was having dinner at my home. My guest was a very rich man who had some thoughts about marrying me. "Only one thing bothers me," he said. "You seem to be married to your career." "Oh no," I assured him hastily, "a happy marriage means much more to me than my work."

I was sure I could be happy with all those millions, plus the twenty-six-room apartment on Fifth Avenue, the estate by a lake in Connecticut, and the lovely house with a huge swimming pool in Palm Beach.

At that moment the telephone rang. A voice that sounded like Marlon mumbled, "I know you would want the news that Marlon Brando is getting married tonight." He rang off. Several hours later, having telephoned every possible person who might know when and where, including trying to track down his close friend, Jay Kantor, I returned to my guest. "I think someone was having me on," I said wearily. To which he replied, "You see what I mean about your work." Ah well, they say that it keeps the brain alive longer if you keep on working.

Marlon was paid $50,000 for his first Hollywood film, $1 million for *The Godfather*, $2 million in 1979 for *Apocalypse Now*. In between he made some good and some bad movies. *Streetcar* was good, *On the Waterfront* excellent—for which he won an Oscar. *The Ugly American* was bad, as was *The Chase; One-Eyed Jacks*, which he starred in and directed, was awful; then *The Godfather* was good, *Last Tango in Paris* embarrassing, and *The Countess from Hong Kong* terrible.

He had always wanted to work with Chaplin, but when the chance came he was brutal to Charlie, who was directing the film. And he was cruel to Sophia Loren, his co-star, reducing her to tears in a love scene. He made fun of the director behind his back, imitating his little tramp walk, and was always arguing about how he should play his role, causing long delays on the set.

He once boasted that he could have any woman he wanted. It was probably true. But it is one thing to have an affair, and quite another to have a good relationship with a woman, or a happy marriage. He married Anna Kashfi, believing she was pure Indian, but he left her after learning that she was pure Welsh. For years afterwards they were in and out of the Los Angeles courts fighting for the custody of their son, Christian.

Wife number two, Movita, eight years older, lasted long enough to give him two children. I am not sure whether he married Tarita, his girl in *Mutiny on the Bounty*, with whom he had two more. In any case she does not seem to be around today.

Like Orson Welles, when I first met him, Marlon as a young man was handsome and slim. I haven't seen him lately but in his movies there is too much fat. And he hates to be fat, or rather he did. He was always dieting, then over-eating. Perhaps now that he is sixty (in 1984) he is reconciled to the blubber. He was always restless, always moving, staying in cheap hotels under different names. His longest stay was, or still is, in the big house, high up in Beverly Hills, owned by Mr. Balzar, the organic food man. (You can bet Marlon does not eat any of *that* stuff!)

You don't hear much about his private life today (now that I have written this he is sure to go off and marry another dark-haired beauty). And as he approaches his seventh decade, I am wondering if he is lonely. Or if he can still have any woman he wants. Or how much longer they will pay him two million dollars for a brief appearance in a film.

Chapter 12

"Are You Now or Have You Ever Been . . ."

Between 1940 and 1947 being a member of the Communist Party in Hollywood had about as much significance as membership in the Hillcrest Country Club. I remember, early in 1940, attending a cocktail party at the home of Budd Schulberg and the place was crawling with members of the party and sympathizers. Mostly writers—Ring Lardner, Jr., who had not yet sold his *Woman of the Year* script to MGM, John Howard Lawson, the first president of the Screenwriters' Guild, the director Eddie Dymtryk. And, among many others, Scott Fitzgerald, who had been visited by the number one Communist from a Southern state (Brimmer in *The Last Tycoon*), who had tried to convert him to joining the party. Scott was drinking heavily at the time and the meeting had ended in a brawl. "In any case," he told me, "I could never be a member of any party and be told what and how to write."

The year before, I had been taken to James Roosevelt's house in the six-hundred block at North Rodeo Drive by Paul Willert, whose father had been the Washington correspondent for the London *Times*. On arriving from London he had tried to get in touch with Scott, who was then on his last binge, and was passed on to me. It was an interesting gathering to honour a man called Bada, a Communist who had escaped a hanging in Spain during the Civil War.

142

The most talkative guest was the actor Lionel Stander, who made no secret of his political beliefs. He bragged about how he had slyly put some propaganda into a recent film. There was a scene where he was waiting for an elevator. There would be a few seconds before it arrived. The director suggested "Think of some business to do there." So he whistled a few bars of the "Marseillaise." I suppose you could call that propaganda.

To understand the fear which swept through Hollywood only a few years later, from 1947 into the early fifties, you must know that in 1946, when the war was over and Russia was no longer our ally, Congress had passed the Smith Act, preceded by a Supreme Court decision that said in effect that the Communist Party was not a legal political party but a criminal conspiracy. There was naturally great concern in Hollywood among the party members and those who sympathized with them.

It was a difficult time. To resign from the party or not to resign? To stay, or to run away? People were split down the middle. Husbands differed with their wives, brothers were against brothers, and business partners disagreed politically with their associates. People believed, and really believed fervently, on either side. Actually, the Communist Party in Hollywood totalled less than two percent of the work force, a figure below the national average. But Hollywood has always been a target for politicians who want publicity.

The actual drive against the entertainment industry had begun with what was known as the *Little* House Committee on Un-American Activities, which was a California state committee. And the suspicion has always been strong that the publicity it received enticed the congressional group in Washington into realizing that this was a fertile field for them to come to Hollywood and investigate.

They were welcomed by the heads of the Motion Picture Alliance for the Preservation of American Ideals. Members included strong rightists such as Adolphe Menjou, John Wayne, Robert Taylor, Ward Bond, the director Sam Wood, and several right-wing writers.

After the Rosenbergs were executed following their conviction on the charge of selling secrets to Russia, this group had a good excuse to proclaim that there was a Communist conspiracy in America. A fear grew that the Communists were plotting to overthrow the government of the United States. And if you were a fellow traveller, or a financial contributor to liberal causes, you were just as dangerous as if you were a party member.

Also, there was a right-wing rumour that anyone who was anti-Communist would be unable to get work. This was the time when the emergence of television was causing anxiety in the studios, with many workers laid off. Someone had to be blamed for all this, and the Communist Party was a convenient victim.

To combat the expected persecution, another group was formed in Hollywood, "The Committee for the First Amendment" —the right of free speech—founded by William Wyler, John Huston, and the writer Philip Dunne, with the Henry Rogers Public Relations Company to pass the message to the public. Among several hundred who signed on were Mrs. Eleanor Roosevelt, several judges, Edward G. Robinson, Humphrey Bogart, Danny Kaye, and this reporter. Of course we were all labelled Communist sympathizers, even Mrs. Roosevelt. Hedda Hopper had a field day referring to us as "Demmies," which sounded like Commies. As you may remember, the group called by the press "The Unfriendly Ten" all received prison sentences after invoking the First Amendment. If they had used the Fifth Amendment, which gives the right not to incriminate oneself, they might have got off.

Previously, Mr. Rogers had organized a planeload of Hollywood celebrities to go to Washington to plead for the Ten. Of course to no avail. In fact Humphrey Bogart and Danny Kaye were so intimidated by the reception they received that as soon as they returned to Hollywood they disassociated themselves from the group.

It all seems so long ago now, and some of the details are blurred in my mind, but I remember that Gary Cooper, a right-wing Republican, was so grateful to Carl Foreman for the good script he wrote for him in *High Noon* that he decided to go into production partnership with Carl even though he was blacklisted. But so much pressure was brought on him that finally Gary backed out of their company. John Wayne even accused him of Communist propaganda in *High Noon* because in the final scene, disgusted with the townspeople who had let him down, Gary had thrown his sheriff's badge on to the ground.

Carl had been interrogated by the committee in Hollywood and, rather than face the call to Washington before J. Parnell Thomas, he took off for England, where he wrote scripts under a different name, so there was no one to step forward and claim the Best Writer Oscar for *The Bridge on the River Kwai*. Later, under his own name as a producer with headquarters in London, he made such winners as *The Guns of Navarone* and *Born Free*.

Dalton Trumbo and many other writers who had been black-listed also wrote successful film scripts under assumed names. Kirk Douglas and Otto Preminger were the first to break the blacklist by giving Mr. Trumbo credit for writing *Spartacus*. But two fine actors, Larry Parks and John Garfield, never made it back. Larry went into real estate and made a fortune, more than he made from *The Jolson Story*. Garfield died in the bed of a lady who was not his wife. Edward G. Robinson, a liberal who contributed to worthy causes, testified voluntarily in Washington but for many years was relegated to B movies.

As for Miss Hopper, she made the intentional slip of referring to MGM as Metro-Goldwyn-*Moscow* because of her hatred for the new boss, Dore Schary, a well-known Democrat. It made the first edition of the *Los Angeles Times*. And then, with the threat of a lawsuit, disappeared.

But in all wars there is some humour. Robert Taylor, who had starred in *The Song of Russia* during the war, when we were still cozy with the Russians, flew to Washington and New York to tell the investigating committee that he had been suckered into making the movie, with its fadeout, an American flag with the Russian flag superimposed on it. He cited this as proof that Hollywood was trying to indoctrinate the people that Russia was about to take over the United States.

And fiercely patriotic Darryl Zanuck sent word that if any of the Commie writers tried to enter his studio, he would personally man a machine gun on the roof of the main building, and mow them down.

Howard Hughes was just as rabid. RKO had made *The Las Vegas Story*, written by Paul Jarrico, who was among the blacklisted. Hughes insisted that his name be taken off the credits. Paul sued Hughes, who took the matter to court, one of his rare appearances in that milieu. And Hughes won. He also fired another RKO writer, Adrian Scott, one of the Ten who went to jail.

Mr. Hughes personally investigated everyone who worked at the studio, and if he found the slightest tinge of pink, he or she was dismissed. Dore Schary, with his liberal views, lasted a few months with Hughes, then went on to bigger and better things as head of MGM production, finally ousting Louis B. Mayer. I remember Oscar Levant chiding me for printing this possibility. "But they can't fire L.B. He *is* MGM." But they did, mostly because the studio profits under Mayer had sunk to a disastrous level, and the money men decided to put in a younger, more innovative man.

Of course today none of the right-wingers in Hollywood will admit that there ever was a blacklist. Even Ronald Reagan, who was President of the Screen Actors' Guild from 1947 to 1952, and again in 1959, becomes vague when asked about this blot on Hollywood history.

SHEILAH GRAHAM
NOTED HOLLYWOOD COLUMNIST

LECTURE SUBJECT:

TOWN HALL

WEDNESDAY MORNING, NOVEMBER 8 ❖ 11 o'clock ❖ **HOTEL CLEVELAND**

SUBJECT: **HOLLYWOOD UNDER A MICROSCOPE**

Management ·· PARLOR 80, HOTEL CLEVELAND   -:-   -:-   PROSPECT 8000 - MAIN 6499 - CEDAR 2229

20. Sheilah's nationwide lecture tour in 1940: "Surrounded by my paragraphs"

21. *Left:* Scott and Sheilah, early in 1940. 22. *Below:* Lunching at Twentieth-Century Fox with Deborah Kerr during the filming of *Beloved Infidel,* in which she took the part of Sheilah: "Was she too much of a lady to play me?"

23. Gregory Peck and Deborah Kerr in *Beloved Infidel,* 1959: "I swooned when he said, 'I love you, Sheilo'."

24. Sheilah with John Wayne and Lauren Bacall on a tanker off Hawaii for *Blood Alley* in 1955: "Me trying to be funny"

25. Beautiful Ava Gardner: "I have come to know her better."

26. Laurence Olivier: "The greatest actor of our time, in *Fire Over England*"

27. David Selznick, Leslie Howard, Vivien Leigh and Olivia de Havilland before signing for *Gone With the Wind*

28. Alfred Hitchcock, Grace Kelly and Jimmy Stewart: "Snapped on their way to attend a premiere"

29. Ingrid Bergman: "Fresh from Sweden, taking a non-alcoholic drink in Hollywood"

30. A very young Katharine Hepburn with Joel McCrea at the beach

31 and 32: Party time in Hollywood...
[31]: Sheilah's children Wendy (12) and Robert (9) with Gordon Scott and Chimp on the set of *Tarzan's Hidden Jungle* and [32] *Above:* Judy Garland, Mickey Rooney and Ann Rutherford making faces at a party. 33. *Left:* Sheilah with Dean Martin and Jerry Lewis at Ciro's "Jerry was trying to be funny."

34. Milton Berle: "Mr. Television." 35. *Below:* Ronald Reagan in cowboy outfit at the Beverly Wilshire in 1974 when he was Governor of California

36. Sheilah with Darryl Zanuck at her third wedding reception, Valentine's Day 1953: "A command performance." 37. *Below:* Tilly Losch in *Duel in the Sun:* "There were no survivors."

Chapter 13

The Monster

Of the two disasters that threatened Hollywood in the late forties, the House Committee on Un-American Activities and television, the latter was considered more dangerous. They were afraid that television would make Hollywood a ghost town. But at the beginning it was written off as a fad that would soon pass. Who would want to stay at home to watch a small blurred screen when they could go out and join the crowds in the ornate cinemas and see such films as *Killer McCoy* with Mickey Rooney, or Clark Gable and Deborah Kerr in *The Hucksters*, or *Easter Parade* starring Fred Astaire and Judy Garland? In the same year, 1948, Deanna Durbin appeared in *Something in the Wind*, Jimmy Cagney in *The Time of Your Life*, and Cary Grant and Myrna Loy in *Mr. Blandings Builds His Dream House*, to name a few of the choice offerings from the major studios.

In 1947 there were only seventeen television stations in America, broadcasting to 136,000 sets. In the next year, Milton Berle, song writer, vaudevillian, radio star, and night club performer, was hailed as "Mr. Television," the king of the burgeoning entertainment medium. "Uncle Miltie," as he came to be called, would receive a $6 million contract paid, at his request, over a period of thirty years.

The speed with which television took over brought panic to the studios. It seemed to make no difference that contract players were forbidden to appear on the snowballing enemy. In those first years it didn't matter how bad the shows were. People watched because

147

it was a novelty. Also, there were enough big names *not* under contract to lend lustre to the casts of the live television plays.

Robert Montgomery, who was much better than the happy-go-lucky rich playboy he usually played at MGM (he proved it as the killer in Emlyn Williams' *Night Must Fall*), left Hollywood in the late forties, to concentrate on television in New York. From 1950 to 1954 he produced, directed, hosted, and sometimes acted in "Robert Montgomery Presents," an anthology series for television.

He became active in politics and in 1952 worked to help General Eisenhower become President of the United States. He was appointed the President's adviser for his appearances on television, including the make-up, deemed important, as Richard Nixon would learn later. Nixon's unshaven appearance in the debate with John F. Kennedy is credited with losing him many votes, and just possibly costing him the election for President.

With the loss of audiences in the movie houses—the TV people knew that the way to keep them at home in front of the small screen was to put on good programmes at eight P.M.—the studios drastically reduced their contract lists. Twentieth Century–Fox closed down for a while. New methods were tried to bring back the lost audiences: 3D for the horror films, such as *House of Wax,* and bigger screens. I emceed the debut of the huge Cinemascope screen for the premiere of *The Robe,* starring Richard Burton and Jean Simmons.

There were even "Smellies." I distinctly remember *The Scent of Mystery* giving forth a perfumed odour. But none of this brought back the ringing sound of cash at the box office during the Golden Years before television. Soon only 15 million Americans went to the movies, as against 135 million watching television.

Because the Hollywood studios would have nothing to do with what was stigmatized as "The Monster," early television drama series such as "Playhouse 90" and "The Robert Montgomery Show" were performed live in New York and kinescoped, a bad photographed reproduction, for the rest of the country.

Performers who had not been too successful in films became over-night stars in television: Jackie Gleason and Art Carney in "The Honeymooners"; Jack Webb in "Dragnet"; Hugh O'Brian as Wyatt Earp; James Arness as Marshal Dillon in "Gunsmoke" (the thirty-year-long series that was first offered to John Wayne); Lorne

Green in "Bonanza." Robert Stack's FBI series, "The Untoucha-bles," refused by Van Johnson, made Stack a millionaire.

Film stars who were not under contract to the studios, such as Eddie Cantor, Jimmy Durante, and Groucho Marx, became more popular. And Lucille Ball in "I Love Lucy," with her then husband, Desi Arnaz, set a new standard for television by *filming* the show with the now prevalent three-camera method before a live audience in Hollywood.

Milton Berle had the same idea, to film a show so that it could be preserved and shown again, and eliminate the mistakes and pitfalls, impossible for the live shows. He took his idea to Louis B. Mayer. "We will call the show *The MGM Follies,* and use your con-tract players as guests and MGM as the sponsor to promote your movies." He received a fast turndown. He went to Harry Cohn. "We will call the show *The Columbia Follies.*" Mr. Cohn's reply: (bleeped). Jack Warner, being somewhat sharper than his fellow tycoons, con-sidered the matter, but then said no. And not even *The Zanuck Follies* could persuade Darryl.

Actually, because of mishaps and fluffs, the live shows were more fun to watch. Like the Pallenberg Bears from the Ringling Brothers and Barnum and Bailey Circus. Uncle Miltie was doing his monologue down front, and introducing the first act, the Pallenberg Bears, who were back of the curtain waiting to come on. But appar-ently the trainer of the bears had forgotten to take them out for a walk around the block before the show.

"There I was," said a reminiscing Mr. Berle, "telling jokes, and I hear expelling sounds coming right in over the mike. *Plaah!* The cameras are shaking because the guys can't hold them from laugh-ing, and the audience is screaming because in the middle of my lines you can hear *Plaah!* They were all hysterical, and I'm afraid of censorship." Mr. Berle, famous for dialogue that is not in the script, went in front of the curtain and shouted, "Stop ad libbing back there!"

The curtain opened, and from the MC came: "Ladies and gen-tlemen, the Pallenberg Bears from the Ringling Brothers and Bar-num and Bailey Circus!" Berle continued: "Instead of staying with me, the cameras went to a wide shot. And I had to cross over to the bears. You can imagine the size of polar bear frisbees? There were ten of them, and I had to keep stepping over them. And it was being shown live!"

The next act was the late Jack Cole, with an East Indian dancing team who performed barefoot with bells on. They could not clean up the stage fast enough, although Miltie stalled on his introduction. So the dancers were slipping and sliding all over the place. I will slide over the reaction from the crew and the audience.

Unexpected disasters in those early days of television could be laughed at. But not the first issue of *Red Channels*, a magazine for television with so-called facts on the political affiliations of performers who had to be cleared by the sponsor of the commercial product before they could appear. These were the late forties and early fifties, and the witch hunting was in full swing. John Garfield was taboo, also Gertrude Berg, who had her own television success, "The Goldbergs," at that time, but was fighting the fanatics who demanded that she get rid of her co-star, left-wing Philip Loeb. Eventually they prevailed, Mr. Loeb's career was ruined, and the mentally-ill son he was supporting in a private hospital was transferred to a state institution. Philip Loeb then committed suicide. (In Martin Ritt's 1976 film *The Front*, starring Woody Allen, Zero Mostel portrays a blacklisted comic who commits suicide in a hotel room. The incident is based on Loeb's death.)

"I couldn't even get Edward G. Robinson on my show," said Mr. Berle, "even though he had been cleared of Communism after he went to Washington." But the taint was there. Also there was an unwritten sponsors' law that you couldn't have blacks and whites at the same time on television. When Mr. Berle had Lena Horne on his show in 1949, and at the end he put his arm around her and said, "That's wonderful, Lena," they received hundreds of thousands of letters of protest.

"And that scared the sponsor. So one week I had a dynamic dance act that opened the show, four black dancers, The Four Stepbrothers. As I came in for rehearsal, the man from the William Morris" (agents) "office said to me, 'The Stepbrothers are out.' I said, 'Why?' He said, 'They're just out.' I called the agency that handled my sponsor—Texaco. I knew they had never seen The Stepbrothers and I said, 'You must give me a reason why.' They refused.

"It's now Tuesday afternoon, the Tuesday of the show. No Stepbrothers. I said, 'You'd better bring them back.' They said, 'We don't want them.' I said, 'If you don't want them, I'm not going on.' It's now twenty minutes to eight, twenty minutes to the start of the show. I said, 'I'm here but I'm not going on until I get a reason why. A letter or a verbal reason why The Stepbrothers are not allowed on the show.'

"Of course I knew why. But I didn't know where it came from, the sponsor or NBC. Somebody. Well, I wouldn't go on. Fifteen minutes to eight and I wouldn't go on. I didn't leave the building, but I went downstairs. Ten to eight. Five to eight. And then I heard shouting: 'They are on!' I think that broke the barrier for the black situation."

That was not the only innovation Mr. Berle brought to television. He is responsible for the cue cards, the teleprompter, and, alas, he invested in and promoted the laugh machine. "That machine has made it easier—and you can quote me—for the comedy shows to seem more successful." But it's not good for the writers. If someone says the joke is not good enough for a black-out, the writer can say, "What are you worried about, the machine will love it."

As Bob Hope reminded me, in the beginning there was a big hassle about showing the Academy Awards on television. It was the enemy, it was fighting motion pictures in the cinemas. But when they discovered how much money they could make by selling their movies to television, well, everybody was in love with television and the big wedding happened. But for a long time Hollywood was still a depressed area. Chiefly because studios were still making the kind of films that people could see for free on television.

Even for the top television stars the pay before, and sometimes after, 1950, was comparatively low. In 1948, for instance, Mr. Berle was paid $2,500 a week although he had been making $15,000 a week in night clubs. It was all NBC could afford, they told him. But a year later he was raised to $25,000 a week. And $40,000 a week the following year. His $6 million exclusive deal gave him the right to produce, direct, and write his shows and other NBC shows. But he was not happy. NBC used him mostly as a performer and he could not work anywhere else.

After many years the deal became a straitjacket. "They were paying me at the rate of $200,000 a year for thirty years," he told me, "A lot then but nothing today. When Redd Fox moved over from " 'Sanford and Son'." (copied from the British show 'Steptoe and Son') "to ABC, they gave him $6 million just to move over."

In 1957 Mr. Berle told General Sarnoff, the head man at RCA–NBC, that he would take a forty percent cut every year to make the contract non-exclusive. The General agreed. And by the time the contract ended in 1981, it had cost the star more than $100,000. "But it was worth it. I was free to work anywhere I liked." Jackie Gleason's contract was for ten years, but unlike Milton, he worked it through and kept the money. He wouldn't tell me how much. And neither would Bob Hope.

But if you are interested, I will tell you what *I* was paid: one hundred dollars when, in the late forties, I was asked to do the commentary on television for a wrestling match starring the man-mountain known as Gorgeous George, because of his long blonde curls. The camera panned from the ring to me when I was talking, to George when he was wrestling. Mostly my commentary consisted of: "Oh my God," when one or the other, or both, seemed to be hurtling into my lap.

Afterwards, I interviewed Gorgeous George in an upstairs room. The director crouched under the television camera and gave me strict instructions to look at him, and him only, during the interview. It was a two shot. So there I was, asking questions, but staring straight at the producer under the camera. George, of course, was looking at me when he answered them. My friends who had seen the show thought I had gone mad. Another thing I remember about that first show was the make-up, strong whites and reds, but the lips were dark purple, almost black.

I thought my television career was over after that ghastly beginning. But I was still trying. I took an idea to ABC Television on Vine Street in Hollywood. The man I had to see was on the phone. He was talking to Groucho Marx, begging him to come to his network. Every now and then he waved a hand to me, as if to say, "I haven't forgotten you," while I was thinking, "I wish he would want me as badly as he wants Groucho." Ah, now he was ready for me.

"My idea is this," I said rather weakly—the long wait had taken away some of my confidence. "I will ask the studios to give me clips from the films about to go into release and hopefully allow me to interview some of the people in them." He shook his head. "They will never give any part of any film to be seen on television."

As I arrived home, utterly depressed, the phone was ringing. It was Fred Wile, a top executive at NBC-TV in Hollywood. "How would the best columnist in Hollywood like to do a weekly show for the best television company? It will be on the West Coast only to begin with, but I'm sure it will soon go coast to coast." Well, what do you know. I caught my breath and asked, "How much are you paying?" "Fifty dollars a week." I wasn't sure I had heard it right. "Fifty dollars?" "Yes, fifty dollars." I should have been insulted, but the main thing was to get a foot in the door. "I'll do it for seventy-five," I said. It was a deal.

Helen Mack, a former actress who had produced my radio show, was in shock. "You should not have accepted," she said. "It will hurt your reputation." But after six weeks we had a sponsor, Max Factor. Pay: $600 a week. We had some fairly respectable guests. Jose Ferrer, then making the film *Cyrano de Bergerac,* demonstrated on me how to kiss with an oversized nose. Jimmy Durante always said yes to requests, and Bob Hope appeared too. This was in 1951.

In October 1954, another call came from NBC-TV. This time from New York. Tom McAvity, head of programming: "Would you be interested in a daily fifteen-minute network show from Hollywood? It will be seen in New York at ten-thirty in the morning. We will want some gossip, and a filmed life story of a star to be used in five daily segments."

In a daze I asked, "How much are you planning to pay?" "$5,000." I was on the point of saying, "A month?" "A year?" when he added, "A week." Then I (almost) fainted. Coming to, I heard him say, "We want you to set up your own company and have your own staff. And arrange for the filming." The show would start at the beginning of January 1955, nineteen years after I had started my syndicated column.

My children had a Christmas without a mother in '54 because I wanted to get as many life stories filmed and in the can before the live starting date. Bing Crosby was hoping for a second Oscar for

The Country Girl. To win the Award, stars who would do nothing for you at other times said yes to every request. To have Bing Crosby on my show for a whole week was a great coup. I was so excited that I called Mr. Wile to give him the news. "But you can't have him," he told me. "He has an exclusive contract with CBS." If only I had kept my mouth shut. I settled for William Holden, also a big name then, who was in the same film.

Bob Hope was under contract to NBC, so that was no problem. He stood still for a whole day of filming. Marjorie Main, then a big star because of her "Ma and Pa Kettle" movies, insisted on doing her life story at her home. She was being massaged on a table in her sitting room when I arrived with my director and camera crew. Marjorie had a great idea, she said. "How about lying down with me, and they can film us together on the table while you ask the questions." I declined with thanks. Many weary hours later I staggered home, but not before she had second thoughts about whether she should have done the show, and could it be cancelled? No way.

In addition to the filmed life story of a star, I also had a brief live interview. When Jack Benny called to tell me he liked my show, which was high praise from the master, I grabbed him for a live appearance. He arrived at seven A.M. sharp for the rehearsal. "Coffee," he demanded immediately, and then took charge, telling us what he would say, and what he would not say. At this distance I can't remember either. But what I *do* remember about Jack, and most of the stars I knew, was the care and preparation, whether as a guest or for appearing on their own shows on television or in a theatre.

Marlene Dietrich, for instance, was over in London for a one-woman show many years ago in Golders Green. She went to the theatre the day before the show, going over the lighting, testing the microphone, and rehearsing over and over with the orchestra. I learned that you don't remain a star unless you supervise every detail.

Red Skelton, then at the height of his popularity, was a live guest on my show. It wasn't an important appearance for him, a few minutes for the housewives of America, but he had planned everything in advance, a résumé of some of the funny characters on his television show. Years later I saw Red in Zurich. He was taking his son, dying of leukaemia, on a trip around the world. One of the cheaper British newspapers accused him of using the boy for publicity. It was cruel and unjustified.

Dean Martin and Jerry Lewis, a law unto themselves, defied the studio ban against appearing on television. During their filmed story for my show they assured me they would never break up their successful partnership as Abbott and Costello had done. But they broke *me* up with their antics. One of my failings is that I am always trying to be funny. I actually tried to top Dean and Jerry! They made mincemeat of me. I expected we would get a higher rating, but we actually lost a point.

I took my young daughter with me when I filmed Edward G. Robinson at his home. The five-part interview took place in his art gallery, against the background of his French Impressionist collection. My daughter, regarding a pale Bonnard nude, remarked, "That lady needs a tan." *Everyone* in California had a tan!

Mr. Robinson had other problems apart from the House Committee on Un-American Activities. His wife, Gladys, one of the important Hollywood hostesses of the thirties and forties, demanded and received half of the paintings at the time of their divorce. Later, Eddie was able to buy some of them back from the Canadian collector who had bought them from her. At a price. He also had ongoing trouble with his son, Manny. One time, Manny arrived at the Robinson house at three in the morning and beat up his father, who nevertheless shed some tears when the son died.

I took both my children with me, Wendy, twelve, and Robert, nine, when I filmed the Gordon MacRae family in their pool with my kids. Gordon had starring roles in the movie versions of *Oklahoma!* in 1955 and *Carousel* in 1956. Later that year *The Best Things in Life Are Free* marked the beginning of a long hiatus in his film career. Twenty-three years on, in 1979, he tried for a movie comeback in *The Pilot*. There had been a drinking problem, although he was able to manage personal appearances and concerts. For many years now he has been one of the advisers at Alcoholics Anonymous.

When Rosalind Russell kicked up her heels in *The Girl Rush*, a 1955 musical with a Las Vegas background, it gave me an idea for a contest on my television show. "If your legs can match Rosalind Russell's, send a photograph of them to me at NBC-Burbank." The prize was a date with Liberace, then at the height of his piano-playing fame.

I was flooded. Legs of all shapes—long ones, short ones, fat ones, thin ones. All wanting to walk with Liberace. One facetious male sent a photograph of the front legs of a horse! It did *not* win the first prize, but it was Miss Russell's favourite dinner-party story. The winner of the best legs was brought to Hollywood for a night out with the glittering star.

In spite of his bejewelled hands and startling costumes, Liberace offstage has always been a pleasant, modest man. He often had me for tea at the home he shared with his mother in the Valley. On departing she always gave me a bag of her home-baked biscuits. There were two unusual features in the Liberace home, both in the shape of a piano: the pool and his bed. I was glad that the guest toilet was normal, and not in the shape of his trademark, the candelabra on his piano.

I felt a personal loss when Miss Russell left us in 1976. Of all the women I knew in films, she was my favourite. I had met her in 1936 on the set of *Craig's Wife* at Columbia. Her role was that of a wife obsessed with the cleanliness of her home, always scrubbing and polishing after the servants (like Joan Crawford in real life, who starred in the 1950 remake). In those years most of Miss Russell's roles were dramatic. She had saved her comic talent for entertaining guests at parties. Until one evening when someone said, "Roz, you should do this in a movie." *His Girl Friday* is one of the all time great comedy performances. She was crisp and bitchy in *The Women*. She was amusing in *My Sister Eileen*. And marvellous in *Auntie Mame*.

I had spent one evening with her during her honeymoon with Freddie Brisson. It was during the war. Captain James Addams, whose daughter Dawn would come to Hollywood later, was testing planes in California for the Royal Air Force. He was flying to Santa Barbara to bring the Brissons back to Los Angeles and asked me if I would like to ride with him. I said yes, as I always do. It would give me a chance to visit my friends Alan and Helen Hooker the following day in nearby Ojai.

Captain Addams' war machine was built for fighting the enemy.

For better manoeuverability it was extremely narrow. It rattled and slipped up and down and sideways. I was terrified. When the pilot turned to talk to me he found me praying, which rather shook him up. I had to rest in a bedroom at the Biltmore Hotel before I felt steady enough to join the Captain and the Brissons for dinner.

About a year before Rosalind died, I visited her in the Beverly Hills house she had bought early in her successful career. She had always been slender and she was still well-dressed, but her face and figure had been distorted by the cortisone injections for her crippling rheumatoid arthritis. "I went to sleep one night and when I woke up my hands were as big as hams," she told me, without self-pity. And there was none when she said, "There isn't a day when I am without pain."

While she had given up making films, she was active in the National Program for the Arts in Washington and very active in supporting research to find a cure for arthritis. Within six months of her death her husband, Freddie Brisson, married again. I wished that he had waited a bit longer.

After almost a year, I begged NBC to drop my television show. It was too much, having to get up at five-thirty to be ready to perform at seven-thirty for viewing in New York at ten-thirty A.M. One morning while driving to the studio there was a huge red glow in the sky—they were testing the atom bomb in far-away Nevada. I was writing seven columns a week, plus a radio show three times a week, and two monthly magazine pieces, in addition to running a big house and two children and trying to survive a difficult third marriage. The last did not survive.

As I collapsed into the Scripps Clinic at La Jolla, near the Mexican border, there was a phone call for me, from NBC in New York. "We are putting on a new weekly half-hour show. We want you on it to do a five-minute interview with a star." "Not now," I said. "Perhaps in a few months, when I am rested." "The Perry Como Show" was a hit from the first note, and you never add to or tamper with success, not even for an interview with a movie star. I could have been very rich.

Since then I have appeared on many talk shows, including a spot on the Huntley-Brinkley news show. They asked me to describe Khrushchev's visit with his wife to Hollywood. I referred to them as the Ma and Pa Kettle of Russia. Twentieth Century–Fox gave them a star-studded luncheon at the studio, and later Shirley MacLaine and the girls from *Can Can* gave them a live performance of the famous dance. It rather shocked them. In his welcoming speech, Spyros Skouras said that the United States was a great country where a poor Greek immigrant, like himself, could rise to be President of Twentieth Century–Fox. When it was Khrushchev's turn he said, through his interpreter, that Russia was greater than the United States because a poor peasant like himself could rise to be President of an even greater company, the USSR.

Chapter 14

The Glamour Maker

"THE GLAMOUR HAS GONE." That is all you hear in and out of Hollywood. The glamour has gone. But what is glamour? Is it fake eyelashes? Paint and powder? Publicity? Confidence? "It's security," said Ross Hunter, the producer who changed Doris Day from the freckled girl next door to the chic, sophisticated lady of *Midnight Lace* and *That Touch of Mink,* and Lana Turner from a sweater teenager into the worldly performer of *Imitation of Life.*

He is the man who went on to tell Ann-Margret that she would never be a star unless she combed her hair. And who fought Jacqueline Bisset until she agreed to wear a red wig in *Airport,* "to bring out the blue in your eyes." He is also the man who would like to remake Elizabeth Taylor into the glamorous beauty of her long-ago film *A Place in the Sun.*

But in today's Hollywood of computers, robots, strange little men from outer space, and $40 million spectacles, there is not much room for a producer who would like to bring back the human glamour that was synonymous with Hollywood. It has been more than a decade now since Mr. Hunter produced his last film, a remake of *Lost Horizon,* which was not a success. So he has turned to other media, television and the theatre.

I have known Ross ever since 1953, when he signed on as a producer at the Universal studio. When I visited him in his elegant home in the Trousdale Estates (very expensive) overlooking the City of Beverly Hills, he was preparing an out-of-town revue, *Ladies of the Silver Screen,* with some nostalgic names—Dorothy Lamour,

159

Virginia Mayo, Kathryn Grayson, Vivian Blaine, Betty Garrett, and Patti Andrews of those singing sisters.

"It was Annie Sheridan who started me off as a producer. 'You'll never be any good as an actor,' she told me. I had been playing bits in B pictures—'and Ross, no one knows women and glamour better than you do, so why not drop the acting and go in for production?' She was then starring with Cary Grant in *I Was a Male War Bride*. She told the director I was her dialogue coach, and that's how it all started."

"But how did you learn so much about women?" I asked. "From my mother. She said, when I was a very young boy, 'Look, if you have a shirt, make sure it is clean. When you go out of the house make sure that your hair is combed. Make sure you are proud of yourself.' So I thought, if I'm going to be a producer, I'm going to take all these beautiful women and make them *really* beautiful. I'm going to find out what their blemishes are, what is wrong with their faces, and if there is anything I can do to enhance what they basically have."

For instance, when Maureen O'Hara was making an early desert film for Mr. Hunter, the sound boom was throwing a shadow across her neck, making it look sallow and wrinkled. The producer found a branch of a tree—he did not explain where he found it in the desert—and held it for take after take so that it obliterated the shadow.

Doris Day was a plump podge in 1948 when I saw her on the set of her first movie, *Romance on the High Seas*. She had made a name on radio singing in that husky, slurpy voice. But she was decidedly not film-star material—a fat girl on a chocolate box. She had been a last-minute replacement for Betty Hutton, to the dismay of the director, Michael Curtiz, who was giving her a bad time. In her following films she would be the perennial tease, almost yielding, but not quite. "I knew Doris Day before she was a virgin," quipped Oscar Levant. Blue-eyed, blonde, wholesome, and as boring as a breakfast cereal, until *Pillow Talk*, produced by Mr. Hunter and released in 1959, for which Doris was nominated for the Oscar. (Sudden thought: Would Doris Day have made it under her real name, Doris Kappelhoff? Or Hedda Hopper as Elda Furry? Or Sheilah Graham as Lily Sheil?)

"How did you manage the transformation?" I asked Ross. "Well, I had to get her away from being the girl next door. If the public wants to see the girl next door, they will go next door and ring the door bell. First of all she had to lose weight. The next thing was to team her with a glamorous star: Rock Hudson. Before my movie *Magnificent Obsession,* in 1954, Rock had been mostly in B films, or rough John Wayne westerns, or Arabian tits and sands. I knew that he was really a handsome hero in shining armour just waiting to carry off his lady love. So I put him in a tuxedo and I had Jean Louis dress Doris—do you remember that sensational, nothing, white dress?—I gave her a fabulous hair-do, and I did something about her skin."

"What was the matter with her skin?" "All those freckles. And how she loved them. And how she loved those darned old dresses. And how the studio boss loved her in them. I had to fight them both. Doris sobbed, 'What do you mean, you're going to take me out of these dresses?' The studio was sure that sophisticated comedy wouldn't sell. They'd had some success with the girl next door, and they didn't know it was over. I wanted actors and actresses to be glamorous, romantic symbols. I wanted the average man and woman to have something to cling to. To say, 'If Doris Day can look like that, maybe I, who am the girl next door, can also look that way.' "

As I told you, in those day of strict censorship you could not have two people in the same bed, even if they were married. In *Pillow Talk* Mr. Hunter put Rock and Doris in separate bath tubs, but you saw them together on each side of a split screen. And when Doris lost her soap, Mr. Hunter had her hand go through the screen into Rock's tub. Of course that was too naughty for the censor and was cut.

In 1958, Lana Turner was in trouble at the box office because of the scandal of her association with the gangster Johnny Stompanato, who was stabbed to death by Lana's daughter, Cheryl. "She and I were old friends from my acting days," Ross told me. "I wanted to help her and to give her more fascinating roles than the insipid parts she had been getting.

"In *Imitation of Life* " (a remake of the Fanny Hurst story starring Claudette Colbert), "Lana would play a glamorous mother whose daughter had a friend who, although black, passed for white. This was in 1959, a touchy subject then. Again I had to fight the front office. They said it wouldn't do any business in the South. So the minute I finished the picture I made a tour of the South and I went on every radio and television show."

"Were you harassed?" "Not at all. They were happy to see a black picture that was glamorous instead of the typical black picture that was dirty and slimy. *Imitation of Life* was one of the biggest grossers at Universal." "How much did it bring in?" "Oh God, way over $50 million." "How much did it cost?" "$1,100,000."

On the producer's advice, Lana had taken a small salary plus twenty-five percent of the profits. This and two other films she made for him, *Portrait in Black* and *Madame X,* made Lana richer by four million dollars. The interest on her percentage, plus the advance she received for her recent autobiography, is now supporting her comfortably in her Century City co-op apartment. Recently, she became a born-again Christian. She says she is happier now that she has found God. She is no longer drinking—it had been a problem —or smoking.

Mr. Hunter's worries—with the studio bosses, the Hayes Office, and later the Johnston Office—were more often with the star. Jacqueline Bisset is an example. He brought her to Hollywood from Europe to play a leading role with Burt Lancaster, Dean Martin, and Helen Hayes in *Airport.*

"Jackie, that beautiful lady, she fought me all the way. She has one of the most gorgeous faces in the world—those eyes! But she has black, straggly, thin hair. And she loves it that way. She loves it all over her face. I said, 'Honey, I want to see your face. And another thing, I don't like your hair, it's terrible.' But when I suggested the red wig—titian really—she said, 'Oh no, I'll look awful.' 'Let's test it, and if you don't like it, we won't use it.' She had to admit that it made her glamorous."

Airport was Mr. Hunter's most expensive picture. It cost $10 million to make and broke even at $23 million. As of this writing, he claims that it has grossed $200 million. He assured me he had nothing to do with *Airport 1975.* Like some of the sequels of previous hits, it has not been successful.

Elizabeth Taylor was a glamorous star when she made *Giant*

with Rock Hudson. The film was directed by George Stevens, but Mr. Hunter was responsible for Rock getting the co-starring role in the Edna Ferber story. William Holden was first choice for the part, but Ross made the Warner people look at *Magnificent Obsession,* the film that had made Rock a romantic star. There was no further talk of William Holden.

I knew that Ross had never made a movie with Elizabeth and I asked him, "Now that she has lost some of her beauty, would you like to?" "Yes," he replied, "but only if she would allow me to do what I'd like to do with her. First of all, I would raise those low-cut gowns, and no dresses slit to the knee. She's a tiny girl and it cuts her in half. Then I would cut off all that hair. Fourth, I'd take off that Cleopatra make-up and just let her gorgeous face show."

Elizabeth still has an aura of glamour, of untouchability. An image of stardom. Of being something special. Of being confident. Perhaps it's because she still acts and lives like a movie star. Actually, I think that the most glamorous person in Hollywood is still Cary Grant. Which proves that glamour does not only apply to women. It's Cary's inner security. It's how he regards himself, as Mr. Hunter told me he tried to teach Sandra Dee.

Sandra was fourteen years old when he discovered her. "I picked her up right in front of 1175 Park Avenue in New York. I saw this tiny glamorous baby standing on the street corner. She was waiting for her mother. I walked up to her and said, 'My name is Ross Hunter. I'm a Hollywood producer. I would like you to come to my office in New York.' She said, 'Yeah, sure.' She thought I was trying to pick her up. She eventually took my card.

"Her mother called me. They came to my office. I told them that if Sandra would follow my instructions, I could make her a star. I brought her to the head of my studio. 'I don't like her,' he said. 'Why not?' 'Because she has no tits.' 'Neither did you have when you were fourteen!' 'How dare you!' They wouldn't put her under contract."

So Mr. Hunter put her under personal contract. He paid her three hundred dollars a week, then loaned her to MGM to play Paul Newman's sister in *Until They Sail.* In *The Reluctant Debutante* she was the deb daughter of Rex Harrison and Kay Kendall. "After that I put her in this little picture and that little picture. And then I put her in *Imitation of Life* and *Portrait in Black* with Lana." He also installed her in a pink and white house in Beverly Hills, with strict instructions on how to behave.

She must never go out in public unless she was well dressed. Her hair must be beautifully done. She must always look like a movie star. "And for seven consecutive years her movies were in the first ten at the box office." "But what is she doing now?" I asked Mr. Hunter. He sighed. "Unfortunately, she is still living with the ghost of Bobby Darin. She was fifteen years old when she married him, against my advice. I told her, 'You haven't even learned yet to neck in cars. You don't know what it's all about. But he does. He's well versed in that area.' "

Sandra and the singer, famous for his recordings of "Mack the Knife" and "Dream Lover," were divorced long before his death in 1973. Three years before, in 1970, the once glamorous "baby," who is now in her mid-forties, made her last Hollywood film, something called *The Dunwich Horror*. No, not with Mr. Hunter.

To my question, "Who is the most glamorous person you have ever met?" Mr. Hunter ignored Garbo, Dietrich, Oberon, Gable, Cooper, Taylor, Grant, etc., and replied, "The Queen of England. Now there's a lady who has inner security. She doesn't need the false eyelashes, the fake paint and powder. It would be a crime to hide her lovely complexion. She is more beautiful than I had imagined."

The occasion of the encounter was the Royal Command Performance in London of Mr. Hunter's *Airport* film. "When the Queen stopped in the line to talk to me she said, 'I want to tell you, Mr. Hunter, that I liked your *Flower Drum Song* very much.' And then, in a whisper, 'But I *loved* your *Pillow Talk.*' "

Chapter 15

Beloved Infidel

During my time in Hollywood, when you sold your story to a studio you forfeited all your rights as to how it should be presented on the screen. I believe it is somewhat different today, when the author is usually asked to write the script. But in my day, once you had signed the contract, which gave the studio everything for all eternity, you could save yourself some anguish by hiding somewhere until the resulting film had run its course. Even Ernest Hemingway knew better than to offer suggestions. Although with the filming of his book *For Whom the Bell Tolls,* he put in the word for Gary Cooper and Ingrid Bergman to play the leads. But that was all. And, for a change, he approved of the finished product.

I thought I was lucky when Jerry Wald, who had his own production company at Twentieth Century–Fox, bought *Beloved Infidel,* a book mostly about my time with Scott Fitzgerald. When his writer gave him the finished script, Mr. Wald sent it to me, as a courtesy. We both knew he did not have to do that, but I was an important columnist and it was safer not to upset me.

However, I was upset. The script had little resemblance to the book or the people in it. And when Mr. Wald called me one morning at seven-thirty (we were the earliest risers in Hollywood) and said eagerly, "Well, what do you think of it?" I replied, "I think it is awful!" Slight pause, while he turned on a tape recorder. "Alright," deflated, "tell me now, don't wait until the preview."

Half an hour later I was put on the studio payroll for two weeks, during which time I was to go over the script and bring it back to the book, for which they had paid $100,000, plus five percent of the profits. Mr. Wald said he approved of my changes and passed them on to his writer, who promptly consigned them to his wastepaper basket.

I had not intended to write about my years with Mr. Fitzgerald. We had been so private that only his friends knew of our association. The idea for a book had started in the early summer of 1957, when the editor of a top women's magazine called on me. "I would like you to write your story for us. About why you came to America. What did you hope to find here? And did you find it? And, of course," casually, "anything you would like to write about Mr. Fitzgerald will be fine." I had just gone through a difficult divorce from husband number three, and wasn't sure that I would have the time or inclination to write such a book. Also, I was planning to take my children to Europe, and to cover the Hollywood-financed films that were being made there.

"I'll make it easy for you," said the editor. "Give me one week in New York and you can tell the story into my tape recorder." He came every day to the Warwick Hotel, where we were staying, and while my children went to the movies or played in Central Park with the woman I had hired to take care of them, I poured my life into his machine. He would have it typed while I was in Europe.

By the time I returned, the magazine had closed, and his job with it. The words, my words, had been typed, but they were also on his property, the tapes. It was somewhat of a tussle and in the end I paid to get my words back, with a legal guarantee that he would never use what was on the tapes.

Mr. Wald now enters the scene. He was on a literary kick. He would like to be remembered for more than his *Peyton Place* soap opera success. A producer had made a film on the early years of Ernest Hemingway. Jerry decided that he would bring the life of Scott Fitzgerald to the screen. He asked John O'Hara to write it for him.

"Not me," said John. "You should talk to Sheilah Graham." "Why her? What did she have to do with Fitzgerald?" "She knows more about him than anyone here." Wald was surprised but asked me for lunch. This was shortly after I had returned from Europe and was trying unsuccessfully to retrieve the one written copy from that magazine editor.

"You can forget about him," said Mr. Wald expansively. "I will get you a contract for the book with Simon and Schuster. One of their top editors, Jack Freeman, is a friend of mine. And, of course, I will make the movie. So start writing." I wrote 100,000 words in three months, all from the top of my head, and without correcting a comma sent it to Mr. Freeman.

I had written one book, *Gentleman Crook,* a murder mystery, in 1933, before I went to America. There was an advance from the publishers, Rich and Cowan, of £25. And that was all. But I was able to go to New York as a British author.

"You need a collaborator," Mr. Freeman wrote to me. "You need someone to put all this into shape." He suggested Gerold Frank, who had written two bestsellers, Lillian Roth's *I'll Cry Tomorrow* and Diana Barrymore's *Too Much, Too Soon.* Both had been bought for films. Gerold was in Hollywood and we had several discussions about the book, which I was calling *Beloved Infidel,* after the poem Scott had written for me.

Gerold wasn't sure that he wanted to work with me. His two ladies had both been alcoholics and he wondered whether his reading public would welcome a book about a man who was also an alcoholic. "This book will bring you more prestige than anything you have done so far," I urged. I told him of Jerry Wald's interest. We would sign the contract with Simon and Schuster.

And then Mr. Freeman died. The woman editor who had taken his place hated the whole idea of *Beloved Infidel.* "I think it would be in terrible taste," she said, minimizing me to a speck of dust. When I reported her words to Gerold he too backed out of the project. I returned to Hollywood a very depressed lady.

But, writing my column, being with my children, living in a lovely house, swimming, playing tennis, having some money in the bank (not too much left over from the divorce), and being an optimist by nature, I soon perked up.

On the phone to Mr. Wald I said, "Jerry, you have always believed the Scott Fitzgerald story would make a good movie. Why don't I write an original script, just for you?" "Come right over," he said. And when I arrived he had two of his top screen writers to listen to me. Of course he would buy the film rights, but first, he said, it must be a book. He would call Donald Friede of World Publishing. He also called the *New York Times.*

That Friday Mr. Frank had gone to a theatre in New York with his wife. Leaving the play, he bought the Saturday morning edition of the *New York Times,* which came out on to the streets after eleven in the evening. Heading the page devoted to films he read in big black letters: "Jerry Wald Buys *Beloved Infidel.*" Which he had not quite. Jerry in his eagerness and enthusiasm had jumped the gun. But Mr. Frank did not know that.

Gerold's call in the morning to me was preceded by one from Mr. Friede. World Publishing was eager to give me a contract. He assured me he would guide me all the way. But I had been shaken by that woman editor at Simon and Schuster. Was *Beloved Infidel* really in bad taste? How far should I go in writing about a man who had once threatened me with a gun, an alcoholic, who had an insane wife in a sanatorium, but whom I had loved, and who was now considered among the best of the American writers?

All those hours of discussions with Gerold tipped the scale. He understood the story. He realized the dilemma. Yes, we would do the book together. At that point I should have hired an agent to handle my part of the deal. But I have always been an idiot about money, always believing that it would be there as I needed it. And strangely, it has been.

So when Gerold suggested that his own publishers, then Holt and Company, should also be my agent, I agreed. Good God, you never have your publisher as the agent. You get an agent to deal with the publisher. Especially as I already had a verbal promise from Jerry Wald to buy the film rights. But I agreed. Holt would get ten percent of the film, and Gerold would get fifty percent of everything. Also, I would handle the details of the film contract with Mr. Wald.

We had already discussed that. "How much do you want?" he had asked me. It had been my dream ever since coming to America to own a cottage in Connecticut. That was what I wanted for *Beloved Infidel.* "How much do you think a cottage in Connecticut would cost?" Mr. Wald had asked cautiously. I thought about $50,000.

(Today that "cottage" would cost $400,000.) So the price had been vaguely agreed upon. But now I had a collaborator. And Mr. Wald had put himself in an awkward position with his premature announcement.

As my present-day agent, Douglas Rae, said recently, "You should have been an agent." A woman friend said, "You need an agent like a hole in the head." But I do. I am still so amazed when publishers want to buy my writing that I would happily do it for next to nothing—well, almost. It was not long before other studios were aware that Mr. Wald did not have a contract. MGM and Warners were both making offers. But I owed the book to Jerry, and after much haggling: "$50,000 and five percent of the profits. Look, I'm giving you an annuity for your children. . . ." Like hell he was. I stood firm. "$100,000 *and* five percent of the net profits." Of course in Hollywood you rarely see the net profits. A good agent would have made it one percent of the gross.

But first the book had to be written. Gerold was a meticulous researcher. He interviewed dozens of people who had known Scott, and I learned some things I had not known, such as Scott telling Nunnally Johnson, the writer and producer, "You won't come to visit me again" (at Malibu) "because I am living here with my paramour." It's a good thing Scott isn't here now!

I gave Gerold the hundred thousand words I had retrieved from the magazine editor, and I repeated most of it, word for word, into *his* tape recorder. I learned a lot from my collaborator, chiefly how to put a book together, but also how much a good editor can contribute, and we had a great one at Holt. As Edmund Wilson told me after reading my solo effort, *College of One,* I really should have written the first book alone, then worked with the editor as I have with the nine others that have followed.

Time magazine murdered the book, adding "vulgar" to "tasteless." The cheaper British press murdered *me.* And I suffered, notwithstanding the high praise from the *New York Times* reviewer: "I hope it has a million readers," and Cyril Connolly in the London *Sunday Times,* and the *New Statesman* and the *Times Literary Supplement.* And Edmund Wilson in the *New Yorker,* in page after page of glowing comment, saying that of the ever-mounting books about him so far, it was the best account of Scott Fitzgerald.

The reviews for the film were something else. While it was being made I had deliberately absented myself from Hollywood. There were enough productions in London, Paris, Rome, Madrid, Athens to fill my seven columns a week. But after two months I had to return to put my children back in school, and *Beloved Infidel* was still shooting at Twentieth Century–Fox.

They were doing the scene with Scott at the Los Angeles airport, where he was going with me to Chicago to help me fight the sponsor of my radio show, who loved my gossip but loathed my British accent. The sponsor's idea was to have someone else read my five-minute interpolated segment, which was part of an hour-long vaudeville show emanating from Chicago. I was going there to prove my right of speech. And Scott was coming to support me. He ended up punching my sponsor—but that is a different book.

I watched Gregory Peck—as Scott—reacting to my realization that the liquid in his glass was not water but gin. When I had tried to move it away from him, Scott had grabbed my arm and flung it violently away. It was my first experience of seeing him drunk. Gregory was playing it as the gentle person he is in real life. After the first "take" I told him how it had really been. My shock. Scott's anger. "Oh no," he said, "I wouldn't play it that way." Recently he explained to me why he had merely smiled, retrieved the glass, and continued drinking.

"I hadn't wanted to do the film at all," he told me. "I didn't like the script. It should have been a love story, not rags-to-riches. Also I knew that I was nothing like Scott Fitzgerald, so I decided to play it as any American writer. It could have been John Steinbeck, or William Faulkner, or Hemingway."

Deborah Kerr had liked the book and had telephoned her agent from her home in Switzerland asking him to get the woman's role for her. She had chiefly liked the beginning, the girl leaving the orphanage, and later being presented at Court, coming to New York, and then meeting Scott in Hollywood. But the early years were cut, for otherwise Mr. Peck would not have appeared in the picture until a good way in. There had been some argument about that and he had insisted on bringing in his own writer.

Actually I thought they were both wrong for the roles. Greg was too tall and self-contained for Scott, and Deborah was too thin and too ladylike for me. (I had some second thoughts about the latter after reading Stewart Granger's autobiography in which he implied that he and Deborah had an affair in a taxi in London.) Marilyn Monroe or Jean Simmons would have been better in my part, and for Scott, Richard Basehart, the poetic fool in *La Strada*. But when I had suggested this to Mr. Wald, he replied, "Oh no, I plan on having much more important stars."

He invited me to the preview in Long Beach, an hour's drive south of Los Angeles. I sat alone, not wanting his other guests—the director Henry King, the cameraman, his secretary—to watch me while I watched my life unfold on the screen. Some highlights of the film had already been shown to several members of the press in Hollywood. And the word was that *Beloved Infidel* might win the Oscar. Those highlights were the good parts of the picture.

I sat there in the darkness absolutely frozen. Why didn't I feel anything? It was supposed to be my life up there. Why didn't I cry when Scott died as I had almost twenty years before? Why didn't I giggle at the end when Deborah was kneeling on the sands of Malibu to the accompaniment of the theme song, "Oh My Beloved Infidel," an imitation of "Love Is a Many Splendored Thing," which was a steal from Puccini. The music presumably was wafting Scott to his place in heaven.

The lights went up. Mr. Wald and the director hurried over to where I was sitting, still frozen. "Well, what do you think of it?" said Jerry with false joviality. "I didn't feel anything," I said flatly. "Ah, that's because you are too close to it." That made me angry, which returned me to life. They were both so pathetically eager for me to like it. But I thought the film was terrible. "It's too long," I said, for want of anything else. This annoyed Mr. King. "I love every foot of it," he cried. "I won't cut a thing."

I hoped I was wrong, but the critics agreed with me, although some of my colleagues tried to be kind. Scott's daughter had read the book and had telephoned me praising it. I dreaded what she would think of the film. But she never saw it in a theatre. Years later she caught it on television and adored the whole thing. "I thought Gregory Peck was so like Daddy!" I recently told this to Mr. Peck and he was pleased. I had asked him what he thought of the film and this was his answer: "I thought I was splendid!"

Beloved Infidel is always being shown on television, and when Kirk Douglas caught it the other evening, he phoned Gregory and told him, "You were very very good; you were wonderful." Even I like it better on television.

As for my five percent of the profits from the picture, I received just one statement from the studio, and was delighted to read (this was a year after the release of the film) that so far it had made $3 million. While I was figuring out how much my five percent would come to, my eye wandered to the other side of the page. *Beloved Infidel* had cost *$5* million and was $2 million in the red. Of course it was not. Most of the film had been made at the studio, and the two stars were fulfiling an early commitment before their price had gone up. In fact very few that I knew ever received a dime from a net profit. Mr. Wald died three years later at the age of fifty-one.

CHAPTER 16

Hollywood Abroad

IN THE early fifties and during the sixties, my Hollywood went abroad. And I went with it. I was known as "the Jet Age Columnist," the first of my profession to follow the films where they were being made. Most of the stars were delighted to see me. So many of them were afraid of being forgotten so far away from Hollywood. The films were being made in Rome, Paris, London, Madrid, Athens, Dublin, Venice, and Haifa. My favourite city of course was London, and with so many Hollywood-financed films there in the sixties I could also catch up with old friends.

In 1954 I was in Rome, where an Italian company was making *Helen of Troy* for Warners, with Robert Wise directing. At the time I completely ignored the brunette maid and concentrated on La Belle Hélène, Rosanna Podestà. But later I was to remember the maid: Brigitte Bardot.

I was in Rome again in 1961 for most of the shooting of Elizabeth Taylor's *Cleopatra,* which had been transferred from the fog and bad weather of London. I was in Greece for Sophia Loren's *Boy on a Dolphin,* with Alan Ladd; in London for Laurence Harvey's *Room at the Top,* with Simone Signoret, in 1958; in Madrid for Sam Bronston's *King of Kings* in 1961, with Jeff Hunter—"I Was a Teenage Jesus," *Time* magazine cruelly critiqued it.

Two years later in Spain again for *55 Days at Peking,* starring Ava Gardner and Charlton Heston, and in Rome again for Sophia Loren's *Yesterday, Today, and Tomorrow,* for Joe Levine and his American Embassy Productions. In London I looked up my old friend Carl

Foreman, who had completed his first big epic as a producer, *The Guns of Navarone*, with Gregory Peck and an all-star cast. (I was saddened by Carl's death last year.) Those two charmers Peter O'Toole and Omar Sharif were also in town, doing publicity in London for their film *Lawrence of Arabia*, for Sam Spiegel with Columbia studio money.

My producer friend Jimmy Woolf escorted me to the Shepperton set where Leslie Caron was starring in *The L-Shaped Room*, for director Bryan Forbes. Also coming up on his agenda was *Seance on a Wet Afternoon*, written, directed, and co-produced by Bryan, starring Richard Attenborough and Kim Stanley. And I had a cocktail at the Connaught Hotel with Sean Connery after he was signed for James Bond. I was sure he was wrong for the role, as was the author, Ian Fleming, although he did not say so publicly.

The sixties. What a marvellous time it was for me to be in London. The Beatles were making their first movie, *A Hard Day's Night*, in 1964, financed by United Artists. I was almost crushed to death at the premiere at my old stamping ground, the London Pavilion. And the year before I had met Richard Harris while he was making *This Sporting Life*, the film that made him an international star.

I had forgotten how good Laurence Olivier was in his 1962 *Term of Trial*, with Sarah Miles, released by Warners, until I saw it again recently on television. I imagine it was easier for him to play such robust roles as *Henry V* and *Richard III* than the mousey schoolmaster husband of Simone Signoret in that film.

I attended the London invitational preview of Tony Richardson's *Tom Jones*, starring Albert Finney. "It's a dis*ah*ster," Tony intoned at the end. "It's a dis*ah*ster!" How wrong he was proved. I also met Michael Caine at Joe Levine's party following the 1964 premiere of *Zulu*. He had fooled me as the upper-class British officer with his Eton-Oxford accent—as we know, Michael was a cockney from way back and still is, even though he is now living in a posh home in Beverly Hills. Michael is one of the more articulate actors I have known during my nearly four decades of writing about Hollywood. He is an expert on the film world. I visited him recently to chat about why Hollywood had gone abroad in the fifties and sixties, and why it had returned in the seventies.

"Of course, I wasn't there then," he said. "But you're right, American films went abroad partly because it was too expensive to make them in Hollywood. But chiefly it was because there was a very good structure for foreigners in England—the Americans didn't have to pay any taxes there. But in the seventies they all moved back to America when the socialist government decided to tax the foreigners the way they tax the British."

"Now they've gone back again to England, not to live but to make movies," I said. Michael agreed: "Because they have the best technicians at half the price of Hollywood. Today you can't get a foot of studio space in England."

In the sixties, I reminded Michael, the Americans with their money came to England as executives only, and made pictures with British talent. Another inducement to make films in Britain was, until recently, the Eady plan. The United States government does not give a cent towards the making of movies in Hollywood. But the British Eady plan gave the producers who made films there a return on the percentage of what was earned in Britain, providing they made the film with X number of British performers and technicians. In the sixties, fifteen percent of the profit from American-financed films would come from England, plus the Eady money, ten percent, for making the film in England. In recent years, until the British government cut it off last year, it had been only two and a half percent.

All the Bonds were British, and I admitted to Michael that I was wrong in thinking that Sean Connery, an ex-truck driver from Glasgow, would be miscast as Ian Fleming's suave 007. The ability to mix the right cocktail and wear the right clothes was less important than his projected macho image.

I had met his successor, Roger Moore, in Hollywood when he took over from James Garner in *Maverick.* I found Roger easier and more pleasant to talk to than Sean, who mostly worked on a closed set. In the early days he had been delighted to have a hundred and fifty-six journalists and photographers asking to visit him on the set of *From Russia with Love,* his second Bond, following his smash hit in *Doctor No.* I felt that for him, as for Marilyn Monroe, who had also been pushed around at the beginning of her career, being difficult with the press was a form of revenge.

"And this was when the best British actors all came along," said Michael, "O'Toole, Bogarde, Finney, Harris, Terence Stamp, myself (modestly), and Julie Christie. American money made *Darling* and Julie won the Hollywood Academy Award as the best actress. And we had some good directors: John Schlesinger, Lewis Gilbert, Stanley Kubrick *(Doctor Strangelove* and *2001: A Space Odyssey).* Kubrick went to England in the sixties and has lived there ever since."

I mentioned that MGM had made *Doctor Zhivago* in Spain, and that it was all American money. "Yes, but with all British technicians." And the same for *Lawrence of Arabia* in Jordan. "Of course it was because they got them cheaper. But were they better?" "Better? Cheap is no good unless you've had the people at the end of the day who have done a really good job. Cheaper is good only if you get the same quality. And what you get in England is the same quality of technicians as in America. Only cheaper." Me: "Plus someone who also speaks English."

Talking of *Doctor Zhivago,* Madrid has some of the world's best restaurants, Horchers in particular. Haifa had the worst. Otto Preminger had invited me to Israel in 1960 to cover *Exodus,* which he was directing in Haifa. The only good restaurant there was German. And that is where, on my first night, Paul Newman took me to dinner. His wife, Joanne Woodward, was there, not to work but to be with him. She and I are knitters and we had a great time comparing patterns for sweaters and such.

What fine careers Paul and Joanne have made for themselves, although it started badly for Paul with *The Silver Chalice* for Warners in 1955. How he loathed that picture. I can still hear him complaining. But talent, as I have said, will always survive. It's a pity that *Gandhi* and *Tootsie* both came out in the same year as *The Verdict.* In any other year Paul would have won the Oscar for his fine performance.

Returning home I stopped in London. It was May and the buds on the trees were as big as golf balls and Princess Margaret was getting married to Tony Armstrong-Jones. I covered the wedding for my syndicate. Mostly I watched the Queen. She was very serious and I wondered what she was thinking. Did she approve?

Five years later, for *Doctor Zhivago,* I stayed in Madrid much

longer than I had in Israel for *Exodus,* and I had some good talks
with the *Zhivago* stars. Mr. Sharif dined me at Horchers. What food!
And I talked at length with Julie Christie, who was then in the midst
of her affair with Warren Beatty. Would they marry? I did not think
so. Neither did she.

"But whether I marry or not," she said, "I want to have a child
by the time I am thirty." She is now forty-three, and she has neither
married nor had a child so far. Omar was married then and long
separated from the Egyptian film star by whom he had a son, Zerek,
who is now in his twenties. But, like Mr. Beatty, Omar has always
preferred to play the field with the ladies. I doubt whether either will
ever have a legal, live-in Mrs.

In Madrid I tried and failed to see Ava Gardner, who was then
living in the same apartment house as Juan Peron, the ex-dictator
of Argentina. Ava would not talk to the press after a trusted associate had written a searing account about her for a London Sunday
newspaper. She also stated at the beginning of each film that she
would walk off the set if she saw anyone from *Paris Match.* A photographer of theirs, perched in a tree, had used a long lens focused on
her bedroom during her affair with Walter Chiari, the Italian actor.

Both Clint Eastwood and Richard Chamberlain had to leave
Hollywood for Europe to become million-dollar-earning stars.
Richard went to London to shake off his Doctor Kildare image. His
stage *Hamlet* was highly praised, as were his Lord Byron in *Lady
Caroline Lamb* and Mark Antony in *Julius Caesar.*

Clint is now on the $3 million per picture plateau. *A Fistful of
Dollars,* an Italian film for an Italian company made with Italian
money in 1964, for which he was paid $15,000, followed by *For a
Few Dollars More,* was the beginning of his successful career in Hollywood. But with success came some problems in his marriage, which
often happens when the man or the woman becomes rich and famous.

Gregory Peck and Anthony Quinn were making *Behold a Pale
Horse* in Paris. And, of course, I was there. Tony and I were having
a chat between takes when he was called to the telephone—"To kill
a rumour," he said to me. I was worried. A mutual friend had told
me that Jolanda, the wardrobe lady on a previous film, who had

already presented Tony with a son, was again pregnant. I had used the information in my column. But because they were not married I had timed the item to appear the day *after* I was to visit the set. Had my syndicate mixed up the dates? It had.

Tony returned like a raging bull. "It's not true," he stormed at me. I wanted to run but the exit was some distance away. I followed Tony as he sat down on the hospital bed (he was playing a wounded soldier), and said, "If it's wrong I'll certainly make a retraction." "Of course it's wrong," he bellowed. And then more softly, "I'm on the point of getting my wife to give me a divorce, and now you've spoilt everything."

To cut an embarrassing retraction short, Jolanda *was* expecting a baby and it gave me some satisfaction to retract my retraction. They have been married for many years now and have three sons. I saw Tony recently in New York, where he is starring in the musical version of his stage and film success *Zorba the Greek.* He told me he would like to live in America again and is now hoping to convince Jolanda.

During the sixties in London, I saw the Israeli actor Topol playing Tevye onstage in *Fiddler on the Roof.* He departed abruptly for Israel during the Six-Day War in 1967, feeling that his presence there would be useful. Of all the Tevyes I had seen, including Zero Mostel's in New York, I believed that Topol's was the best. And when the film of *Fiddler* was being discussed, I campaigned for him in my column, which he read where it was syndicated in Tel Aviv. In his recent autobiography, he gives me credit for helping him to get the role.

The most uncomfortable visit I made to Europe in the sixties was to Paris, where William Holden and Audrey Hepburn were co-starring in a comedy titled *Paris When It Sizzles.* Most of the heat was coming from the producer and the director because of the delays caused by Mr. Holden's drinking. He and they had thought his alcoholism was under control, after he had undergone a devastating cure that consisted of the nurse giving him a glass of his favourite tipple every hour on the hour. Soon he would start retching just hearing the footsteps of the nurse. As you know, he died years later at his home in California, where he fell and hit his head. Poor Bill. He was a gentle, caring person.

CLEOPATRA

The most interesting and the longest of all my journeys abroad was my coverage of *Cleopatra* in Rome. I was there so often that when two of the publicity men on the film wrote a book about their experiences, they put my name on the production sheet with the names of the members of the cast.

Because Elizabeth Taylor did not want to do the picture her price had spiralled, not to the publicized $1 million, but $10,000 a week for as long as she worked in the film, which would add up to *$2 million*. Elizabeth and the producer, Walter Wanger, were the only hold-overs from the $7 million disaster of the filming in London. Stephen Boyd was scrapped as Antony, and Peter Finch as Caesar. Also the director, Rouben Mamoulian, was fired. The decision to start the whole thing again was taken during Elizabeth's recovery from the pneumonia she had caught in London that had almost ended her life.

For some time before this illness, which necessitated a tracheotomy—a cut in her throat to allow breathing through a tube—she had been extremely unpopular. She had broken up the marriage of her best friend, Debbie Reynolds, who had been her chief bridesmaid at the marriage to Nicky Hilton. Elizabeth had been Debbie's matron of honour at the marriage to Eddie Fisher. "How cold-hearted," cooed virtuous maids and matrons. And what a forlorn figure of a man Eddie had looked when photographed leaving the hospital in London. Mr. Elizabeth Taylor. Her lap dog.

But now he was settled in his own magnificent office at Cinecittà. Eddie's main job for his salary of $1,500 a week was to make sure that Elizabeth reported to the set. And what a set it was! Six hundred extras milled around and there were dozens more to carry the high platform on which Cleopatra would arrive in Rome.

The new director, Joe Mankiewicz, was a busy man. He had not only been rushed into the job, but he was rewriting the new script every evening for shooting the next day. He had a break whenever the weather turned nasty, which held up the filming on the huge outdoor set. But Joe still managed to find some time to continue his romance with the secretary whom he would later marry, and with Elizabeth—their friendship had started three years before in London when he was directing her in *Suddenly Last Summer*. In fact, the talk on the *Cleopatra* set was that the reason she was flirting with Mr. Burton was to make Joe jealous. But Richard did not know that, and he was flattered when the most beautiful girl in the world seemed to have fallen in love with him. He certainly did not expect either of them to take it too seriously. He often had an affair with his leading lady, and his wife, Sybil, always understood. So why should this one be different?

Mr. Mankiewicz had not wanted to direct the film. He had spent six months writing a script based on the Alexandria stories by Lawrence Durrell, and had been ready to start it at Twentieth Century–Fox in Hollywood. A six-figure bait in dollars had persuaded him to put *Justine* aside, all of which was adding to the cost of the film, which would eventually reach $44 million, unheard of at that time, and threaten the studio with bankruptcy.

Darryl Zanuck was already in trouble with his New York boss, Spyros Skouras. Television had caused a downward dip in profits, and Skouras did not take kindly to Darryl's high cost of loving his ladies and putting them in his films. Both executives were frantic at the reports from Rome of the dollars pouring into a barrel that had no bottom, for a picture that had started there in October 1961 and would take another year to complete.

Miss Taylor was being difficult. She disliked the six-day work schedule usual on all locations, and she decided she would not show up on Saturdays. "What can they do, fire me?" She knew they could not. She was often late to work, especially as the affair with Burton hotted up. His understanding wife, Sybil, had been advised to leave, but whenever she returned, Elizabeth would cry all night. With those violet eyes all red and puffy she would be unable to work the next day, so six hundred extras would be idle. It was worse when Richard invited a dancer from the New York Copacabana night club to visit him. After work they went on the town, and then *he* would be three hours late to the set.

Elizabeth's contract provided for approval of her photographs. But she added another dimension, a large pair of scissors. "I don't like it," she would say, cutting the negative into shreds. It all depended on her mood. She would say yes, and then no, to the same thing. And never ask for another opinion. Certainly not Eddie's.

This was one of her periodic times of disliking me, which depended on what I wrote about her. But I wanted to interview her. She was front-page news all over the world, and in my role as a purveyor of gossip, the shenanigans with Richard were the story of the decade. Especially after Elizabeth forced Eddie to return to New York, where he was hounded by the press into making a phone call to his wife in Rome. "Go on, call her," they urged, not believing his statement that there was nothing wrong with their marriage. "Tell them, dear, that everything is great between us," he gurgled. In four-letter language she told him where to put their marriage.

In my efforts to see Elizabeth, I was repeatedly discouraged by a certain Julio Ascarelli, who was in charge of all the publicity emanating from Rome. He was the most negative man I ever met. I was used to much more co-operation in Hollywood, New York, and London, but he was terrified of Elizabeth's tantrums and would not engender another on my behalf. So I went to Walter Wanger, who took me to dinner at George's, one of the best restaurants in Rome. He enthused about how marvellous everyone was, and what a great picture *Cleopatra* would be. I took his comments with the proverbial grain of salt and made a great show of writing down what he said. But Miss Taylor's answer was still no.

So, failing Elizabeth, I asked for Burton. But he too was afraid of her and would not risk talking to someone she disliked so much. Oh, he would say, "Good morning," or "Afternoon," and then walk quickly away. Finally I cornered Mr. Wanger in his office and said, "It doesn't really matter whether Richard sees me or not. I have enough material on this picture, especially the senseless waste, to fill a whole week of columns."

What I did not know at this point was that a meeting of the studio stockholders had been scheduled for the following week. It promised to be a stormy session. They had read the accounts of what was happening to their investment. Mr. Wanger called me later, all sweetness and darling. "Because I like you so much, I have arranged for you to see Richard tomorrow afternoon at the Grand Hotel."

We talked in the curtained alcove behind the enormous lounge in the hotel. Ninety minutes of pleasant chit-chat ended with his answer to my question, "Are you planning to ask Sybil for a divorce?" "What, divorce my wife to marry Elizabeth? NEVER!" He really meant it at the time, not reckoning with Miss Taylor's determination when she is in love with a man.

But I was still annoyed at Ascarelli and at Elizabeth's refusal to see me. I enlisted the help of an Italian press agent I knew, and we drove into Cinecittà, hoping to catch Elizabeth coming or going. Not a sign of her. We settled for a surreptitious entry into her dressing room. It was worth a fat paragraph. There were wigs on stands all over the place, and all her fabulous fifty-pound (in weight) costumes hanging up side by side, with metal supports to support the twin doves that King Solomon raved about.

Stopping at Ascarelli's office, I could not forbear teasing him. "I've seen her, I've seen her," I shouted. He turned pale. He did not have to ask who I had seen. "When, where?" he spluttered. "Never mind when or where, I've seen her!" I was so happy at his discomfiture that I felt as pleased as though I really had seen Elizabeth.

Actually, if I had wanted to be lazy there really was no need to see anyone in the film. There was enough going on there, and enough people who would talk, to keep my readers titillated for the duration. Elizabeth had two secretaries to cater to her whims, her personal hair-dresser, make-up man, and sundry hangers-on, in addition to Eddie when he was there. Richard had as many people on his or the studio's payroll—the latter I imagine. Plus a butler-secretary, and Richard Manley, through whom everything had to be cleared.

Rex Harrison was the only one without an entourage. But sexy Rexy was so distant and aristocratic-looking that I left him alone, although I did mention in my column the passionate love affair he was having with Rachel Roberts at the Grand Hotel in Rome.

Charlie Einfeld, then head of publicity for Twentieth Century–Fox in New York, was angry when informed that Elizabeth refused to see me. With so much money at stake, and with all my newspapers wanting to inform the public about *Cleopatra,* it was incomprehensible to him why Elizabeth would not co-operate and talk to me. God knows, I tried, but her answer was always no. Near the end of the filming they suggested taking me to a far-off difficult location on the chance that she would relent, but for the first time in my journalistic career, *I* said no. Besides, I already had managed to get a fine interview with Richard.

During the last months of *Cleopatra,* and with millions of dollars disappearing at an uncontrollable rate, the head office in New York demanded some economies. It always made me laugh, or cry, when a studio wanted to cut down on expenses. The first ones to go were usually the secretaries. How much could you save from them? For *Cleo* they cut down on the number of cars—there had been about sixty. Press agents had to share rides with crew members. Mr. Harrison's dressing room trailer was taken away. He screamed bloody murder, and threatened to return to England. And a press agent who wanted to be with his pregnant wife, who was about to give birth, had to pay for his own ticket to New York. And alas, no more free dinners for *anyone.*

They did not dare cut the salaries of the stars or the director. Besides, they had already received most of it and the rest was in escrow. During this period of economizing, Mr. Mankiewicz was heard to remark, "I'm the oldest whore on the block. We're all prostitutes." In fun, of course. Mr. Skouras, in a fit of petulance, had even fired Walter Wanger, who refused to leave. "They can't do that to me," he said in his modulated Dartmouth College voice. *"Cleopatra* is my baby!"

Near the completion of the film, the action was transferred to Ischia, where Elizabeth had the only suite at the Regina Isabela Hotel. There was one room for Richard, which Sybil, on a final visit to him, described as "an ice box." Only Elizabeth was needed for the final scene in Alexandria. This had been a problem, because Egypt was still at war with Israel and Elizabeth had become Jewish after her marriage to Mike Todd. Richard insisted on going along "to protect her," he said, from the Egyptian and world-wide press that followed her there. At that time he master-minded Elizabeth's publicity—usually without her, as she avoided talking not only to me but, except for the *New York Times* and the London *Times,* to any of the press who buzzed around hoping for some scraps.

Finally, *Cleopatra* was in the can. But Elizabeth would not allow them to announce that at last her role was finished and they could all go home. She was afraid that the message would bring Mrs. Burton back to reclaim her wandering husband. However, Sybil and

Eddie had had enough. Two divorces were slated, while Elizabeth and Richard went to their His and Her chalets in Switzerland. Mostly hers. Mankiewicz returned to Hollywood, where he fought with Mr. Zanuck, who insisted on cutting the picture. Mank then gave up on the film, which he said "was conceived in a state of emergency, shot in confusion, and wound up in blind panic." The splashy premiere did not help. One reviewer wrote: "*Cleopatra:* an elephant which produced a mouse."

I was interested in Mankiewicz's evaluation of the Elizabeth and Richard romance: "They were not really lovers. Just two actors who did not know when the show was over." Mr. Wanger's summation of Elizabeth: "From early childhood she had lived in a world of fantasy. She doesn't know any other world."

In my opinion Elizabeth can be charming, but sometimes she acts like a spoiled child. Mr. Burton, drunk or sober, was *always* charming. He was a good actor. But he was not going far in Hollywood until his affair with Elizabeth coated his ability with a sexy image. He had always seemed cold on the screen, but as the lover of Liz he was raised to her million-dollar plateau. According to Mr. Fisher, that is what Richard had set out deliberately to do—to use Elizabeth to get rich. It took him some time to realize that Elizabeth was colder and more calculating than he was. Starting as a beautiful sixteen-year-old, she has always used men as matchsticks to light her ego.

She learned something from each husband. When young Hilton left her on their honeymoon to play golf, or gamble, she learned that not all her tears could stop him. Michael Wilding, her second husband, gave her a course in English foul language. Mike Todd made her greedy for jewels, and taught her to respect a man who would knock her about. When Todd was married to Joan Blondell, he had broken her arm during an argument. We will pass over Mr. Fisher. "It was a mistake," she had admitted to Mr. Mankiewicz during the filming of *Suddenly Last Summer* in London three years before *Cleopatra.*

I can't imagine Mr. Burton beating her physically. With his extensive abrasive vocabulary and fine delivery, perhaps he did not have to. But even he was unable at last to handle the bad publicity, and he would be screaming and swearing at everyone, even at

Roddy McDowall, the go-between for the Burtons and the Fishers. Mankiewicz, on returning to America fed up with the whole project, told one of the wire services, "The Elizabeth Taylor–Richard Burton thing is a cover-up for the real story, which is that *I* am in love with Richard, and *Elizabeth* is just the cover-up!"

One of Miss Taylor's problems is that fundamentally she is a puritan who believes that if you have an affair with a man you ought to marry him. Not all of them, of course. Not that used-car salesman in Hollywood, and she knew that Mank was on to her and would never give her the important ring. As for her affair with the intellectual columnist Max Lerner, I suppose he did not want to make the same mistake that Arthur Miller had by marrying Marilyn Monroe.

Elizabeth loves the flurry and excitement of the courtship, but not too long after the marriage she becomes bored. When asked, "How are things going with Eddie?" she reportedly replied, "When I walk into the house and hear him rehearsing, 'Oh My Papa' one more time, I'm going to scream the place down!" And later, after her marriage to Senator John Warner, she said, "If I have to make one more campaign speech, or kiss one more baby, I'll go mad!"

A year before the latter break-up I believed their marriage was on the skids. A neighbour near Senator Warner's Georgetown house in Washington told me, "They are in the pool, day and night, always quarrelling." Another sign of trouble was when Elizabeth returned full time to her acting career. This is a sure clue that the marriage is over. When everything seemed fine with Mia Farrow and André Previn, I knew it was the end for them when she returned to America and her acting career.

These career stars miss the excitement and the applause. Not so much the money, but that too is pleasant. Naively I had thought that Elizabeth, as the wife of an important senator, was setting her sights on the White House, to be the First Lady of the land. But attending all those political parties in Washington, having to talk to all the wives, was a taste of what could come—too boring.

It would take a Proust to understand and describe how Elizabeth changed from the gentle, sensitive, shy girl I first met when she was twelve years old, making *National Velvet* at MGM, to the self-centered woman of today. Louis B. Mayer had presented her with the horse from the film. I remember her bubbling with excitement telling me how she was caring for the mare, and how desolate she was when Nibbles, her pet chipmunk, had died. It would take another book to go into all her marriages, all her films, all her illnesses. Besides, it will be more interesting to bring you up to date on the person she has been in the last decades.

The Regency Hotel has always been her favourite place to stay in New York. She went there originally when her press agent, John Springer, asked me if I knew of a hotel with a back door where the Burtons, then newly married in 1964, could leave without wading through a crowd of autograph seekers. The Regency was fairly new. It is on the corner of Park Avenue and 61st Street and has a side-street back door, so you can leave through the garage.

Their secretaries went on ahead to inspect the rooms they would occupy, with their hundred and twenty-five matching, initialled, pieces of luggage. There was one whole suite for Elizabeth's clothes. The staff loved the Burtons, especially Elizabeth, a great tipper. The hotel maid received a hundred dollars every time she unpacked for Elizabeth, and another hundred when she repacked.

One night there was a robbery at the hotel. The burglars were looking for Elizabeth's vast collection of jewels. But they were not in the hotel. They were in the vault at her bank. In the evenings when she sallied forth in all her glittering splendour, four guards protected them and her. Sometimes there were two guards all night outside the bedroom where they or she slept. Superstars have always been afraid of kidnappers.

When the Burtons first went to the hotel, Richard had taken the manager aside and given him some good advice. "If you want to get along with my wife, say yes to everything she wants." One night, at three in the morning, Elizabeth had a sudden yearning for cheesecake. Not ordinary cheesecake; it had to be Lindy's cheesecake, which was famous all over the show business world. She called down to the kitchen, "Please send up some Lindy's cheesecake." "We don't have any," she was told. "I must have it," said Elizabeth. They awakened the manager.

Jacques Camus is no longer at the Regency. He is managing another fabulous hotel, the Westwood Marquis, in California. During lunch with me he revealed the saga of the Lindy's cheesecake. "I got dressed and went to the kitchen. Lindy's (on Broadway) had been closed for two years, but I couldn't disappoint one of our best customers. So I took our own cheesecake out of the ice box, and brought it up to her, and said it was from Lindy's.

"Was it a present?" "Oh no, it cost her fifty dollars. And all she ate was a tiny slice and sent the rest back!" Incidentally, the Burtons rarely used the back door of the Regency. They preferred to feel their fame by plunging into the crowds waiting for them in front of the main entrance.

I think the biggest change in the Elizabeth of yesterday is her present passion for publicity. Where Richard Burton had to force her to give interviews, now she will do almost anything for publicity. She recently went so far as to open a new bank. Perhaps she owned it. And that fire engine she had pick her up at the stage door when she was starring in *The Little Foxes* in New York! She said she needed it to be rescued from her fans. And the performance at her fiftieth birthday party in London, which of course Richard attended—*he* always loved publicity—where he said, "I love you," in Welsh. Later Richard told the world that they had gone to bed that night, "for old times' sake." After which she popped into bed with her fiancé, the Mexican lawyer Victor Luna, while Richard did likewise with *his* soon-to-be wife, Sally Haye.

Then, to extract still more publicity from their association, they were co-starring onstage in Noel Coward's comedy *Private Lives,* to the most devastating reviews I have ever read. Of course it was the money, a guarantee of $70,000 a week each. They had realized for some time that their million-dollar days were over in films.

Don't get me, or Elizabeth, wrong. She has made some good movies. I think the best was *Cat on a Hot Tin Roof,* with Paul Newman. But she was essentially a film product, not a stage actress. I say "was" because some of her last films, including *The Blue Bird* and *A Little Night Music,* were unsuccessful. She has not made a movie since *The Mirror Cracked* (1980).

The Blue Bird was made in Russia and directed by George Cukor, who admitted to me that there had been many problems, not all of Elizabeth's making, "although," he said reluctantly, "she was inclined to be late. But she's such a darling." (George either loved you or loathed you, and if he loved you, you were either adorable or a darling.)

"One big problem was the Russian crew. They would change technicians every day. I'd say, 'Raise this,' and I'd go there and there would be a man I had never seen before. It was maddening. And the cinematographer had never shot colour before.

"That's when I called in Freddie Young from England. He brought an English crew and after that we had absolutely no problems." They were in Russia for eleven months and the cost was enormous. "But I was unaware of that," said George, "because the Russians supplied half the money, so it didn't matter too much when Elizabeth held up shooting by being late."

Elizabeth's voice is too high-pitched for the theatre, although I hear she has been taking lessons to bring it down. Perhaps the theatre and occasional television will now be her main area for work. You have to give her an A for trying. And the media, yearning for something outrageous and colourful in a rather drab world, went out of their way to be generous when reporting her live appearances, until *Private Lives,* and then they came down on her.

Richard, of course, would have kept plodding on: films, theatre, television, whatever. I saw him again in his revival of *Camelot.* He still had that great voice, and no one has been better in the role. Not Laurence Harvey, whom I saw as Arthur at the Theatre Royal in Drury Lane, and not even Richard Harris, who sang better, but lacked the stage magic that Mr. Burton had.

Chapter 17

Meanwhile, Back in Hollywood

MEANWHILE, BACK IN HOLLYWOOD, Alfred Hitchcock was getting away with murder in *The Birds,* with a new blonde lady, Tippi Hedren. *Torn Curtain,* starring Julie Andrews, was another failure. In fact, after his success with *Psycho* in 1960, the old master seemed to have lost some of his touch, at the end of a great career that had started in England with *The Pleasure Garden* in 1925, and in Hollywood with *Rebecca* in 1940.

John Ford was once asked what he thought of Mr. Hitchcock, to which I was told he replied: "Hitchcock lives on his reputation as a director of suspense. He's a great technician, but only rarely does he achieve suspense, except in the last few minutes of the film." And when a New York critic wrote of Hitchcock's *Rear Window,* "It had me on the edge of my seat," Ford remarked, "He must have had haemorrhoids." "Suspense," said Mr. Ford, "has only two elements. A nice guy gets into trouble and the audience is screaming for them not to call the cops. Or, it's a monster rampaging, an awful man, and the audience wants the cops to get him." Many of us would disagree with this judgement by one director of another. For my part I have enjoyed more of Mr. Hitchcock's films than those of Mr. Ford, except for his *Stagecoach,* with John Wayne. The others I have found too sentimental.

As two former Brits, Hitch and I would chat about the old country, mostly about the food. Hitch adored kippers and had cases of them flown from Scotland to him in California. He did not care too much for actors, which was another bond between us. In all my thirty-eight years in Hollywood, most of my close friends were the writers or people outside of the film industry.

In Hollywood, Billy Wilder was still angry with me because I had disliked his 1961 movie, *One, Two, Three,* which he had made in Munich with James Cagney. I had written that there had been too much shouting, that it was all on a monotonous level. The director, who had fled from Nazi Germany in 1933, would then not allow me on his sets, or on the junkets that went to Europe for other films. He had won every kind of award for writing, directing, and producing *Sunset Boulevard* in 1950. But in his later years, like other formerly brilliant directors, his films had not been up to his standard —another example is *Kiss Me Stupid.*

John Huston was in a Hollywood cutting room with *Freud,* which he had directed in Vienna, with much grief and frustration from Montgomery Clift in the title role. Monty had great difficulty remembering the strange medical terms. He had not been a hundred percent well since the auto accident he had suffered while filming *Raintree Country* with Elizabeth Taylor in 1957. There were also problems with his homosexuality. I believe he wanted to be "straight," but his inclinations were the other way. He was embarrassed the last time I saw him. It was in an elevator on Central Park West. He was taking a young black man, obviously gay, to his apartment.

In Hollywood, Paul Newman, in between marching in Washington for civil rights (he is now actively campaigning for a nuclear-free world), was preparing to star in *Hud* with Patricia Neal, who would win the Oscar as Best Actress for her part. Two years later she would suffer the devastating stroke that kept her in a coma for a month. She always credited her husband, Roald Dahl, with bringing her back to physical normalcy. Her only disability today is a slight limp and difficulty in remembering names. She has been living in America doing TV commercials for a pain-killer tablet, which, however, did not kill the pain of having to divorce Roald Dahl. It was the old story of a husband falling for the wife's best friend, said Pat.

There is no such problem for Mr. Newman and his wife, Joanne. She acts, he acts, and often he is her director. They both have a sense of humour, which you need for marriage, and he is still the lover after more than twenty-five years. I remember him telling me that their best times together were when they could leave the children at home, rent a room in a hotel, and stay in bed for a whole weekend, with brief interludes for food and the beer he loves.

There was only one time that the marriage wobbled a bit. I was told this by one of their close friends, a woman. According to that source, Joanne was worried about her acting career. In 1957 she had won the Oscar for her performance in *The Three Faces of Eve,* but taking time out to give birth to three daughters had caused her career to stall somewhat. She thought Paul should pause in his own acting life and pay more attention to hers. It was too much to ask.

True reason or not, for a brief period they parted. In Paris I learned they were staying at separate hotels. Joanne, always honest, has stated on television that of course there were arguments in their marriage. At the beginning of his auto-racing career she was naturally worried. She has now accepted that Paul, who has turned sixty, is careful but stretches himself to the limit to win. He has learned to tolerate her passion for the ballet.

I won't go into all their movies—his: *Harper, Cool Hand Luke, Butch Cassidy, The Sting,* etc.; hers: *The Three Faces of Eve, The Long Hot Summer, The Fugitive Kind, Rachel, Rachel,* which Paul directed. You have seen most of them. Especially, I hope, Paul's winner, *The Verdict.* It's hard to have everything in this life, but I think Paul and Joanne have most of it.

When Cary Grant returned to Hollywood from Paris, where he had made *Charade* in 1961 with Audrey Hepburn, he resolved that he would not go abroad again to work in the winter. His glorious tan was all but faded, and when you have lived in California as long as he has, more than fifty years, you become used to the warmth of the sun. After starring with Leslie Caron in *Father Goose,* on location in the warm Caribbean, he made one more movie, *Walk, Don't Run,* with Samantha Eggar, in 1966. Neither film caused a queue at the box office.

My relationship with Cary has been up and down. Sometimes he loves me, sometimes he does not—most often the latter. The memory of that marvellous dream about him soon after I arrived in Hollywood must have faded, because by the time he was making

Gunga Din at RKO in 1939 I had annoyed him in my column to the point where he was going to tell me off in front of my visiting boss, John Wheeler. I prudently kept Mr. Wheeler away.

But there was a friendly time when he would advise me, using his own philosophy of life: "Never have any doubts. Always believe that whatever you want will be there." "Even a parking space?" I joked. It was almost impossible to find one in Beverly Hills. "Yes, even that." I tried it out at once, driving to the Premier Food Market. I looked down the street. Every space was taken. And then, as I came within two feet of the market, as if by magic, the car right in front of it moved out, and I went in.

"Think thin," he always told me during our days of speaking to each other. That was a bit harder, but I *felt* thin, which was almost as good.

And when I was in the hospital having an operation on my eye, with both eyes bandaged, he phoned regularly, giving the nurses a great thrill. He advised me to exercise my legs in bed, which I could do without moving my head. "I would send you some flowers," he said, "but you wouldn't be able to see them." I almost replied, "But I could smell them."

And that is part of our quarrel. Cary, because of his poor childhood, was extremely careful with his money. I doubt whether he still is with his young fifth wife. The previous Mrs. Grant, Dyan Cannon, gave many examples which I used in my column. She also mentioned in her divorce suit that Cary had used LSD one time. When I visited him at a studio he told me that he was taking lysergic acid "under the supervision of my doctor. It has the effect of making all of nature beautiful." I almost wanted to try it, but I have always been cautious of taking other people's medications.

Recently I was lunching at Les Ambassadeurs in London. An American woman came over to my table and told me that she had been reading one of my books on the plane coming over. "And guess who was on the plane? Cary Grant! When he saw me reading your book he was very complimentary about it." "Oh come now, you know he wasn't," I replied. This was one of the "loathing" periods. "Tell me what he really said." She hesitated, then, "He said, 'Don't read it, it's full of lies!'"

I had to laugh. And it's about time I gave Mr. Grant his due, that he is just about the best thing that ever came out of Hollywood. He gives the place a better image. It can't be all that bad if Cary prefers to live there. He will be remembered for a long time as one of the greats of the film world. So what if he is a bit stingy—and mind you, he is a multi-millionaire from all his movies, most of which he owns outright.

There are still some government officials in Washington who say nasty things about Jane Fonda, because of her anti-establishment causes and her antagonism to U.S. involvement in Vietnam in the sixties, and they will not forgive her for visiting there during the war. Her father, Henry Fonda, was also a Democrat, but he never went as far as his daughter to proclaim his beliefs. While I would sometimes see his name on certain Democratic committees, he did not go about making speeches, perhaps because he was naturally a reticent man.

Henry made several films in Europe. I remember chatting with him in the sun outside a sound stage in Rome, where he talked more than he ever had to me, about his painting. He was a fine painter, and, what with his busy career, his five marriages, and his family, he did not have much time for politics. But he worried about Jane, afraid her career would suffer because of her strong opinions. And he worried about his son, Peter, who was often "busted"—Peter's word—on drug charges.

Roger Vadim, the first of Jane's three husbands, had tried and failed to transform her into another sex-pot like Brigitte Bardot, who had been his previous wife. In the sixties Vadim, as her film director, did more harm to her career than her politics did.

It is hard to believe now that Jane was quite plump—150 pounds, she told me—before she made her first Hollywood film— *Tall Story*, with Tony Perkins, in 1960. Until *Klute* in 1971, for which she won the Oscar playing a highly paid prostitute, she was better known as Henry Fonda's daughter, and for her politics, than as the fine actress she is today.

In fact, Jane is now one of the top film superstars in the world. Not only that, but her exercise books have been bestsellers on both sides of the Atlantic. And if you do not believe her rules you can look at her body, all muscle and no fat.

Jane lives modestly in Santa Monica with her similarly anti-establishment, anti-war husband, Tom Hayden, and their children, who include Vanessa, from her marriage to Vadim. Unlike some others, all speeches and no action, Jane uses most of her multi-million-dollar income to support the causes they both believe in so strongly.

Politics have always been important in Hollywood. I don't essentially mean politics *inside* the studios, which have been going on ever since the movies migrated from New York to Hollywood, and Jesse Lasky joined with Cecil B. De Mille to form the Famous Players–Lasky Corporation in 1914. I mean the right-wingers in Hollywood on the stump for the Republican Party, such as Charlton Heston and John Wayne. For the Democrats, Shirley MacLaine, Angie Dickinson, and Lauren Bacall, and, more recently, Warren Beatty and Robert Redford. In many ways Washington, like Hollywood, has always been full of the pursuit of power mixed with the same kind of gossip and scandals.

John F. Kennedy was a senator when he came to Hollywood in the late fifties. I was introduced to him at the Biltmore Hotel, at a fund-raising dinner for his hoped-for presidency. My column was appearing in the now defunct *Washington Star*. "I read your column every day," said the senator diplomatically. I thought, if he wastes his time reading a movie column, I won't vote for him. But I did, when I considered the dreadful alternative, Richard Nixon. After I voted for Kennedy, I was annoyed when Louella Parsons received an invitation to his January 1961 inauguration. She was a Republican and had voted for Nixon, as Hedda Hopper had. Louella had accepted. Hopper, a more rabid right-winger than Louella, was not asked. I did not really want to go. I dislike blaring political affairs, but I felt I should have been invited. I called the White House, spoke to a Kennedy aide, and explained my injured feelings. An invitation was forthcoming. But I never wrote about Washington politics in my column. It was not in my line of work, which, unlike Miss Hopper's, was concerned only with what went on in the world of films.

However, I have always been vitally interested in politics, and I attended the cocktail party Dore Schary and the writer Leonard Spiegelgass gave for Adlai Stevenson when he was rumoured to be a candidate for the presidency of the United States. The large crowd included the Misses MacLaine and Bacall.

I asked Adlai: "Are you planning to try for the nomination?" "Absolutely not," he replied. "Not even if you are drafted?" "Absolutely not!" Never believe a politician. He fought for the prestigious job right down to the wire.

Chapter 18

Ronnie

Frank sinatra is one Hollywood actor who changed his politics. Another, as you know, is Ronald Reagan, who had been a vociferous Democrat, and switched to being just as fervent a Republican in 1960. Frankie, who is often at the White House now, was also a welcome visitor there after Kennedy was elected. He made the mistake of getting too close to the President, and invited JFK to be his guest on a yachting cruise in the Mediterranean. On the advice of Kennedy's cabinet the invitation, at first accepted, was subsequently cancelled because, rightly or wrongly, Sinatra's name was mentioned too often in connection with the Mafia. In a fit of pique Sinatra switched to the Republican side and took Dean Martin and Sammy Davis, Jr., with him. I was revolted by the sight of Sammy kissing Nixon.

The first time I was aware of Ronald Reagan was in 1937. There was an item in Louella Parsons' column that she was taking a group of young actors and actresses, among them Mr. Reagan and Jane Wyman, on a personal appearance tour to the major cities of America. While she was well known and they were not, the plump Miss Parsons, with her malapropisms, would have cut a comic figure onstage, but by introducing the youngsters as future stars of Hollywood she had a plank on which to reach her audiences. (In the same column as this announcement she had changed Mary Pickford's book *Why Not Try God* to *Why Try God!*)

Jane Wyman was the only one of the group to become a major star, capping her career in 1948 as the deaf mute in *Johnny Belinda*, for which she won the Oscar. In the same year she divorced Mr. Reagan after eight years of marriage. When asked what had caused the break-up she replied, "He talked too much." But that was not the only reason. It was the familiar Hollywood story of one partner on the rise and the other remaining more or less stationary.

I was told that at a party soon after the divorce in 1948, Ronnie was discovered behind a curtain sobbing as though his heart would break. He had not wanted the divorce and the separation from their two children.

During the marriage with Jane, and for some years after the divorce, Ronnie was a good Democrat. It is hard to remember now that in 1950 he made speeches, raised money, and campaigned for Democrat Helen Gahagan Douglas (the wife of Melvyn Douglas) against Republican Richard Nixon, during their bitter contest for a seat in Congress.

In 1964 he would campaign just as hard for Senator Barry Goldwater in the Republican bid for the presidency of the United States. Ronnie's speech for Goldwater on the evening before that election brought him national attention, even though Goldwater lost. It was his first step on the road to the White House. A new voice had been heard, an optimistic, confident voice.

President Reagan always sounds so definite—but as events have shown, he can be persuaded to change his mind. For instance, during the fifties he wrote an article for the *Hollywood Reporter* in which he stated, "I will never run for public office." He had also told Ann Sheridan, "I will never ever appear on television." So you see, he can be very flexible. I always believed that his second wife, Nancy Davis, was responsible for his change from Democrat to Republican. I remember the first day in the late forties that Nancy, the newly signed starlet, sat with me at the beginners' table at MGM. She was very quiet and seemed a cut above the usual beginner. I didn't write much about her. Not even when she married Ronnie in 1952. Readers would be interested in what Marlene Dietrich had for breakfast, but not what Nancy Davis, a bit player, had for her wedding reception.

As a child, Nancy had been adopted by Dr. Loyal Davis, a well-known brain surgeon in Chicago who had married her widowed mother. The family had a summer home in Arizona, next door to the Goldwaters. They were all rigid right-wing Republicans. That was all Nancy ever heard during her vacations, and that was all Ronnie heard when he visited her family after their marriage in 1952, following his five-year term as president of the Screen Actors' Guild. In those early years he was a great union man, fighting for the thousands of underpaid actors and actresses in Hollywood. Later he would call it his "bleeding heart" period. But the people he helped remember it gratefully.

After World War Two, which Ronnie had spent in nearby Culver City as a captain in the army making propaganda films for the war effort (his weak eyesight prevented active service), he determined to help the GIs who were finding it difficult to adjust to civilian life. He joined the American Veterans Committee, a serious organization that did not want to compete with the more flamboyant American Legion, some of whose members were addicted to wearing funny hats at conventions.

Because Ronnie had a reputation as a good communicator, he was appointed chairman of the Valley chapter. He was a tall, handsome figure in his wrap-around camel-hair polo coat, his hair as dark chestnut then as it is now.

Reagan's group was accused of being too radical. It was the beginning of the witch hunt from Washington. Actually the group was low-key, politically moderate. But the American Legion and another group, the Veterans of Foreign Wars, were concerned because the Valley chapter of American Veterans was taking members from them by appealing to the young GIs. So they branded it radical, which, at that time, was as good as calling it Communist.

The vice chairman of Mr. Reagan's chapter was a poultry farmer in the Valley. He was worried, and called a meeting. About sixty men attended and he told them: "I've deliberately not invited our chairman to be present, because our chairman is too far off to the left. So I am resigning my post as vice chairman, and also from the American Veterans Committee. I know what you came into the organization for, but I feel that Mr. Reagan will get us all into trouble. I would recommend that you get the hell out while you can." That was the end of the Valley chapter of the American Veterans.

Ronald Reagan too leftist for the leftists! In fact, at that time

Ronnie was so far left in his thinking and actions that reportedly an associate went to him and said, "Look, we want your money, we want your help, and we appreciate your speeches, but would you mind if we took your name off our lists?"

Today, no one is willing to say whether it was Reagan's fault, as the outgoing President of the Screen Actors' Guild in 1952, that such a bad deal was made with the Producers' Guild regarding residual payments to the actors in the films that would be sold to television. As Bob Hope said, "They gave away billions of dollars for a few millions to benefit the Motion Picture Country Home." All those films from the beginning of sound to 1952 that are shown over and over on the small screen result in no payments to the people who worked in them. Mickey Rooney, for instance, receives nothing from all the films—about seventy—he made before the 1952 agreement with the producers.

But I am sure that if the responsibility for the bad deal *was* Reagan's, he believed, on the advice of his associates, that he was doing the best possible for his union. As he believes, no doubt, about the policies he pursues as President.

During his later years at Warners he was known as the actor who usually did pretty much as he was told. He might grumble, but he accepted the roles, the directors, and his co-actors. And in 1954 he even accepted a chimpanzee, Bonzo, as his co-star.

I doubt whether Ronnie has ever struck a woman. He certainly had trouble striking Angie Dickinson during his last movie, *The Killers*, a 1964 remake of the earlier Burt Lancaster film. It was the only time that he played a villain, which he prefers to forget. "Sorry, it's in the script," he said, swinging feebly. "Come on, hit me," Angie kept saying. "I can't do it," said Ronnie. As you know, in films they rarely hit each other. They fake it. But he could not even fake it, and a less squeamish hand was inserted to strike the blow. I saw *The Killers* recently on television, and I couldn't tell the difference.

The President has always appreciated kindness. In his early B-picture years at Warners, he was mostly ignored at the studio that had stars of the calibre of Jimmy Cagney, Paul Muni, Humphrey Bogart, Errol Flynn, Pat O'Brien, and Bette Davis. He was grateful to the junior press agent assigned to him, and thought he was underpaid. He went to the publicity head and demanded a fifty-dollar raise for him. The PA, Johnny Flynn, is now head of publicity for Warner Communications.

As I have mentioned, Ronnie's resignation from the restricted Lakeside Country Club pleased Jack Warner, his Jewish boss, and perhaps helped Ronnie to some better roles, as in *King's Row* and *Knute Rockne: All American,* a football story with Ronnie as the Gipper, and Pat O'Brien exhorting the players, "Go out and win for the" (dead) "Gipper."

Hal Wallis, who produced that picture, attended a reception in Hollywood for Mr. Reagan when he was campaigning for the President's job. "Everyone lined up to shake hands with Ronnie and Nancy, and when I got there I said, 'Are you going to win one for the Gipper?' and he replied, 'I'm sure as hell going to try.' " Hal added: "He was always great to work with. He was easy. No problems."

My first awareness that Mr. Reagan was seriously thinking about a career in politics was in the winter of 1965. After that speech for Goldwater there were ever growing rumours that an élite, rich group of businessmen in California was urging him to run for governor of the state. I had not talked too much before that with Ronnie. As I told you, I was not interested in writing about the lesser personalities unless they did something unusual. But a movie actor running for governor? That was unusual.

I cornered him at the Golden Globe Awards at the Ambassador Hotel. He was chatting with the Robert Taylors. "Are you planning to run?" I asked him. "No, I'm not," he replied. "I'm an actor and I'm going to stick to acting." Mr. Taylor smiled facetiously. "Aren't you going to ask *me* whether I plan to run?" I walked away, but I used both comments in my column.

When the talk of Reagan for governor persisted, I asked him to have a drink with me in the bar of the Beverly Wilshire Hotel. He came alone. Sitting tête à tête in the darkened room, ignoring the noise of the other drinkers (I forget what, if anything, we drank), he had a different answer to the question, "Are you going to run?" He said, "If the people want me to run, I will." It was as good as saying, "I am running." He used the same answer to the later question from the media, "Will you be running for the presidency?" "If the people want me, I will run." You probably remember that it was not so much a vote for Reagan as a vote against a second term for President Jimmy Carter, who might have made it if he had managed to get the American hostages out of Iran in time.

On my recent visit to Hollywood I stayed at the Beverly Wilshire Hotel, which brought back memories of my talk with Ronnie in the bar. How different it was for him the last time he stayed at the hotel, which has been the number one place for Very Important People ever since Hernando Courtright took it over. Prince Charles and Prince Philip have occupied the Royal Suite, as also have King Olav of Sweden, Emperor Hirohito of Japan, and, more recently, Prince Andrew and Princess Anne.

This time Ronnie was not just an ordinary citizen sitting in the bar with a columnist. This time there were one hundred and eighty people from the media to cover the visit of the President of the United States and, in addition to the Royal Suite for the Reagans, one hundred and sixty rooms were occupied by his entourage, the security people, and the press. I tried to figure out the cost of it all with Helen Chaplin, publicity director and aide to Mr. Courtright.

"Well," she said, "each suite has two bedrooms and four bathrooms, a his and her. The normal price would be $1,000 a night for each suite. But there is a discount for diplomats, celebrities, politicians, State Department officials, and, of course, for visiting heads of countries." Even so, I figured the cost of a presidential visit is in the neighbourhood of $50,000 a night.

From one of the chefs in the hotel I learned, "When President Reagan visited us while he was the governor, he had his food sent up to him from the regular kitchen. But as President he brings his own chef, and food is cooked separately for him." From another source I learned that he also travels with his own taster of food. He had the latter with him when he and Nancy were in Europe, and this caused some comment. Almost as much as Nancy's black satin knickers! Incidentally, the British aides with Queen Elizabeth and Prince Philip on their visit to the Reagans in California were amused to find a taster making sure that none of them would be poisoned.

No wonder Ronnie has been heard to say wistfully, "I can no longer walk around the way I used to." Certainly he cannot since that attempt on his life. And when he retires from public life, he will still be shadowed by several Secret Service men. But from a distance, he hopes.

In the old days, when he was just an actor, the Reagans enjoyed entertaining small groups at their house on San Ofre Drive—the Robert Taylors, Jane Powell and her boyfriend of the time, and Nancy Sinatra and her then long-time escort, Ross Hunter. They would sit around chatting about what was going on in Hollywood, and after dinner there was usually a movie to see in the den.

When I asked Bob Hope, in the fall of 1982, whether *he* thought his friend would run again for the presidency, he quipped, "I think so. Actors like reruns." Bob has been popular with the last nine Presidents of America, regardless of their being Democrat or Republican. He has campaigned for them all. "It started with Roosevelt," he told me. "Then there was Truman, Eisenhower next, then Kennedy and Johnson, Nixon, Ford, Carter, and Reagan." Eisenhower was, and Ford is, his golf partner.

When I mentioned the Lakeside Country Club incident, it reminded Bob: "About thirty years ago, when I saw Ronnie walking out of the Lakeside golf shop, he said, 'D'ye notice anything different?' 'No, what is it?' 'Contact lenses.' " He still wears them and they give that extra glisten to his eyes. But what I did not know until Bob told me was that both he and the President are rather deaf.

"I didn't know it about Ronnie until I was campaigning for him in Peoria. After dinner we sat together and talked. I asked him, 'What time do we have to get up tomorrow?' 'I think about nine o'clock,' he replied. 'We are due at the meeting at ten.' 'Oh,' I said, 'I must remember to take my Niacin.' 'Oh,' he said, 'you take Niacin too?' " I interrupted to ask, "What is Niacin?"

"It's a little pill that excites the veins around the ears. It opens them up. Ronnie got his deafness from an actor in a picture firing a gun close to his ear. It caused him to lose some hearing. I got mine in a rifle range in Palm Springs during the Vietnam days. I fired a gun without wearing plugs. My ears rang for ten minutes afterwards. What Niacin does is to keep the circulation going around the ears. And because of this great pill we can hear everything."

Then I said that the President sometimes looks very flushed on television and I wondered if it happened when he was angry. "Oh no," said Bob, "he's a very amiable person. He rarely loses his temper. The rosiness is rouge. Do you expect him to appear without make-up?"

There was another question that I did not ask Mr. Hope. Does he or doesn't he? For years I, with many others who have known him for so long, believed that he dyed his hair. It isn't enough to be blessed with a low hairline, but Ronnie, being in his seventies, wants to project a younger-man image. And he does. He looks years younger than white-haired Tip O'Neill, who actually *is* younger. But he *does* do something to his hair. He is telling the truth when he says he does not dye it, for he uses a strong rinse, which is why it is sometimes darker or lighter. How do I know this? A friend of a friend reported a slight dark brown stain on the white fabric head protector on the presidential plane.

Talking of planes, when Ronnie did all that travelling on behalf of the General Electric Company, his talks to their salesmen around the country had to be spaced out. He was fearful of flying and always went by train. Many people are afraid of flying, some get over it and some don't. But when Ronnie was campaigning for the governorship of California, it would have given the wrong image to travel to the many cities in the state by train. He *had* to fly. Nowadays when I see him on television, jauntily running up the steps into Air Force One, I wonder what is going through his mind, and if he still is secretly afraid of flying.

Regardless of his political career, Ronnie has a $200,000 memento to remind him of his career in the movies. Not long ago, the executives of Warner Brothers presented him with a documentary they put together from thirty-five of the films in which he appeared from 1937 to 1957, but not, of course, including *The Killers*.

When I saw the brochure, I noticed that every film segment depicted Ronnie as the star. For instance, the 1939 *Dark Victory* had starred George Brent and Bette Davis, but Ronnie's name is first in the brochure. In the same year, Dick Powell had the lead in *Naughty But Nice*. Ditto for Dick in *Going Places*. You would not know this from the brochure.

In 1942 Errol Flynn starred in *Desperate Journey*. I saw the war film recently on television. Reagan, in his Navy uniform, looked handsome, but he was the best friend, not the star. This reminds me of a remark made by Jack Warner during a *Brother Rat* story conference in 1938. "No, no, Wayne Morris is the star. Ronnie is the best friend."

Even in the clip from the *Knute Rockne* film, with Ronnie as the Gipper, appearing for about twenty minutes, he is depicted as the star. I wondered what Pat O'Brien had to say privately about this. But Pat, with several of the others who were in the films with Ronnie, made glowing remarks in the documentary about their President. They all like him; they all have affectionate memories.

I have been told that the documentary, titled *A Funny Thing Happened on the Way to the White House,* will never be shown publicly. But if you are a friend of the "best friend," you will have seen it in the projection room of the presidential home. Ronnie shows it all the time. He is proud of those twenty years.

Book Three

Chapter 19

Children of Hollywood

I HAVE KNOWN Morgan Mason since he was a baby. He was charming then, and still is. When he was quite small, James Mason, his father, told me he hoped that when his son grew up, he would become a song writer "because they make so much money." I don't know how much Morgan earns as a vice president of the Rogers and Cowan Public Relations Company, but for a lad still in his twenties he has done very well for himself. During the first Ronald Reagan campaign for the presidency, Morgan was in charge of supplying the entertainment at the fund-raising dinners and meetings. Most of the Rat Pack sang for him—Sinatra, Dean Martin, Sammy Davis. His reward was to be the deputy chief of protocol, provided of course that the boss was elected. The chief of protocol has to be a married man or woman because of the entertaining involved.

According to his mother, Pamela, Morgan would rather have been the President than his deputy chief. "But if he could sit close enough to the President," said Pamela, "people might think he really *was* the President. So he occupied the suite of rooms for the chief of protocol, two doors from the Oval Office." At that point Mrs. Walter Annenberg, the wife of the former ambassador to the Court of St. James, had not yet been chosen for the top protocol job.

Morgan took over her office and was sitting behind her desk, giving interviews and getting enormous amounts of publicity, as he does when he opens his big (his mama's words) mouth. When Mrs. Annenberg arrived to take up her position and found that Morgan had taken over her office, she demanded, "Who the hell is this upstart, this youngster, who is running everything, ordering the secretaries around, and changing everything?"

Morgan also had a GI driving him around in an Army car. The man had been assigned to him during the inaugural celebrations, when Morgan was in charge of the security for all the stars who came to the galas. He picked them up at the airport and made sure they were in secure housing. He had continued to use the car and the driver.

Mrs. Annenberg, settling into her new job, demanded, "Where is my car and driver?" She was told that it was not part of the Protocol Department. "Then why has *he* got one?" "Well, he's always had it." "Oh did he?" she said angrily. Then, "I don't want him as deputy in my department." Whereupon Reagan offered Morgan two other jobs. Would he like to work in the State Department? "No." How about with Weinburger in Defence? "No." Morgan accepted something called "Special Assistant to the President in Charge of Political Affairs." No one quite knew what it meant or what the duties involved were.

Not long afterwards, Morgan was relieved of his rather vague position. But I haven't given up on Morgan. He was born in the United States, which makes him eligible for the presidency, and I think that one day, say in about ten years, he will be running for the highest office in the land.

James Mason, who remarried several years ago, remained close to his children. Morgan had a brush with acting as the child of Elizabeth Taylor in *The Sandpiper*. At the age of sixteen he was assistant to Herbert Ross, the director of *The Last of Sheila,* a Raquel Welch film.

My introduction to another Mason child, Portland (shortened to Porty), was at the Mason pool. She was about two years old then and refused to join us in the water. I put this down to the fact that at the age of three months she was swimming for her life under the supervision of a famous teacher in Hollywood who believed that babies should be thrown into the water soon after they were born, as it was natural for babies to swim like fish. It took Portland several years to believe her. She is a writer now, blonde and beautiful, lives in a cottage on her mother's estate, and on warm days swims in the family pool.

Not many of the children of Hollywood stars follow in the footsteps of their famous parents. Many have tried and mostly failed, but with some notable exceptions: Jane Fonda and her brother, Peter, and two of Lloyd Bridges' sons, Beau and Jeff. Jeff told me that he was destined to be an actor from the age of four: "My mother would sit me down and say, 'How do you express happiness?' and 'Sadness?' " Carrie Fisher, the daughter of Debbie Reynolds and Eddie Fisher, has made a fine career for herself, and Kirk Douglas' son Michael is not only a good actor but a fine producer—*One Flew Over the Cuckoo's Nest, The China Syndrome,* and *Romancing the Stone.* John Carradine's sons have made names for themselves in the acting field, as have Judy Garland's Liza and Maureen O'Sullivan's Mia (Farrow). But by and large the children have not inherited the talent of their actor parents.

Raised in an artificial atmosphere with the trappings of success —palatial homes, swimming pools, expensive cars, exclusive schools—children of the stars had to be aware of the precariousness of Hollywood fame, where you were only as good as your last production, admired now, slighted tomorrow. Many collapsed under this insecurity inside the home, while the world outside clamoured for the smiles and autographs of its celluloid favourites.

Several committed suicide. Others are still sticking around, the greater number playing bits in television and hoping that their surname will convince a producer to give the all-important break. A smaller group ignored Hollywood and forged an identity elsewhere. And there are those who have written books.

"Promise me you will never do a Christina Crawford on me," said Anthony Quinn to his oldest daughter, who has the same first name, Christina, when he learned she was planning to write a book about her life. This was a few years ago and I haven't seen the book yet, so perhaps she changed her mind. But Tony had some reason to be worried. In London recently, having tea with me at the Hyde Park Hotel, he told me, "My problem was that I simply didn't know how to be a father."

When I talked with his daughter in Seattle, where she was

running a business called "Quinn Enterprises," she assured me she would try not to be bitter about her now sixty-nine-year-old, but still virile, father. "None of us in Hollywood really had parents," she told me. "They were always on the verge of a divorce. Even if the mother is not an actress, she doesn't have time for the child. The mother has to be devoted to the actor father, the parent who earns the money. If she isn't she doesn't last long. Actors don't have any time for the children, not if they want to make it big.

"The damage could be avoided if the parent would make one small concession. To listen to the child. Until I was five years old my father and I were very close. Then we separated and didn't come together again. I had a nervous breakdown when I was nine and another at fifteen. I laugh a great deal since I left Hollywood. Leaving there changed my life. In Hollywood no one wanted you when you were getting older. Not if you were over thirty. You were shipped out and no one cared where you were."

Miss Quinn's parents (Tony was married to Katherine De Mille, C.B.'s adopted daughter) were divorced in 1965 after twenty-seven years of marriage. A brother, aged two, had drowned in the family pool. I remember Tony's anger against his wife, who was inside the house when the tragedy happened. He accused her of being negligent. But it was not her fault; a maid was supposed to be watching the child.

"Was that the beginning of the trouble between your parents?" I asked. "That made it worse, but it started before that. The early years before my father made it, we lived moderately, in a small house, but as his career improved, it went worse for us. He wanted more and bigger roles, and there was no time to listen to us. It took me quite a while to get it all together, but now I have a good life in Seattle."

I asked Tony, "What about your other children; did they have the same problem with you?" "Some," he admitted. "Let me tell you about my son, Duncan. First he worked as a chauffeur, then as a bullfighter, and then he decided to be an actor. He took lessons with Stella Adler and Uta Hagen in New York, and then with Jeff Corey in Los Angeles.

"He had a part with me in *Children of Sanchez,* but found it hard

38. The Fox lot: "For the way it was when I arrived in Hollywood, follow the dotted line; for the way it is today, follow the unbroken one."

39. *This page.* Shirley Temple in 1936: "When small is big." 40. Sheilah with Pamela Mason and Portland Mason: "If you want to know about James, ask Pamela."

41. *Opposite page. Above left:* The 1940 Academy Awards—Spencer Tracy and Victor Saville. 42. *Above right:* The young Henry Fonda and Tyrone Power as the James Brothers in 1939. 43. *Below:* Clark Gable: "One of MGM's top moneymakers, but he had to toe the line."

44. Gary Cooper and Patricia Neal: "Love in the Forties."

45. Paul Newman and Joanne Woodward: "Love in the Seventies."

46. *Right:* Richard Burton in
1969: "Off duty on the set of
Anne of a Thousand Days"
(Courtesy Hal Wallis)

47. *Below:* Richard Burton
with, left to right, Elizabeth
Taylor, Mr. and Mrs. Cary
Grant, his last wife Sally Haye
and Hernando Courtright

48. *This page. Right:* Claire Trevor: "The Queen of the Bs." 49. *Below left:* Sheilah with Roger Moore on the Pinewood set for the Bond film *The Spy Who Loved Me:* "The long and the short of it." 50. *Below right:* Michael Caine: "He fooled me."

51. *Opposite page.* Sheilah with Shelley Winters on location for *Journey Into Fear,* at Windsor: "How about that diet?" 52. *Inset:* With Telly Savalas in Berlin, where he was filming *Inside Out* in 1975: "Everyone's favorite uncle." 53. *Below left:* With Pat Neal at Gypsy House in the seventies: "Two innocents abroad." 54. *Below right:* With Omar Sharif in London, 1970: "Pressing the flesh"

55. Sheilah, Jessie Matthews and Anna Neagle at the London publication party for
Jessie's autobiography: "Three elderly Cochran Young Ladies"

playing with his father. He said, 'He's my father, he keeps me from realizing myself.' I had to beat him up in one scene, but I couldn't. I didn't want to lose my son's affection. So I merely bawled him out. He was angry. 'I'd rather you had beaten me,' he said. 'The scolding was a comedown.'

"When they wanted an actor to play my son in *Caravans,* Duncan seemed the logical choice. It took a lot of persuading, but he finally agreed. He was too serious about it. I told him, 'Don't eat your guts out, enjoy the money, pretend it's Christmas.' Afterwards I had a heart-to-heart talk with him. 'You've got a lot of talent,' I told him, 'but you're making it rough on yourself. It should be fun, like making love.' He said they were accepting him only because of me. I said, 'Forget that, go in and do your thing.' He was offered $50,000 to do a play but he didn't feel confident enough to accept. Duncan suffered enormously being my son. 'Why haven't I made it big?' he says. 'Why aren't I important?' "

It was different for one of his daughters. She is married and has three children. "She got lucky." His youngest daughter, Valentine, lives in Los Angeles and is an actress. "I think being my daughter helped her get some roles. Not big yet, but I think she'll make it." And wistfully he added, "I don't think she resents me as a father.

"I think we had a good family life until the mid-fifties," Mr. Quinn continued. "We had lived modestly in Los Angeles. We never went to parties. We had an old car. But when I bought a beautiful town house in New York, it was too rich for them. They could take my failure, but they could not relate to my success." His three sons with his second wife, Jolanda, are delighted that Daddy is rich. That is all they have ever known. Daniel, now a handsome twenty-year-old, has embarked on an acting career. "I spanked them," said Daddy. "I never did that to the others, but it made for a good family life."

I wondered why there were so many problems for Hollywood parents. "We created around our children a protective cocoon. We over-sterilized them. We gave them too much." I reminded him of the boy who was climbing a tree in Beverly Hills. Another boy came along and said, "Hey kid, who do you take your tree climbing lessons from?"

There is the story about the son of Steve McQueen. After Steve divorced his first wife, Neile, and married Ali McGraw, his son was upset. The boy had read that Steve had gone around saying how much he loved Ali, more than anyone before. The boy was angry with his father for that.

It's a good thing Bing Crosby is not alive today to have read his oldest son's book about him. While Gary stated that he was reconciled with his father shortly before his death, he wrote of a cruel childhood that included harsh punishments and severe beatings for the slightest disobedience.

The children in a Hollywood divorce usually take the part of the mother. Although when Yul Brynner's son grew up he preferred to live with his more famous father, who had earlier left his mother, Virginia Gilmore, an actress.

Why have so many children of the entertainment world committed suicide? Recently I heard that the twenty-nine-year-old son of Louis Jourdan had killed himself, and many years ago when Michael, the son of another Frenchman, Charles Boyer, shot himself, Charles became an old man overnight. He had adored Michael, an only child. In talking with him it was always, Michael said this, Michael said that. Some time after the tragedy, Charles told me that his son had wanted him to finance a film for him. He had refused. "If only I had given him the money," he cried to me. Many years later, when his beloved wife, Pat, died, Charles took his own life.

Gregory Peck was unable to work for two years after the suicide of a son from his first marriage. How proud the late Dan Dailey was when he brought his small son to Twentieth Century–Fox when he was a top star there. I watched while they did a tap dance together. But the boy had barely reached adulthood when he ended his life. The son of Jim Arness also committed suicide. Where was the marshal of Dodge City? The daughter of the talk-show host Art Linkletter jumped to her death from a window in his home. Art blamed the drugs she had taken and has campaigned against them ever since.

The son of Mary Tyler Moore, the star of her own show on television, recently ended his life, which contributed to the end of her marriage to Grant Tinker, now the head of television programming at NBC. And why did the son of the successful producer Ray Stark—his grandmother was Fanny Brice, the Ziegfeld star—jump to his death from a high window at the Gotham Hotel in New York?

Ray Milland's son, Daniel, blew his brains out in the bedroom of his Beverly Hills home. And Paul Newman's son, Scott, who was hoping to be as good an actor as his father, was found dead in a hotel from too many pills and too much alcohol. The daughter of Jennifer Jones and the late David Selznick jumped twenty storeys to her death. Robert Taylor had been dead for several years when his twenty-three-year-old son died of an overdose of drugs. The answer to why they and others were unable to cope as the children of the famous was revealed to me in part by some of the parents I talked with.

Shelley Winters is the only person I know who can out-talk me. So when I visited her at her home to discuss the problems of bringing up a child in Hollywood, I let her do most of the talking. Shelley has a daughter, twenty-seven-year-old Vittoria, from her marriage to the Italian actor Vittorio Gassman. In her recent autobiography there was barely a mention of Tory, as her mother calls her. By special request. For years they were barely on speaking terms, but I believe there is now more understanding of the demands of the mother's career and of the daughter's problem in establishing her own identity.

"My daughter changed her name because she didn't want anyone to connect her with Hollywood," said Shelley. "She dislikes Hollywood and everything connected with it. She has never wanted to be an actress. You couldn't pay her to be in a picture. She says it's not a profession for mature people. She hates the pressure of show business. As a child she was always angry with me when I was on the phone talking business with my agent. But what could I do? It was my work. She was embarrassed about being the daughter of a movie actress. Once, on a Sunday, we were sitting at an outside café waiting to see a movie. A kid came over and said to Tory, 'Aren't you Shelley Winters' daughter?' She looked away and said, 'Not on Sunday.' "

But while Shelley did not say too much about her own child, we discussed the problems of some of the others. The reason Joan

Crawford was so strict with her children was because of her own childhood in an orphanage. There was no love there, only discipline. She was expected to be perfect. She once told me that someone had given her a doll when she was a child. The doll always obeyed her. It never answered back. That's what she expected from her adopted children. She didn't know how to be a mother.

Alan Alda had never really lived in Hollywood since his childhood. His father, Robert Alda, was a film star in the forties—in 1945 he portrayed George Gershwin in *Rhapsody in Blue*. But when Alan was starring on television in "M.A.S.H." (what you see now are reruns) he left his home in New Jersey late on Sunday to report Monday morning to the studio in Hollywood and flew East after work on Friday for the weekend at home with his family.

He did this for eleven years, until he decided it was too much travelling and called it quits for the popular show. But he had to return to Hollywood for the two-and-a-half-hour "M.A.S.H." TV film. It had the biggest audience for any show ever on American television. Alan had polio when he lived in Hollywood as a boy. I don't know whether this had anything to do with his determination to raise his children away from Hollywood. As of this writing, Alan is hoping to revive his TV series based on his successful movie *The Four Seasons,* and in case it happens he decided to buy a second home—in Hollywood.

Echoing the complaints of other star parents, Shelley reminded me that "When you are working in the movies you have to get up at five in the morning for the make-up and hairdressing. When you come home at the end of the day you're too tired to talk to your children. You can't give them the time they need and all you really have to give them is time. God gives you children until they are sixteen. After that you can lose them."

Jerry Lewis has four sons. One of them was ready with an answer when I asked him what it was like being the son of Jerry Lewis. "Okay now, but terrible when I was at school. The other guys were not impressed, or said they weren't, at my having a movie star for a father. They played all kinds of tricks on me. When a big bully tried to throw me down a staircase, I called my father and said, 'Dad, they're trying to kill me!' Wouldn't you know he had his tape recorder on, and whenever he thought I was getting out of line, he would play it for me." The Lewis boys have always been closer to their mother, and were unhappy when Jerry obtained a divorce to marry another woman, especially when he stated publicly that he had been searching for her all his life and expected to live happily ever after with her. Richard Burton had said the same thing about Elizabeth Taylor.

Gene Kelly's daughter, Kerry, was in the same class as my daughter at the Hawthorne School in Beverly Hills. When I tracked her down she was living with her husband, Dr. Jack Novick, and their children in Ann Arbor, Michigan. I called her. "Was it good or bad for you to grow up in Hollywood?" "It was good, and not so good," she replied. "When I was a child everyone knew that I was in analysis. But *everyone* in Hollywood seemed to be in analysis, including my mother, Betsy Blair" (whom Gene had married when she was seventeen, "so I can mould her into the perfect wife," he told me).

"My father," continued Kerry, "was the exception. But when I told him that I wanted to make psychiatry my life's work, while he didn't believe in it, he was curious to know why I was so interested, and why for so many people in Hollywood it was an ordinary way of life. He read all the books he could find on the subject, then gave them to me. And while I'm sure he will never go to a psychiatrist, he now believes that analysis can help some people."

With both parents in the acting profession, I asked Kerry whether she had ever wanted to follow them. "No, I never wanted to be an actress. Like any other child I was mostly happy, accepting the life style of my parents as the norm. As for me, they were determined I should have an ordinary childhood."

But there was nothing ordinary about the Sunday gatherings at the Kelly home, then on the residential section of North Rodeo Drive in Beverly Hills. The most glamorous stars in Hollywood— Frank Sinatra, Judy Garland, Lena Horne, Bogey and Baby—would stop by for a chat and a drink, followed by the showing of a movie. "I loved it. I'd sit on the stairs and peek at them through the railings." Kerry laughed at the recollection.

"As you know, I went to a public (elementary) school. And I never had what my peers, the other children of movie stars, had. I had less pocket money, and less of everything, and I didn't realize there was anything unusual about my parents until I saw other people's attitude towards them."

Their divorce was friendly. They had joint custody of Kerry, who went to live with her mother in England and stayed there for fifteen years. In the summer, and during Christmas and Easter vacations, she lived with her father in Hollywood. After a while she got tired of doing nothing in London and worked as a set and costume designer. But she wanted to work in analysis and signed on to train at the Anna Freud Institute in Hampstead. That was twenty years ago, when she was twenty-three.

"Jack had signed on the year before," said Kerry. "We married in 1970 and came back to America when we were offered good jobs here. We have a good life. We both work at the same clinic in Ann Arbor. I was an only child, and like most only children I always wanted lots of kids." The oldest girl is now ten, the boy is eight. The baby is three.

Would she ever want to live in Hollywood again? "Oh no. To use a cliché, it's nice to visit but not to live there. It's funny, everyone here asks me what it was like to live in Hollywood. But they are more interested in believing their fantasies than in the reality."

Deborah Kerr is one of the few among the parents I questioned who thought that Hollywood was a great place to bring up children. To hear Deborah tell it, the film capital "was a paradise for children. They remember Hollywood," said their mother, "as always full of sunshine." But her two daughters now live in London. Francesca is married to an actor and lives in Hackney. "They took over a dilapidated house and redid it with the aid of a government grant." Melanie—now in her mid-thirties—has been living in Hampstead. She works as a sociologist as applied to medicine and is solely concerned with helping working class women. She believes they have too many breakdowns from too much work, inside and outside the home.

Were Deborah's children ever interested in becoming actresses? "No, although Francesca, when she was younger, thought it might be fun until she realized it would be too disciplined a life for her. You have to be totally dedicated, as I am. Acting is an extension of myself."

The father of the children, Tony Bartley, was a World War Two hero. He came with Deborah to Hollywood in 1944 and they lived in a beautiful house in the Pacific Palisades. But to be just the husband and escort of a movie star bored him. After the divorce Tony returned to England and Deborah married Peter Viertel, the writer, whose mother, Salka, was a close friend of Greta Garbo.

"How did your daughters feel about having a movie star mother?" I asked Deborah. "Melanie didn't have an opinion about it until she saw me in *King Solomon's Mines*. She was only four and I was afraid she would be scared. Afterwards she said, 'I liked it very much, but why did you keep on screaming and falling down?'

"Francesca was not at all hung up on being the daughter of a film star, and if she had really wanted to act, I mean with all her heart, I would have helped her. Before her marriage she was a Jack-of-all-trades. She worked in a boutique, and as a production assistant on Sam Spiegel's *Nicholas and Alexandra*. Before she had a child, she felt she had to work at something. She said it was ingrained in her because she was brought up in Hollywood, where everyone works, especially the women."

I told Deborah that Anthony Quinn and Jerry Lewis had believed that the children of Hollywood stars felt more secure when the father was the star and the mother took care of the home. She agreed. "It's not so bad when the father is an actor. It's harder if the mother is famous and pretty. There's always the comparison, 'She's not as pretty as her mother.' "

How was it when her career had taken her away from the home? "They had a good nanny—nannies are sometimes missed more than the working mother. I tried to keep my children unspoiled. While some children went to school in a chauffeured Rolls or Cadillac, mine went in the school bus. Thank God they are no longer teenagers, with all that alcoholism and drugs about." Did they feel nostalgic about Hollywood? "No, but they love getting out the scrapbooks, recalling the house and the lovely garden and the sunshine."

When I suggested talking to her daughters the next time I was in London, Deborah shuddered. "Oh no. I'm sure they wouldn't talk to you. I have always sheltered them from any publicity concerning my career. Let's leave it that way."

Would you like to know how it was with *my* children in Hollywood? As soon as they reached high school age, thirteen and fourteen, I sent them to boarding schools in the East. After that they chose to attend college in the East, Bryn Mawr for Wendy, Columbia for Robert. Otherwise they might have believed that everyone had a swimming pool, a tennis court, and parents who were worried about whether the next production would be as good as the last.

CHAPTER 20

THE SILVER NOSE

WHEN I WAS a child living in the East End of London I was afraid, and yet fascinated, by photographs of Chinamen lying on their bunks smoking opium through long-stemmed pipes, called hookahs. They lived mostly in Limehouse and Wapping, two districts I was cautioned to avoid.

After leaving the orphanage, while dancing at the Cottage in Bow, my sophisticated friend Sophie (I was sixteen, she was fifteen) assured me that the young man who played the drums took hashish "to pep him up," which led me to believe that all drummers were on that drug.

Having lived through the marijuana sixties, I was still surprised on my recent visit to find how deeply the drug habit, mostly cocaine, has polarized Hollywood society. Those who *do* cocaine and those who *don't.* Those who go upstairs as soon as they arrive at a party and those who stay downstairs. But mostly the downstairs, non-user people send regrets and don't come at all. They might have to work with the "snorters" but they won't socialize with them. Which is why "Tichi" Wilkerson, the efficient, attractive owner of the *Hollywood Reporter,* was being truthful when she said during a recent interview on television that the reports of large numbers of cocaine users were highly exaggerated, and she personally knew no one who was taking the stuff. She obviously makes it her business to avoid them.

During my time in Hollywood it was booze added to sleeping pills that caused the "accidental" deaths—Marilyn Monroe, Robert Walker (Sr.), probably Judy Garland (although the verdict was "natural causes"), and others less well known. Earlier, in the twenties, the handsome star Wallace Reid had died of addiction to morphine at the age of thirty-two. And while the death certificate of Mabel Normand, the silent screen comedienne, gave pneumonia and tuberculosis as the cause of her departure at the age of thirty-six, it was known at the time that she was on heroin.

This, added to the other scandals of that era—Fatty Arbuckle was proved innocent of the death of Virginia Rappe, but the trial ruined his career; and the mysterious murder of the director William Desmond Taylor, one of Miss Normand's lovers, created a public outcry—caused Hollywood's self-censorship of its morals.

It began with the Hays Office, which all members of the Producers' Guild joined and obeyed. No kiss was to last longer than three seconds. No couple to be in the same bed. The only rebel was Howard Hughes, who resigned from the organization because of the exception taken to Jane Russell's cleavage in *The Outlaw*. How quaint that seems today, with the frontal, sideways, and back view of explicit sex on the screen.

The first I knew that marijuana had entered the higher echelons of Hollywood was when Robert Mitchum was arrested in 1948 and charged with possession of the weed. He was recently on the "Today" television show and I was shocked when he stated that a director he knew in Hollywood was spending $20,000 a week on cocaine. Apparently the cocaine habit has penetrated every stratum of Hollywood society, with the pushers having access to the lunch rooms and sets of the film and television studios, and to the most exclusive homes.

In one elegant residence, when the front door opens you are confronted with a golden bowl on an antique table with silver straws alongside, for you to take a sniff before you join the others, who presumably have done likewise. In another expensive home, the users must wait until dinner is served, and the small dishes on the table that usually contain salt, or nuts and mints, are filled with their favourite white powder. If a silver straw is unavailable, they can roll a dollar bill, or a hundred-dollar bill, into the shape of a straw and use it to "snort" the cocaine up the nose.

In time the cocaine burns the cartilage of the nose, which users call the silver nose. It is sometimes difficult when filming to shoot a scene because the lack of membrane irritates the nose and makes it water. A well-known host on television is always rubbing his nose, giving rise to the rumour that he is a user.

Even worse than the cocaine habit is what they call freebasing, combining cocaine and heroin. Used with alcohol it can be fatal. It helped kill John Belushi, the American comedian on the successful television show "Saturday Night Live." He reportedly spent $100,000 a year on cocaine and heroin. Richard Pryor (*California Suite, The Muppet Movie, Live on the Sunset Strip*) is lucky to be alive after setting himself on fire while preparing the combination. Richard Dreyfuss (*American Graffiti, Close Encounters of the Third Kind*), who crashed his car into a Hollywood lamp-post, is now on a two-year programme to rehabilitate himself from the drug.

But it would not be fair to make Hollywood the chief culprit for the cocaine habit. It is rampant in the large cities of America. In Washington, D.C., lawyers and lobbyists pass the little white envelopes to Congressmen, one of whom was caught snorting in his office by a startled visitor. And recently in New York something like 116 pounds, with a street value of millions of dollars, were confiscated before they could be distributed.

Los Angeles and Miami have open season for bringing in the cocaine from South America. There is barely a week when the authorities have not found abandoned boats and planes, with traces of cocaine. Miami is *the* capital for the drug that is sent all over the United States.

In Los Angeles, which supplies the film world, they are trying to do something about it. There is a self-help group called "Cocaine Anonymous." There are also several centres for detoxification of the drug. Studios are attaching cards to the paychecks, demanding, "Are alcohol, drugs and cocaine causing problems in your life?" And if you are really serious about dropping the habit and can afford it, you can spend three weeks at the expensive Beverly Glen Hospital in West Los Angeles, and undergo therapy designed to help you lose the craving. As someone said recently, "Cocaine is God's way of telling you you're making too much money."

Today there are not many arrests in Hollywood, or anywhere in the United States, on the charge of smoking marijuana. It's a long time since Peter Fonda was "busted." And I believe marijuana is no

longer a misdemeanor in several states. Some doctors prescribe it
for cancer sufferers to lessen the pain of chemotherapy. At one time
it seemed that everyone was taking it, especially in the colleges and
universities, the professors as well as the students, and you can be
sure that it was very prevalent in Hollywood.

Apparently, marijuana heightened whatever mood you were in,
sex, sadness, anger, happiness. But sometimes, for beginners, it did
nothing and they soon dropped out. I don't know what cocaine does
to the user, and mild intake is apparently not dangerous. But why
would anyone want to take the risk of becoming an addict? Perhaps
it's a question of joining The Club. In Hollywood it used to be an
invitation to the A-list party givers, being seen at the right places
with the right people. Now it's "Going Uptown," "Having a Blow,"
"Seeing the Lady," all of which mean Doing Cocaine.

CHAPTER 21

PARTY TIME, THEN AND NOW

ALAS, THE A LIST in Hollywood has gone the way of glamour. A party today is a sad copy of the private and industry parties of my time in Hollywood. The Basil Rathbones always gave a party on Christmas Day, and the producer Sam Spiegel always had open house on New Year's Eve. In the late thirties, one of the top hostesses was the Countess di Frasso. Her affair with Gary Cooper was long since over and he was now married to the Long Island socialite Veronica Balfe. I never heard of a Count di Frasso, but presumably he existed somewhere in Europe. It was strictly the A List for the Coopers, top stars and the top in every area, which included visiting society from the East.

Dolores del Rio, the exotic actress from Mexico, mingled Hollywood society with rich businessmen and their wives. She was married to Cedric Gibbons, the art director of MGM films, and for a short while was the mistress of Orson Welles. She divorced Cedric in 1941, but like so many powerful single women in Hollywood, she continued to give large parties until she left for Mexico in 1943, where she recently died.

The most expensive parties were given by the movie moguls and the important agents, who could write the whole thing off as a tax deduction. There was always a party after a big film premiere and following the Academy Awards, the latter with a huge gathering of stars, press, and producers with their wives.

In fact the Oscars were originally combined with a dinner paid for by the studios, in the ballroom of the Biltmore Hotel, where, as

223

Scott Fitzgerald wrote on a tablecloth, "The speeches got drearier and drearier at the Big Academy Dinner." When Greer Garson was one of the winners she made such a long speech that the rule of five minutes was instituted for each speaker.

But the parties I enjoyed most were hostessed by Sonja Henie, the ice-skating champion turned film star. I had met Sonja in St. Moritz in the early thirties, when she was winning all those world championships. When her money-making movies with Tyrone Power established her as a star, she gave wonderful parties at her Bel Air home under a large tent, with tables around the swimming pool, boarded-up for dancing.

Unlike some other A-List hostesses, Sonja knew that the secret of a successful party was not only plentiful hard liquor and champagne, but also great food. The smoked fish was imported from her native Norway, the tenderest roast beef, lamb, chicken, the salads and vegetables from California, which grows the best in America. The mouth-watering desserts were always arranged around a huge ice figure in the centre of the long table. And the dance music was not so loud that it killed conversation.

Sonja and I became good friends. My son still has the tiny gold bracelet engraved with his name and my telephone number that she sent him soon after he was born. She would ask my advice on her various film projects and this and that person who was trying to interest her in a business deal. She had a large ranch, about a hundred miles south of Los Angeles, managed by a male member of her family.

Even when she was quite young, Sonja's face was marked with deep lines, the result of smiling non-stop during her skating exhibitions. She was always optimistic and mostly happy in her private life. She seemed to have the best of it all, first with her marriage to the attractive millionaire Dan Topping. I visited them in their beautiful apartment in New York full of priceless antiques, where they lived when she was not working in Hollywood. I don't know what went wrong with the marriage but they remained friends after the divorce. She retired and married an even richer Norwegian businessman. They lived in Oslo, where she died of leukaemia in 1969. As with Rosalind Russell, I felt I had lost one of my few good friends in the Hollywood film world.

Anita Louise, still beautiful in her middle age, gave some good parties during her marriage to Henry Berger, masterminded by Richard Gully, an Englishman, a look-alike for his first cousin, the late Anthony Eden. Richard was, and still is, the arbiter of Hollywood social life. Hostesses are still imploring him to make up their party lists. Among others, he served in this capacity for Jack Warner, Cobina Wright, and Arthur Cameron, the oil millionaire who married Ann Miller, the MGM dancer-star.

Richard and I have discussed the parties of Then and Now. "Today there is no Hollywood society as such," he stated. "In the old days there was not only society, but there were courts. There were monarchs with a whole group of courtiers, and court jesters. Zanuck, for insance, had Gregory Ratoff as his court jester." (Mr. Ratoff directed Ingrid Bergman in *Intermezzo,* her first film in Hollywood.) "Jack Warner had the actor Bill Orr. Even the stars had a court jester. Fanny Brice had a man called Roger Davis."

The monarchs, of course, were the heads of the studios. Jack Warner was very social. The Goldwyns gave beautiful parties. (My first party in Hollywood was at the Goldwyn house in Beverly Hills on New Year's Eve, 1935. I was standing next to Sam when the clock sounded twelve. He turned and kissed me, the first kiss I had from anyone in Hollywood!)

"The Louis B. Mayer gatherings mingled business people with command appearances of his stars," Richard said. "David Selznick gave good parties—all the top people in Hollywood would be there. I understand that Harry Cohn gave some pretty good parties, but I never went there, because I was working for Jack Warner and he and Cohn were never on speaking terms." Apparently they didn't like each other. Harry swore all the time, but Jack was witty. He was corny, but he was an elegant man. He liked the good things in life, although he was tough in business, even complaining about the writers leaving the lights on when they left their offices.

"But Jack was a great spender. He lived in the grand manner, gambling heavily at baccarat in Monte Carlo. He had great style, and Zanuck had style; they were both fun men to be around, and they gave fabulous parties. There were always dinner dances at Romanoff's, or the Crystal Room, after their picture premieres. Of course," added Richard, "there are no more big pictures, not with humans. I mean, who the hell would want to give a dinner dance after that horrible thing" (*One from the Heart*) "that Francis Ford Coppola did? I mean, how can you sit through a dinner dance after a picture that makes you want to go home and throw up?"

Actually, unless you were very important, the guest list often counted for more than the host. With Warner, Goldwyn, and Zanuck, it was a Command Performance. You had to come, and you came when you didn't want to. Your job depended on appearing. Even the rebellious Errol Flynn accepted when the boss beckoned. But when he became disreputable, when he was bloated with alcohol, he was dropped from all the lists: A, B, C, and D.

Today the big parties are a memory of the past. They departed with the glamour that was synonymous with Hollywood. There are only three couples in the whole industry who can put a large star party together now, the Cubby Broccolis, the Ray Starks, and the Irving Lazars—he is the top agent in Hollywood.

Two years ago, when Mr. Broccoli's wife, Dana, gave a party for his birthday, it was like the old lavish days in Hollywood. He was leaving soon for the location shooting of *Octopussy,* his James Bond picture with Roger Moore. As you know, Sean Connery at the time was competing with Roger, returning as 007 in *Never Say Never Again.* Both Bonds were at Dana's party with their respective wives. The four of them shared a table on the terrace of the Broccoli home in Beverly Hills with the Gregory Pecks.

At that party the old guard was present in full force: Cary Grant with his wife, Barbara, the Billy Wilders, the Irving Lazars, Loretta Young—flinging her fringed dress around as she shimmied on the dance floor—Jimmy Stewart and his wife, Gloria, who would soon be leaving for Rome, and Greer Garson with her long-time husband, the Texas oil millionaire Buddy Fogelson. Greer was receiving congratulations for her winning horse, Ack's Secret, at Santa Anita. I have fond memories of Greer and Buddy standing around the piano at my Christmas parties and singing carols, played by my children.

And of course everyone who was still able to walk was in San Francisco for the bash given by the Reagans for Queen Elizabeth and Prince Philip. The Queen's hats have always caused comment in the American press, and you saw her smiling broadly at the fantastic headgear presented in the entertainment. But why, oh why, did she wear that white and navy polka dot hat and suit for her first appearance to the Americans? It made her look twice her real size.

Old-time stars such as Jimmy Stewart and Gregory Peck will sometimes invite as many as forty people to their homes to celebrate a birthday or to repay hospitality. And before her tragic death, Natalie Wood and her husband, Robert Wagner, gave sought-after dinner parties for the younger set.

The Reagan California "Mafia" entertain each other in their homes, the Justin Darts (before his death), the Armand Deutsches —the oil and hotel millionaires. But they don't invite the picture people, and while their parties are elegant all the political talk does not make for a relaxing time.

In the old days, with a live-in couple, an extra waiter, and a hired bartender, you could give a fair-sized party at your home. You could employ a great cook for sixty dollars a month. I remember how startled I was when I had to pay a hundred and fifty dollars a month for a cook-housekeeper. This was after the war and prices for help were going up.

Today, *if* you can get a cook-housekeeper, it's $1,400 a month, and she won't do this and she won't do that. Cooks come from China, Korea, Mexico, Cuba, El Salvador, the Philippines, and they stay in one place long enough to decide if they want to take a degree in gardening, or be a cook or hostess in a restaurant. In fact the domestic world doesn't exist anymore in Hollywood, or in London for that matter.

But there is another difference between the old Hollywood and today's. As in many big cities, there aren't as many married couples and that makes a big change in the social scene. So many women now have children without being married, and so many couples who go together or live together don't want to get married. Whereas in the days of the great Hollywood, you couldn't be caught doing anything like that. Everybody was playing the game—they were all married or getting married, or engaged. It made a difference who went to what party. You never went with someone you shouldn't go with. Nowadays sex and social life are no longer tied together.

Another difference is the lack of women stars on the Hollywood scene. So many of the big films today are for little men from outer space, or for robots. I can think of only three women who deserve the label superstar: Jane Fonda, Barbra Streisand, and perhaps Meryl Streep. And none of them is a shining light on the party social scene. Meryl Streep is a big star today, but she herself has no glamour. But at least she looks real.

And how about some of the male superstars: Burt Reynolds, Clint Eastwood, Al Pacino, Dustin Hoffman? None of them is handsome in the old tradition of Clark Gable, Gary Cooper, and Robert Taylor. Or John Wayne; even when he lost all his hair after contracting a virus in Korea and had to wear a wig, Duke looked more glamorous in his films than the current crop. I caught a glimpse recently of Burt without *his* wig and he was positively plain, and shorter than he seems on the screen. When acting he wears high heels. He has a tremendous ego. Wouldn't you have if you were paid four million dollars for ten weeks' work? But he is amusing and fun to be with. Angie Dickinson, who has co-starred with him, adored working with him, and others have told me how much they like him. But a glamour boy he is not. Perhaps that is what the public wants today. Ah well, we do have Robert Redford and Paul Newman. And Cary Grant is still around, although long since retired. They are all getting on a bit—Robert is forty-seven, Paul sixty, and Cary turned eighty in 1984.

The elegant Mr. Richard Gully had some thoughts on what constituted Hollywood charisma—the quality that Gable had, and Burt Reynolds has not: "It's not only looks, it's the way they dressed, the life style, the kind of women they went with. Most of the leading men today pick up tacky girls. There are no great combinations like Gable and Lombard, Hepburn and Tracy, or Tyrone Power's love affair with Lana Turner." According to Lana, Tyrone was *the* love of her life. But he also liked men—not Errol Flynn, as had been reported. However, two others are still around.

Richard went on: "When Arlene Dahl, for instance, was married to Fernando Lamas, and they walked into a room, everything stopped. I was with them once in New York and people stood on chairs to look at them." (My comment: pretty soon they will be standing on chairs to see their handsome son, Lorenzo, who is now well into an acting career.) "Today," said Richard, "most of them are what I call mismatched. You don't see exciting couples anymore.

But if Robert Wagner and Jill St. John were to get married it would be a wonderful wedding, because they look so beautiful together.

"But take Clint Eastwood. He's charming and handsome, but there's no charisma there. He's a nice man, but he does not have the something that Gary Cooper and Errol Flynn had."

Tom Selleck, the star of the television series "Magnum PI," is very handsome and was much in demand until he made two rather bad feature films. Perhaps his latest movie, *Runaway*, will bring back his number one popularity. He will know by the time you read this book. Anyway, he is still tops with the Reagans. Nancy insisted they meet him on their stopover in Hawaii on their way to China last year. Meanwhile, he still drives around in an old jeep, wearing jeans and an old sweat shirt. It doesn't seem to matter. As Errol Flynn used to say, "I don't have to seduce girls. For Christ's sake, I come home and girls are hiding under my bed." Errol's problem, like Chaplin's and Roman Polanski's, was that he preferred under-age girls, and that gets you into trouble with the law.

Before leaving Richard Gully, I asked him about his close friend Barbara Hutton. He had looked after her during her and my time in Hollywood. "She was a sweet woman, and during the period when she was married to Cary Grant, she was in command of herself. Afterwards she became neurotic, and with all that dieting she was riddled with all sorts of complaints. It was a difficult marriage for Cary. She liked to have all those European titles around, and he couldn't cope with that sort of thing. She had a Princess Tolonya on her doorstep and plenty of English titles that she supported during the war when they could not get their money out of England. It just wasn't Cary's kind of life."

Of all the men she married Mr. Grant was the only one who did not take money from her when they parted, which is why they remained friends for the rest of her life. She was a pathetic woman, the poor little rich girl, the Marilyn Monroe of American society.

Porfirio Rubirosa, her fourth—or was it her fifth?—husband swindled her. Not content with getting a plane and some polo ponies, he took a million dollars in cash when he left Barbara for Zsa Zsa Gabor. The million-dollar baby from the five-and-ten-cent store (Woolworth's) was vulnerable to flattery and she laid herself open to fortune hunters. Incredibly, Richard informed me, she died pen-

niless in a hotel. There wasn't even enough money to pay the final
bill.

The last party I attended in Hollywood was a couple of years
ago at the Bistro in Beverly Hills. It was given for and by Monique
Van Vooren, a New York stage actress (who was later accused of
cashing her deceased mother's Social Security cheque). Greg
Bautzer was there. He is the lawyer who had romanced Joan Craw-
ford and is vaguely portrayed in the film version of *Mommie Dearest.*
My table mate was Henry Berger, the husband of the late Anita
Louise and now married to one of the richest women in America.
The rest of the room was awash with unfamiliar faces.

On the plane returning to New York I read of another Hollywood party, in honour of Mary Roebling, the foremost woman
banker of America. Ah, there were two familiar names on the guest
list: Rhonda Fleming and Irene Dunne. Hallelujah!

Chapter 22

The Movies, Then and Now

Not long ago, in London, I attended a cocktail party in honour of Robert Wise. Later I sat with him and talked about the state of Hollywood today. He has not directed a film since *Star Trek* in 1979, and he wished I had not brought that up. I changed the subject and told him that I see his two great musicals, *West Side Story* and *The Sound of Music,* all the time on television. "Yeah," he said, "I see them everywhere I go." Mr. Wise was not as pleased with his musical *Star,* released in 1968, which had Julie Andrews playing the great actress Gertrude Lawrence.

"What went wrong with *Star?*" I asked him. "We didn't know at the time, but I saw it last week at the British Film Institute. My wife had not seen it before and we sat down and analyzed it. It had too many musical numbers and we didn't get Gertie's character enough on the screen. The numbers were great but there was not enough development of Gertie herself. It was hard to capture her. Too bad, because there was a lot of good work, and I know that Julie was disappointed."

Star cost $15 million and ended with a loss of $11 million. Films were getting more expensive at that time. In 1966 the lavish *West Side Story* had cost around $7 million, which was a lot then. Four years later, *The Sound of Music* cost $8.5 million. Ten years later, *Star Trek* cost $40 million. "It was not one of my favourite experiences," Mr. Wise reminded me. It needed $70 to $80 million to break even. It did not. *Star Trek II* cost a bit more than half of what its predecessor cost, and *Star Trek III* cost $16 million, which is how you make a profit.

To save money, George Lucas made most of his successful *Star Wars* trilogy (*The Empire Strikes Back, Return of the Jedi*) in England. The latter cost $32.5 million and at last count was edging towards $200 million revenues.

What would be a reasonable budget for today? I asked Mr. Wise. "It all depends on the project. A reasonable one might be $8 to $10 million. And it might take $20 million for another kind of story. For a low-to-average film, it's something like $8 million. But even they are going up to $11, $12, and $13 million."

One of the problems in making movies today is what is called the above-the-line costs, and that includes the leading man, the star who gets millions of dollars—like Sylvester Stallone, Burt Reynolds, Paul Newman, or Robert Redford.

"You can see my point," said the director, "that it is difficult to make a fairly modest film if you have that kind of expense." I reminded him that Gable, at the height of his popularity, was paid $5,000, then $7,500 a week, and only for forty weeks of the year. No one in those days was paid for the compulsory lay-off of twelve weeks.

But when I mentioned that Hal Wallis had slammed his fist on the luncheon table and said, "I can make a film today for under $3 million," Mr. Wise agreed. "There are some good small ones now. *Diner* didn't cost too much, and it's been very successful. And a few years ago, a young man named John Sayles wrote and directed a film called *The Return of the Secaucus Seven,* and it cost only $60,000. It wasn't a block-buster but it's a marvellous film which got great reviews in *Time* magazine and the *New York Times.* So far it has earned more than $2 million." His more recent films, *Lianna* and *Baby, It's You,* were also highly praised.

We talked about *Chariots of Fire,* which I have seen several times. The last time, when I took two of my grandchildren, I told them at the end that the two characters played by the stars were now dead. "Of exhaustion?" said the then nine-year-old Sean. If you saw the film you know what he meant. How much did it cost to make? "$5 or $6 million. Reasonable for today. The current profit is well over $50 million. So it can be done."

The producer Ross Hunter agrees. "I had a good idea for a picture called *The Execution.* I took it to the young man in charge of a studio owned by one of the conglomerates. He had done nothing before, he was a messenger boy, a mail boy, and now he's running a studio. He said he would give me $22 million to make the movie. I said I don't need $22 million. $3.5 million will do. He laughed. 'That won't pay for the titles.' I said, 'Young man, I'm twice your age, and you don't know anything about motion pictures.'"

It was almost the same in 1964, when Ross made *Thoroughly Modern Millie.* He had to fight to get them to agree to a $3 million budget. They argued, "Look, we've just made *Paint Your Wagon* and it cost $29 million." (My comment: "And it flopped.") For *Millie* he had five top stars, including Bea Lillie and Julie Andrews, and it was a big moneymaker. When and if he makes *The Execution,* he wants Elizabeth Taylor, Lana Turner, Deborah Kerr, Barbara Stanwyck, and Ava Gardner.

"And with those five stars you can do it on $3 million?" "Yes, because of my system of giving them very little money and a percentage of the profits. Burt Lancaster and Dean Martin took a small salary for *Airport.* Dean, so far, has made more than $8 million. And Burt has made over $9 million." Yes, but when the film is unsuccessful the star has to be satisfied with the small salary. Also, with all the finagling that goes on in the accounting office, the "net" profit, as I have mentioned, usually means no profit.

In spite of the fact that, allegedly, *Star Trek* did not recover its cost, there have been a *Star Trek II* and a *Star Trek III.* This is the era of sequels in Hollywood. *Rocky III* was even more successful than the first *Rocky,* and they are planning a *Rocky IV.* If that is as profitable as the others, there will be a *Rocky V, VI,* and *VII.* There was a third *Magnificent Obsession,* and a second *Sting*—the latter received bad reviews. We have already had *Halloween I, II,* and *III, Jaws II* and *III,* and *Superman II* and *III,* with number *IV* in the works, which sort of knocks out other films. But from the company's point of view, if they have something that grossed $100 million, they say, "Let's make another one."

Annie cost $52 million and so far has taken in a little more than $35 million. There were mixed reviews, and disappointment for

John Huston, who directed it. A budget like this has to earn $70 to $100 million dollars before it can break even. But I believe that *Annie* will in time. Every new batch of kids will want to see it. The Burt Reynolds biggie *The Best Little Whorehouse in Texas* cost around $32 million. There were terrible reviews, and the state of Texas refused to have it shown there. Dolly Parton, Burt's co-star, is very religious and had insisted on changes of language and content. According to the studio, the film made back its budget, but only just.

I wonder whether Warren Beatty's *Reds* will make back its cost of $52 million? To cover interest charges on the original finance, as well as post-production distribution and publicity costs, it would need to take in about $100 million just to break even. I enjoyed the film and thought Warren and Diane Keaton were excellent. But they could have cut thirty minutes from its three-hour length. Whereas *Gandhi*, which was just as costly, won every award for Ben Kingsley and Richard Attenborough and was even longer, but left me wanting more.

As usual with a new idea, Steven Spielberg had a difficult time trying to sell his *E.T.* story. It was refused by most of the studios in Hollywood. The Walt Disney people were offered it first, but when he said, "I want twenty percent of the gross," no deal. No one there now is allowed to mention the two magic letters. Bob Hope's masseur works at the Disney studio and told Bob, "We weren't even allowed to say E-anything." "And," Bob added, "every day when they read *Variety* the whole studio threw up in unison."

Lew Wasserman, the head man at Universal, the nearest person they have in Hollywood now who can be called a tycoon, turned down *Star Wars*, but saw the possibilities of the E.T. kid from outer space. But in case he was wrong, he decided on a comparatively low budget, $11 million. This was possible by making it at the non-union Laird Studios in Culver City.

Mr. Spielberg owns thirty to forty percent of *E.T.* And with his share of *Raiders of the Lost Ark*, *Poltergeist*, *Jaws I*, *II*, and *III*, and *Indiana Jones*, he has to be the richest man in Hollywood. Incidentally, *Raiders of the Lost Ark* was first offered to, and refused by, Twentieth Century–Fox. Ah well, you can't have everything, and their *Star Wars,* which cost $12 million to make, is heading towards $300 million revenues, and more for the next two, especially *Return of the Jedi.* Will there be a fourth? Well, *six* more are planned by George Lucas. Lionel Newman, who supervised the music for those films, was given a bonus of $42,000 to buy himself a Mercedes car. Producers can be generous when they have a hit.

Mike Kaplan was my former editor on *Daily Variety,* and I discussed with him why the number of films produced each year has declined. "It's because they are making bigger pictures," he said, "and the end result is that they stay longer in the theatre. You don't have to worry about replacing them. When *E.T.* or *Return of the Jedi* stays for twenty weeks as opposed to the usual two, it means you don't have to replace that movie for eighteen weeks."

I had thought it was because those pictures cost so much that the producers have little money left for other projects. "No. Most of the studios have revolving credit, so they can get the money they need. The only time they get into trouble is when two or three pictures in a row don't return anything. Then the revolving credit dries up. But most of the really big pictures have been making money." Always excepting *Heaven's Gate,* a $40 million total disaster. And Coppola's *One from the Heart,* which he financed with his own money. It cost him his home and his studio.

I believe it is still basically the story that brings the people to the box office. As Shakespeare said, "The play's the thing." Today we have a highly literate, educated audience that has made a cult out of movies. There is a tremendous college audience. And many colleges today give cinema appreciation courses. While the big feature film action is no longer centred in Hollywood, it is alive across the United States, and in London, and it has really burgeoned in Australia. India, Pakistan, and Sri Lanka have in the last few years been locations for a number of huge productions with stories set in Asia: *A Passage to India* (from E. M. Forster's novel), directed by David Lean; *Kim* (from Kipling's novel), with Peter O'Toole as the General; Steven Spielberg's *Indiana Jones;* a remake of *The Bengal Lancers,* and two television serials, "The Jewel in the Crown" and "The Far Pavilions."

Nostalgia is very "in" right now. It always comes at a time when the economy is bad, and if you lived through the thirties, they were not such good old days. But in comparison to today, you look back and say, "Those were the good old days." Which is perhaps why the *Star Wars* trilogy has done so well. It looks ahead to the future. Anything to forget about today.

CHAPTER 23

Life in the Hills of Beverly

ONE ASPECT of the old days was very good for the stars: income tax was practically nothing. Fifty years ago Joel McCrea paid $35,000 for a ranch in the Valley. He sold it in the mid-fifties for $4 million. Mae West made millions from the property she owned in Van Nuys. And today Garbo lives on the millions she made, not so much from her films, but from the real estate she bought and sold in Beverly Hills.

I'm not sure I would want to live in Beverly Hills today. There has been an enormous increase in crime there. In the old days you would get picked up by the police if you decided to take a stroll after dinner. Today you might be picked up by someone else. A thief or a killer. And it does not have to be at night. I was told of someone who was walking to his garage at four in the afternoon to get his car, when a man suddenly came out of the bushes with a gun. "Your wallet, mister." He gave it fast.

One night I had been out for dinner and arrived back at the Beverly Wilshire Hotel at about eleven o'clock. "I think I'll stretch my legs a bit," I said to the man who took my car. "I wouldn't if I were you," he replied. "We've had a lot of nasty incidents around here at night. It isn't safe for a woman to walk alone." This, in the heart of Beverly Hills! I was shocked, but I did not take the walk.

I was surprised at all the warning signs I saw outside the expensive homes in Beverly Hills. Not only the usual "Beware of Dog," but "Armed Patrol" and "Armed Response." We never had that in the old days. You sometimes didn't even lock your door because

237

there were so many police cars patrolling the streets. To combat the rise in crime, the armed protection systems have a radio gadget in the house, so they can hear from their car everything that is going on inside. They have a plan of the home of each subscriber, and when the intruder says, "Go into such-and-such a room," they know exactly where they are as they are driving to the crime.

These protections are expensive, especially for "Armed Response." This service guarantees to get to the house within three minutes from the time the alarm goes off. The occupants are warned to stay indoors or they could be shot. Michael Caine, who lives high up in Beverly Hills, told me that his alarm had gone off accidentally twice at night. "And it was bloody hell. They were all out there with guns and searchlights. Luckily all the alarms in the house have a two-way microphone attached, so I was able to tell them we were okay." I said, "England was never like this, was it, Michael?"

"Ah well," he replied. "Every place is now like this, London, New York, Chicago, Detroit. Detroit is the only city in the world that has ever declared a curfew because of crime. Imagine, a curfew at ten-thirty in a major city, based purely on crime." I said that perhaps the violence in films and television is responsible for the frightening escalation of life-threatening crime. "Perhaps," said Michael. "My only thought is that Jack the Ripper and the Marquis de Sade never saw a movie or watched television."

While I was talking to Michael, who is the father of two daughters, I wondered what he thought about the explicit sex on the screen, which my generation considers pornography. "Well, you don't have to see it, do you? It costs quite a lot to get in. And it says outside there will be sexually explicit scenes, and if it will offend you, don't come in. So you can go through your life without seeing a pornographic film by accident."

"Well," I said, "I never thought I would avoid something directed by George Cukor, who made the most fantastic films in Hollywood for more than forty-five years. And then in 1979 he makes a pornographic film, *Rich and Famous.*" (Loud interruption from my son, Robert, who was working the tape recorder, and Michael.) "It's not pornographic!" said Robert. "It's not an X-rated film." Michael agreed: "I'm sure that neither Jackie Bisset nor Candice Bergen" (the stars) "would do an explicit sex scene. I haven't seen the movie but I doubt if there is a full frontal view."

When I had brought this up with Mr. Cukor, his young male secretary had interrupted to say, "You don't see genitals, but there *is* grunting and groaning." A peevish "Oh well" from Mr. Cukor. In another scene, said the secretary, the star is picked up on a jet flying to New York, and they go into the toilet and make love while they are landing. As they climax the wheels hit the runway with a bang. Funny? Yes. Pornographic? What do *you* think? What *I* say is, what a pity that *Rich and Famous* was Mr. Cukor's last film. A section of the public must have agreed with me, because it was a failure. As you know, Mr. Cukor died at the age of eighty-three in January 1983.

"What about the sex, violence, and horror on television?" I am back with Mr. Caine. "I think what television has done is to make our kids brighter, and if there is something I think would upset my daughter, I have a key and can turn it off. I remember, when I was a kid, *The Bride of Frankenstein* was the great horror film. Recently I forgot to turn the cable off and came home to find my daughter and her friend watching *The Bride of Frankenstein*, which I hadn't been allowed to see, because in those days it was an H-film—horrific. These young girls were sitting there screaming with laughter. They thought it was the funniest thing. My daughter said, 'I didn't know they had punk rockers in those days!'

"Kids today are different. I'm now fifty and I never really grew up. But the other day I walked through Leicester Square in London, which has been turned into a pedestrian area. All the seats in the square were filled with punk rockers, you know, part of the hair shaved and the rest dyed pink and with pins through their noses. And I sort of aged thirty years from one side of Leicester Square to the other.

"By the time I had crossed over I realized that I was irretrievably out of touch with the youngsters and I was an old man. I had always felt I was still twenty-five, except when I'm running up this hill to the house. And I've always been in contact with my older daughter, who was twenty-eight in 1984. And even with the eleven-year-old I know what's going on, but when I saw all that in Leicester Square I thought, 'My God, I don't understand it,' and I realized at last that at fifty I was an older generation." You can see why I enjoy talking to Mr. Caine. He is honest in his thinking and forthright in his talking.

Actually, all those people who came up in the sixties, now in their mid-forties, are still ruling their own spheres. They were never replaced. No one came behind them. It's still Roger Moore, Sean Connery, Peter O'Toole, Albert Finney. They have not been pushed out by a younger generation. Not in their roles because they are getting older, but also not in doing the things they used to do.

Being seen on television in old movies has helped the older actors. Every movie they made will turn up eventually on late-night television in America, sometimes at three in the morning. It has been very useful in making actors well known in the United States, and they have actually become better known because of television than because of their films shown in the cinemas.

Apart from wanting to keep some of the money he earns, the reason someone like Mr. Caine now prefers to live in California is because no matter where the films are made, Hollywood is still where most of the work emanates from. It is the place to be if you want to get the good pictures that are made elsewhere. Except for *California Suite,* most of his films have been made abroad—*Educating Rita* in Dublin, *The Honorary Consul* in Mexico, *Blame It on Rio* in Rio de Janeiro, and *The Jigsaw Man* in London. Micky Micklewhite has come a long way from the Elephant and Castle (a poor London area).

Crime isn't the only thing that's come to Hollywood. On my last visit there, I was saddened to see for myself that it has not only attracted the crooks, but also the rich Arabs, the Iranians who managed to bring their millions with them, and the well-off Japanese and Koreans. When I say "Hollywood" I also mean Los Angeles and the surrounding areas, including Beverly Hills. But actually Beverly Hills is a different country; it is not the United States. It is a game of wealth and status. I refer specifically to that monstrosity for the very rich, the section of North Rodeo Drive between Santa Monica Boulevard and Wilshire Boulevard.

When I lived there those few blocks were a nice little area. I remember the small cake shop where you could have coffee and a doughnut in the middle of the morning. I bought presents for my children at Uncle Bernie's toy shop, and I chose my lingerie at Juel

Park's. Men came to have their hair cut at Rothschild's, or to buy a cashmere sweater at the London shop. But now the street is jammed with tourists, window shopping and hoping to spot celebrities inside.

Juel Park, of Czechoslovakian ancestry, became a friend and I would often stop by for a chat and to see the latest in her lovely lingerie. I often found Mae West buying it, or I would watch Paulette Goddard and Joan Crawford being measured for their form-fitting nightgowns. Paulette, long ago, actually wore her JP nightgown at a top drawer (no pun intended) party in Hong Kong!

At one of Juel's fashion shows at the Beverly Hills Hotel, I was asked to introduce Miss Crawford and to MC the show. My payment was a pale pink satin nightgown with matching bra and panties. I don't have them now and, alas they would be far too small for me. Perhaps I should follow Miss Bacall's advice and stop eating.

Elizabeth Arden used to be at different locations and much smaller. Now it is a huge emporium, one of the big palaces in the four-hundred block on North Rodeo Drive. Above and below on Rodeo, behind the glass and marble and silver and gold metal, and the enormous glittering chandeliers, "an architectural over-indulgence," as someone described it, are the famous names you see on Bond Street, the Rue de la Paix, and Fifth Avenue: Cartier's, Tiffany's, Van Cleef & Arpels; but because of the many robberies there are only photographs in some of the windows. Other names include Gucci, Hermes, Lanvin, Courreges, Ungaro, Yves St. Laurent, Dunhill of London, and another familiar British name, Vidal Sassoon, the East End wizard who transformed hair and cosmetics into a multi-million-dollar fortune. Have you seen his sexy walk on television?

Where Mike Romanoff first started his restaurant for the stars in the two-hundred block, there is now an open-air cafe for the tourists. Otherwise nearly everything else is on a giant scale in the shopping area. Apparently this is what the Middle Eastern and Oriental customers prefer. I saw similar stuff on the Brompton Road in London. For the Arab trade, I was told.

The commercial section of North Rodeo Drive has an enormous Bank of America at one end. At the other, facing the street from the south is the Beverly Wilshire Hotel, a convenient place to stay for the visitors who shop on North Rodeo and are willing to pay two hundred dollars for a tie and thousands of dollars for the merchandise in the grand boutiques.

Warren Beatty lived for a long time in the penthouse there. I remember when Leslie Caron arrived at the hotel in the late sixties, to marry him, we all thought. They had made the mistake of making a picture together, *Promise Her Anything*. It was unsuccessful, and apparently "anything" did not include a promise of marriage. Not for Leslie; not for Joan Collins, who flew to New York from Israel, where she was making *Esther and the King*, just for a weekend with Warren; or for Natalie Wood, who was sure they would marry when she left Robert Wagner; or for Julie Christie, who was so much in love with him. Warren is just two years shy of fifty and seems quite happy in his bachelor state.

During my stay at the Beverly Wilshire Hotel, I heard that the now ninety-year-old Pola Negri, the famous star of the twenties who is remembered for her passionate love affair with Rudolph Valentino, had recently spent a few days at the hotel. On arriving, wearing one of her famous floppy dark felt hats, she was unrecognized and was annoyed. In her heyday the hotel had not yet been built. Calling for the head man at the reception desk, she said, "I'm Pola Negri, in case you don't recognize me." They did not, but Hernando Courtright has trained his men to recognize everyone, even when they don't. A flurry of apologies ensued.

This reminds me of when Esther Williams ("Wet she's a star, dry she ain't," quipped Fanny Brice) attended a recent premiere in Hollywood. She was about to sit down when a young usher hastened over and said, "This row is reserved for the VIPs." "But *I* am a VIP," Esther said. He shook his head, and the swimming star of the forties and fifties left in a huff. Last year, following the death of her husband, Fernando Lamas, Esther announced that she was returning to her film career.

Natalie Schafer has a house on North Rodeo Drive within walking distance of the bizarre splendors of the shopping area. She always knows what is going on in Hollywood, and I invited myself for tea. We talked sitting around her swimming pool.

"I'm fed up with the idea here that you have to be so young," said Natalie. "You go to an interview and the producers look like boys. And they probably don't remember my "Gilligan's Island," which was practically a television series for children. They don't know who you are. Well, this boy said he wanted to meet me, and my agent said, 'Go down to see him.' And this little boy was sitting behind a counter. He didn't even get up. He said, 'Sit down, Miss Schafer.' Then he said, 'Now tell me, what have you done?' I said, 'You first.' Then I said, 'Thank you very much,' and left."

"They used not to be so young," I said. "Most of the producers were men in their forties, fifties, and sixties, as were the directors —the Frank Capras, the George Cukors. Alfred Hitchcock was still making movies in his seventies." George Eells, who recently wrote a biography of Mae West and was working on one about Robert Mitchum, and who sleeps at Natalie's house because of the crime in Beverly Hills, interrupted us to say that Miss West was forty years old when she first came to Hollywood. She was eighty-five when she made her last film, *Sextette,* in 1978. Mae died before she could star in a new film version of her notorious play *Diamond Lil.*

We talked about Joan Crawford, with whom Natalie had made several films. "I had some good and bad experiences with her," she said. "Some of them were funny because I didn't know anything when I came here. There's the key light. You have to act with the key light on your face. I was playing a scene with Joan and I didn't keep my face in the key light. The director whispered to me, 'Natalie, she's making shadows on your face.' He told me to put my weight on my right foot. I was doing a sort of dance, trying to avoid the shadow Joan was making on my face, but she caught me at it."

It reminded me of when Bette Davis and Miriam Hopkins were co-starring in *Old Acquaintance.* They kept upstaging each other, one coming down on the step in front of the other, so that they almost fell together at the bottom. And talking of Miss Hopkins, when she decided to adopt a child, she sent a friend to the Cradle in Chicago to pick one out for her!

"As you know," Natalie continued, "Joan always drank a lot. She drank all the time we were working. Vodka. A hundred and twenty proof vodka. I always thought it was water in the glass until one day when it was hot and I said, 'Oh, could I have a sip?' I did and nearly fell down."

How accurate did she think Christina Crawford's book *Mommie*

Dearest was? "Well, I remember when Christopher was four or five, Joan came to the set and told me she'd had a terrible time the night before because Christopher was eating candy. There was a big box of candy on the coffee table and he said, 'Can I have some, Mama?' And she said, 'You can have one.' She watched him out of the corner of her eye, while he took one, then another and another. 'I said you could have one and you have disobeyed me. So now you must eat every piece of candy in the box.' He did, then threw it all up. 'You see,' she said to me, 'that's the only way to train a child.' "

Working with Joan Crawford was an education for Natalie. Before that she had worked onstage and toured with Gertie Lawrence, and they were good friends. She thought stars were the same as other people. At Metro, where they had those wooden dressing rooms on the set, hers was next to Joan's, and hers didn't have a long mirror. So one day when Joan was in front of the camera, she went into her dressing room to see how she looked in the long mirror.

The next day when she came back there were two policemen standing there. She asked, "What for?" but nobody would tell her. At about four in the afternoon she was told that because she had gone into her dressing room, Joan Crawford had given instructions to have police on the set!

I told Natalie that I had seen Joan during her London honeymoon in 1929, with the then nineteen-year-old Douglas Fairbanks. They were lunching at the Ritz. Joan's face was smothered in white powder. It was a Hollywood fashion of the time, but I thought she looked weird.

"Doug," said Natalie," is one of the nicest people I have ever known. When we made a movie in England he told me all kinds of stories about his marriage to Joan. He said they always dressed for dinner, she in an elaborate evening gown and he in black tie, even when they were alone."

It was well known in Hollywood that Mary Pickford and Douglas Fairbanks, Sr., had not been happy about the marriage, but Joan was determined to show them where she stood with young Doug. On a rare occasion when they had been invited to dine at Pickfair, Joan untied the strap of her shoe just before they entered the mansion. It was a big party. Inside, with all eyes on them, Joan said, "Oh

Doug, my shoe has come unfastened. Would you fix it for me?" In front of them all, he had to bend down and retie her shoe. The Fairbanks heir at her feet—that was the image Joan wanted to project. They were divorced in 1933.

Natalie did a play with Victor Mature but could not remember the title or the year. "We had a lot of fun. I was crazy about him. As you know, he was very macho and proud of what nature had endowed him with." In *Lady in the Dark* with Gertrude Lawrence on Broadway (this is the play Natalie referred to) he was dubbed "a beautiful hunk of man." "So he came to me one day and asked, 'Do you think I need a jock strap underneath this?' 'Do you really want me to be honest?' 'Yes.' 'Well, I think you ought to pad.' It was hilarious because he became terribly concerned. 'What do you mean, pad?' Victor went to the stage manager and said, 'Natalie thinks I ought to pad. Do you think I should?' 'We did not hear his reply. We were all laughing so much.'"

Victor never took his film career too seriously, which included *One Million B.C.*, *I Wake Up Screaming*, *Kiss of Death*, and *No Time to Die*, among others. He married five times. One wife, Martha Stephenson, committed suicide several marriages later. But Victor seems to be living happily now at his home in Rancho Sante Fe, near the Mexican border. He once told me that he didn't need money from his films, that his family, somewhere in the Mid-West, was rich. He returns to Hollywood now and then to make another film or to inspect his hardware shop, which he started when he was living there. "It and me are thriving," he told me when I phoned him. "I play golf, I swim, and I look after my wife and family."

CHAPTER 24

WHERE ARE THEY NOW?

MANY STARS of my time who are still working have wisely made the transition to television. There are still feature films for Paul Newman, Robert Redford, Warren Beatty, Barbra Streisand, Jane Fonda, and Shirley MacLaine. But most of the old timers such as Jimmy Stewart and Gregory Peck can be seen on the small screen in your living room. It seems to me that "Roots" led the way for the successful and expensive Hollywood-made serials for television. Herman Wouk's "Winds of War," starring Robert Mitchum, ran in segments for a total of eighteen hours and cost forty million dollars to make. It started with Hitler's Germany and ended with the bombing of Pearl Harbor by the Japanese. While it was high in the ratings it was not quite as good as I had expected. Ali McGraw, for one, was miscast, and the actor who played Hitler was even more ridiculous than the real monster. Gregory Peck assured me that he has not retired, not by several shows on television. At one time he seemed to be there every time I turned on my set. He made a good President Lincoln. But even more impressive was seeing him as Monsignor Hugh O'Flaherty in *The Scarlet and the Black,* a three-hour television film made in Italy, with Christopher Plummer and Sir John Gielgud. The latter can still be seen in feature films, full of energy at eighty. Also, he is happy to follow in the profitable commercial footsteps of Orson Welles. As you may have noticed, Sir John has been promoting the wine "that is never sold before its time."

As of this writing, Richard Chamberlain was coming to Broadway in *Born Every Minute,* a new play by Thomas Babe. Richard, the

246

long-ago juvenile Doctor Kildare, shed that image in England, starring successfully in plays by Shakespeare and stories by Henry James. More recently he was delighted to accept a five-figure payment for each of the TV "Shogun" installments, with all those lovely residuals. It is rather like the early days of Hollywood, when stage actors sneered at the idea of appearing in a movie. But when the big money came along, they scrambled on to the financial bandwagon, from John Barrymore down.

Oh, movie actors have now all realized where the good bread is buttered. I haven't seen Greer Garson on television lately, but for a while she replayed her stately lady several times on the small screen. She also took a fling at producing a Broadway play, *The Kingfisher,* starring Rex Harrison and Claudette Colbert. I remember how adamant Claudette was in the fifties against approving a product on television. I wonder if the eighty-year-old star would still say no.

Jimmy Stewart has always been a realist and, his health permitting, he would say yes to a good film offer. He is more likely to be seen in good television plays such as the video version of *The Late Christopher Bean.* Elizabeth Taylor appeared with Carol Burnett on the small screen in "Between Friends." Wise girl.

It was a long time ago that stars were not rushing into the new medium. But "The Untouchables" made Robert Stack a multi-millionaire. You don't have to feel sorry for Van Johnson, who was first offered and refused the series. Van has done well on the road, touring in the big cities of America with proven plays and musicals. In case you have forgotten, Hollywood discovered Van as a chorus boy on Broadway in *Pal Joey.* And yet it was strange that in Hollywood, Van was always shy about standing up before a live audience. There's nothing like a road tour to cure you.

Pat O'Brien was one of my favourite movie actors. After retiring from films, he continued working, but not in Hollywood. In fact that is where he rested from his strenuous tours on the road. Pat was over eighty when he co-starred with his wife, Eloise, in *On Golden Pond* in cities all over the U.S. As you know, he died in October 1983.

Many of the people of the Golden Age in Hollywood have homes in New York. Garbo has been a resident for the last four decades and visits Europe every summer. Marlene Dietrich originally went to live in Paris to be with her daughter and grandchildren, who now prefer life in New York.

Hedy Lamarr emerges there sometimes to do her shopping. I doubt that she had a business manager during the best years of her career, or that she took too many dollars with her when she left. At one time a New York doctor was helping her regain her health.

There are many stars who could have been made richer today had they only chosen the *right* business managers to control the money they earned.

Doris Day was taken for $23 million by the late Marty Melcher, the husband she had trusted. Ross Hunter lost even more with the same manager. Linda Darnell and Robert Mitchum were robbed by their business managers. So was Laurence Harvey, who had given an associate authority to sign his cheques! And, more recently, Sean Connery.

And sometimes there was a diminishing of career when the husband was the producer or the director. Joan Fontaine was an important star when her agent-producer husband William Dozier took her to Universal, with himself as part of the package; some of her films there were not as successful as she'd been used to. Julie Andrews, after a bad start, has been doing better with the films that her husband—Blake Edwards—directs. Mitzi Gaynor, still going strong in personal appearances and night clubs, was never as big a star in films when she made her husband her manager.

Ann Margret is an exception with her TV actor husband Roger Smith as her manager. Her career took off in a big way in *Carnal Knowledge*, the Mike Nichols production. Last year I saw her on television playing Blanche DuBois in *A Streetcar Named Desire* and I was astounded at the depth of her performance. This baby has come a long way.

There have been some questions whether Colonel Tom Parker was a good manager for Elvis Presley. In fact his estate brought a law suit against the Colonel, who counter-sued, claiming he had put his client into the multi-million-dollar class, in spite of the fifty percent deal for himself. A manager usually takes from ten to twenty percent. But Elvis, in real life a shy, soft-spoken man, never tried to change the deal. He was grateful to the Colonel for advising him to make those nine successful films with Hal Wallis. His film career diminished only when he wanted a change from the rock-and-roll singing that his fans demanded.

Poor Elvis. As the pressures of his life mounted, he began to put on weight. How he hated the blubber on the body that had been slim and handsome when I saw him make his first picture in Hollywood, *Love Me Tender*. When I was on location with him in New Orleans I saw what happened to Elvis at the end of a working day. He and the eight or ten men he always carried with him, what they called the Memphis Mafia, had to take the elevator in the building adjoining his hotel and cross over the roof to avoid the mobs out in front, who could have torn him apart. It was really unsafe.

They would have junk food sent up to the suite, and that, with the uppers and downers, and all the one-night concert stands, finally caught up with him. No one ever saw him take a drink, or cocaine or heroin and such, just depressants and picker-uppers, which can be just as deadly.

A recent honest book about Hollywood, *Indecent Exposure* by David McClintick, was sexual only in title. The chief article exposed was David Begelman and his shady dealings while he was the head of film production at Columbia. Every decade in Hollywood has its scandal, and this was it for the late seventies.

It was a mystery to me that a man who was earning almost half a million dollars a year would steal a cheque for ten thousand dollars that he had fraudulently made out to Cliff Robertson. If Cliff had not followed through, Mr. Begelman would probably still be the head man at Columbia. And what is he doing now? Well, he has his *own* production company, which is being financed by some Texas millionaires. Who said vice is its own reward in Hollywood? No wonder so many frauds and con men flourish there. Perhaps because it is a city where it is hard to separate the real from the unreal. Also, it is sure to attract the bounty hunters to a rags-to-riches place where you can be as poor as Burt Reynolds was when he arrived— he could not even afford to pay his half of the rent for a shack. At last report, he was said to be looking for a condominium in New York and is prepared to pay several million for what would be a second home.

Ginger Rogers is an earlier star who is still rich. I remember the

single jar of candy she gave out at the end of her London engagement in *Mame*, to be divided among all the members of the orchestra! That's how you stay rich. In her last movie, *Harlow*, in 1965,
Ginger played the mother. Four years later she took over the lead
in *Hello Dolly* on Broadway. Ginger, as are Arlene Dahl, Joan Fontaine, and Claire Trevor, is a sought-after guest at New York parties.
They add a bit of the old time Hollywood glamour.

Lauren Bacall left Hollywood for New York a few years after
Humphrey Bogart's death in 1957, following her abortive engagement to Frank Sinatra. Katharine Hepburn made all the arrange-
ments for Bogey's funeral. She was a good friend when she was
needed.

As for Miss Bacall, as I have said, she is a strong-minded lady,
and she was admirable in the agonizing years watching her husband
die, day by day. It was Bogey who said, "That's when you separate
the women from the girls." He would have included Miss Hepburn.

Mrs. Bogart was not always playing the hard person we see on
television now, advertising coffee and giving the "look" for which
she became famous with the release of her first film, *To Have and
Have Not*. I recently saw her on television in the 1947 film *Dark
Passage*, and she was appealing and not too sure of herself. This
might have been her original attraction for Bogey, who was even
less secure at that time than she was.

I always envied Miss Bacall her slim model's figure, and one
time when I interviewed her in New York in her West Side apartment, I asked, "How do you do it?" She looked at me coldly, X-
raying the bulges beneath the dress. Then sternly, "Don't eat!" So
I felt rather smug after she gave up smoking (I have never smoked
in my life) to see a visible bulge around her tummy, during her last
months on Broadway in *Woman of the Year*. I have not seen her since
she went on the road with the successful musical, but she looks slim
in those commercials, so perhaps she has gone back to smoking.
Actually, I have always thought it was better to die of over-eating
than of over-smoking.

And what is that dimpled darling on *The Good Ship Lollipop*
doing? As it comes to every popular actor and actress—and even
columnist—Shirley Temple has been writing her autobiography. I

am sure she has been more accurate than some of the other amateur authors.

It has amused me to see how these ladies remember their pasts when interviewed on television—either too many men in their lives, or too few—mostly the latter. June Allyson and Lana Turner were shocked at the very suggestion that maybe they had succumbed to certain gentlemen of their acquaintance. But if you can believe everything she wrote in her autobiography, Shelley Winters, in her search for sex, has left no man unturned.

I remember the muted scandal when Miss Allyson and Gloria Grahame went to Philadelphia to visit Jerry Lewis and Dean Martin, who were appearing in a night club there. Three thousand miles for a platonic visit? A producer told me he had a good laugh when he heard June say during an interview on television that the talk of a romance with Alan Ladd was totally untrue. "I did several movies with her and one of them was during their big, mad love affair. I couldn't even get her on the set!" I told him that June had lisped that the reason Alan and she could never go to bed was because they were each married to somebody else. "I mean, really!" he said in disbelief.

And what about Lana? She said on the "Today" show something to the effect that she had this reputation for being a sexpot, but she never was; she never had much feeling about sex. To which another producer friend replied in disbelief, "Lana said she was a *virgin!!*" adding, "But you know the way I feel about it. I say, 'Good for those gals. Let 'em do whatever they want. But tell the truth in their books. I think it's kind of silly not to.' " Lana actually referred to Johnny Stompanato on television as Mr. Stompanato—that gangster!

This same producer told me that he was in the Russian Tea Room in New York, the very popular show biz place for lunch. "And some of the old gang came over to the table—Kirk Douglas, Nancy Olsen, Tony Quinn—and it was fun seeing them. On the way out I was stopped by the vice president of Putnam Publishing. And he said, 'I would like you to do your story,' and I said, 'No. If I did I would have to tell the truth, and I'm not that kind of man.' "

I remarked that in their books, all those girls were trembling and terrified and so shy. But perhaps that is what the publishers want. For instance, Harper & Row, a prestigious publishing house, signed a contract with Maureen O'Sullivan for her life story. She wrote a truthful account, and the book was rejected. When she told me this she was looking for another publisher.

CHAPTER 25

LOOKING BACK

LOOKING BACK . . .

Looking back, I remember how Lilli Palmer stood by Rex Harrison when Carole Landis took an overdose of pills in 1948, after she realized that Rex was not going to divorce Lilli to marry her. But husbands don't always appreciate the wives who stand by them, and Rex and Lilli divorced not long after.

I was sitting in the Royal Circle behind Rachel Roberts, the fourth Mrs. Harrison, at the London premiere of *Staircase,* in which Rex and Richard Burton were both cast against type as a couple of homosexual barbers. Rachel, who had been drinking heavily since her separation from Rex, was hanging over the balcony shouting obscenities at the man she still professed to love.

A few years ago, she decided on a gruesome revenge. Rex was touring in his big success, *My Fair Lady.* The show was scheduled to open on a Thursday in San Francisco. She decided to ruin his opening night by having her suicide discovered on that day. On Wednesday she took a number of Seconals and Nembutals, with bread to hold them down, dipped in a powerful disinfectant. Then she lay down in the hollow of a tree where the gardener would find her on Thursday. But he changed his routine and came on Wednesday, ruining her revenge. When they told Rex, he said, "I'm not surprised. I always thought she would do it."

I remember visiting Luise Rainer in her Beverly Hills home and noticing that the flowers in a vase on the piano were wilting, just like her marriage to Clifford Odets, the playwright. Shortly after the robbery in the vaults of the Bank of America's branch in London, I lunched with Luise at the Connaught. Her jewels were among those stolen. Luise, who is a worrier, was taking it fairly calmly. After lunch we went to her jewellers near Bond Street, where they wrote descriptions of her gems for the insurance company.

Luise, who had trained with Max Reinhardt in Vienna, where she was born in 1910, was unhappy in Hollywood. She was always at odds with Louis B. Mayer, who threatened to ruin her when she told him she was breaking her contract and leaving the city where she had won two Oscars, for *The Great Ziegfeld* and *The Good Earth*. She faced up to him and said, "Mr. Mayer, I will still be around when you are long since dead." A true prophecy. She sometimes goes to Hollywood with her husband, Robert Knittel, the book publisher, to see their daughter, who lives there. On a recent trip Luise visited the MGM lot, and she was greeted by a banner, "Welcome Home Luise!!"

I remember too when Rita Hayworth married Dick Haymes in a room at the Sands Hotel in Las Vegas. Their "I do's" were accompanied by the clack-clack sounds from the gambling rooms. Her then four-year-old daughter, Princess Yasmin, brought a smile when she demanded, "Mama, may I have a wedding ring too?" Yasmin is now taking care of her seriously ill mother.

And I remember Celeste Holm remarking before Grace Kelly's untimely death (they had become good friends after working together in *High Society*), "Grace is the only actress I know whose life goes in a straight line in both areas, as an actress and as a Princess of Monaco. She takes each step one at a time and is successful in both. She is always radiant. And no one could look like that who isn't happy."

That great lady of the screen Marlene Dietrich has not been well since falling into the orchestra pit during a concert in Paris. I came to know her better during her last years in Hollywood. One day I was interviewing her in her dressing room on the set. In the middle of a question, I burst into tears. At the time I was going through a divorce from my last husband. It was the sort of nightmare that I usually wrote about as happening to others. Marlene took me in her arms and rocked me like a baby. Cold and inhuman? I should say not.

Marlene is lonely for the close friends of her career, who are far away. She discourages the nearby acquaintances in Paris who want to be friendly. When they telephone she puts on a different voice, pretends to be the maid, and says, "Miss Dietrich is not at home."

It is many years ago now, but I remember when Cecil B. De Mille held up the release of the Tony Perkins film *Fear Strikes Out* because it might compete for the Oscar with his circus film, *The Greatest Show on Earth*. Tony, who is right-handed, was brilliant as the switch-hitting baseball player Jim Piersall. It took a great deal of practice to change from right to left.

Recently in New York I lunched with Tony and his attractive wife, the former Berry Berenson, sister of Marisa Berenson, the actress. We talked of the old days in Hollywood when he was a shy, stumbling, round-shouldered beginner wearing steel-rimmed glasses—a barefoot boy. "You advised me," he remembered, "to take life by the tail and swing it!" After leaving Hollywood Tony underwent extensive therapy, which has apparently solved his problems. As you know, he starred in the sequel to his terrifying *Psycho* film. I would not see it, as I did not see the original when I learned what it was about. I have never been enthralled by horror.

Looking back to 1956 in Vienna, Yul Brynner was starring in *The Journey*. He had promised marriage to a girl he had left behind in Hollywood. One day she appeared at his hotel in Vienna, armed with a knife, and tried to stab him in the stomach. Which is why part of the film shows him with a bandaged finger, where he had deflected the knife.

Yul was the most egotistical actor I met in Hollywood. At one time he accused me of writing something about him that he said was untrue. "Why don't you check with me?" he asked. "But I never know where you are," I replied. "All you have to do is to pick up the phone, ask for Switzerland, and say, 'Get me Yul Brynner.' " I know that Switzerland, his tax-free home base, is not a large country, but all the same!

Notes retained from the old MGM make-up and wardrobe department remind me of how Joan Crawford set two world-wide fashions: a big mouth, the opposite of the previous silly little cupid's bow, and large shoulders. Joan had big hips, and her dress designer, Adrian, minimized them with large square padded shoulders. Greta Garbo had a big behind, and Adrian had two measurements for her —thirty-five-and-a-half inches for the upper part and somewhat more for the lower.

Dorothy Lamour, at Paramount, was dressed by Edith Head, who won a dozen Oscars for her dress designs. She told me that Dorothy's bust was the most beautiful she had ever seen. The sarongs took care of the rest. Dorothy lived in the next street to mine in Beverly Hills. Her son Ridgely and my son, Robert, were friends. Ridgely usually came to our house wearing a soldier's tin hat and carrying a toy rifle. I was not surprised to learn that lately he has been earning his living as a security officer.

Charles Laughton was unapproachable for most of the press. But not for me. We had a common bond. We had been students together at the Royal Academy of Dramatic Art (RADA) and shared a dislike for Nancy Price, a character actress who had been one of the teachers. She had cruelly exposed my cockney accent in class: "meeoon." To this day I pause before saying "moon." But while Charles and I were friendly, I never dared interrupt him when he was preparing for a scene. It was the same with Paul Muni. He would go into a corner and concentrate on becoming the character he was portraying.

Zsa Zsa Gabor, with not too much ability as an actress, made herself a saleable product. This is a special talent. When things get too quiet, these people, who are famous for being famous, do something spectacular and receive the publicity essential for their careers. I was amused when Zsa Zsa a year or so ago called a press conference to "settle once and for all" the question of how old she was. She produced a birth certificate. "See, I am fifty-four years old. And that," she said, with the great acting she reserves for her non-working life, "is quite old, no?" No. If the certificate was correct, she married her first husband when she was thirteen years old.

In 1982, when Zsa Zsa let it be known that she was going to divorce her last husband (I've lost count of whether he was the seventh or eighth)—whom she described as the Duke of Alba, which he was not—she confided to the usual friend, "I'm going to divorce him, but I will wait until after Christmas. I don't want to be alone for the holidays." I wonder if he was aware of what would happen after the presents were opened. And actually no one seemed sure that they had married. Her last bout of publicity was less amusing: reportedly moving handicapped people from the front row to the back when she was performing in *Forty Carats.*

What I did not know about Cary Grant in the past is that he is a cat lover. Some years ago he brought a couple of kittens to his bungalow at Universal. Now there are hundreds roaming around there. And Dean Martin suffers with claustrophobia. He prefers to walk up the steps rather than go up in an elevator. Katharine Hepburn has an odd obsession about hair. It has to be newly washed. At one time when I was at Twentieth Century–Fox, I learned that Kate, who was working there, was going around the set sniffing people's hair to make sure it had been washed. It was the same— "Have you washed your hair?"—when she was touring with Vanessa Brown in *As You Like It.*

In recent years the great actress has always seemed on the verge of tears. It was George Cukor, not long before his death, who told me that while she was making the film *Summertime* in Venice, with Rossano Brazzi, her role called for her to fall into the canal. Kate insisted on doing the stunt herself and it resulted in a virus that has caused a weak tear duct in her eye.

Miss Hepburn had never cared about her billing, but the agent for Laurence Olivier irritated her when he insisted that his client should have top billing in *Love Among the Ruins,* their television play. Her solution: "I will be billed first in *this* country, and Larry in *his* country."

I was sad when Steve McQueen died of cancer at the young age of fifty. He did not live long enough to collect the $10 million he was promised for the deal to star in *Superman II,* but he was paid $1 million for just saying, "I will do it." When he died, the producer started a lawsuit to recover the million dollars. There was no written contract, and so I believe he was out of luck.

I remember taking my then four-year-old son to see a "Francis the Talking Mule" film. At the end I told him, "Of course, Robbie, you know that horses don't talk." He looked at me scornfully and said,

"Of course I know that horses don't talk, *mules* do!" J. Paul Getty's son, Timmy, was the same age as mine. Together they learned to swim in the Getty pool at Santa Monica.

We sometimes dined with Paul and his wife, Theodora—Teddy —in the elaborate dining room in his museum overlooking the Pacific Ocean. Timmy and his mother were always guests at my Christmas party, and one Christmas I was startled when in greeting Timmy he missed my outstretched hand. He was twelve years old and a tumour was growing in his brain. Mr. Getty did not care for travelling and was in England when Timmy underwent several dangerous operations in New York that left him blind. Before returning to California, the surgeon suggested some minor plastic surgery "to tidy up the scars." Timmy died on the operating table. Of all Getty's wives, Teddy was the only one who was left a substantial sum in his will, perhaps to make up for his not being there when he was needed.

More recently I remember Richard Burton's birthday party at the time he was courting Princess Elizabeth of Lichtenstein. He was very drunk and behaving badly. The next day he telegraphed his hostess, "Why do we hurt those we love the most, and I do mean you." She wired back, "Because you've had so much experience, and I do mean you."

Years ago I was shocked when Errol Flynn lifted up the visor headpiece on the armour he was wearing for a film. He looked so old and so bloated. Drinking will do it. I remember Errol's trip to Korea to entertain the boys. He took a large suitcase of vodka with him, not for the boys, for himself. Looking back I remember a party at Errol's house, where he had a real rat race—live rodents running in marked lanes, while his guests cheered them on (not me).

And what happened to Betty Hutton, the blonde bombshell of the forties? After reappearing from retirement to play Miss Hannigan in *Annie,* on the road, she has returned to work with some priests in New England. Benay Venuta, the musical comedy star who was married to Armand Deutsch, President Reagan's close friend, kept in touch with Betty and helped her after she left her Paramount contract in 1952. Betty was another film star who could not cope with the razzle-dazzle of a career in Hollywood. For many years she was on pain-killer pills, also benzedrine and brandy. At last report she was well and saying she was content with her life.

I remember when Elke Sommer, a former German au pair girl in England, married Joe Hyams, the author and columnist. Joe was somewhat older than she and their backgrounds were so different that his friends warned him against the marriage: "You're a damn fool, it won't last." But he was madly in love with the blonde actress. "If it lasts six months it will be worth it," he said. It lasted eighteen years, and most of them were happy, before she left him for a young German. Joe is getting over it now, but he was very hurt. Elke's career is not as good in films as it was, but she has been earning a five-figure income doing commercials on television.

I remember when Hayley Mills married the producer Roy Boulting, who was thirty years older. When I saw them together in their flat in Chelsea, Hayley sat literally at his feet, agreeing with everything he said. The difference in age didn't matter, she assured me. He was young at heart, etc. Several years later she left him for a young actor with whom she is raising a family. I wonder whether the pleasure for Mr. Boulting was worth the pain.

And I remember my own pain when I read, "There are no survivors," at the end of the *New York Times'* obituary for Tilly Losch. That beautiful, shimmering person had disappeared so completely. She was twenty-four years old when Charles B. Cochran brought her to London from Vienna, where she was a star dancer and choreographer for Max Reinhardt, to perform the same services for the stars of his 1928 revue *This Year of Grace.* I was one of the Three Graces with Jessie Matthews and Moya Nugent. We were the famous nineteenth-century dancers Taglioni, Fanny Elssler, and Grisi. Tilly soon realized my deficiencies as a ballet dancer, but she was kind and gave me some easy staggering around under the long ballet dress.

Tilly was the toast of London, with her charm and elfish good looks, and was pursued by the young bloods in town. The most ardent was the Honourable Tom Mitford, the brother of all those Mitford girls. And Randolph Churchill tried unsuccessfully to bring her to bed. The richest and most eligible bachelors were the Honourable Edward James and "Porchy," Lord Porchester, the heir to the Earldom of Carnarvon. Tilly married James, then she married Porchy. The first marriage was a disaster for Tilly, but she seemed to be in love with him. I would see her, night after night, dashing into his limousine outside the Pavilion stage door.

"Was it his money?" I asked Tilly many years later. "I don't think so," she replied thoughtfully. "I really found him irresistible." I was in Hollywood when I read about the scandal of their divorce. I was outraged that he had had detectives follow her all the way to the top of the Empire State Building to watch her rendezvous with Prince Serge Obolensky, formerly of the Russian Imperial Guards and the ex-husband of Vincent Astor's sister.

A few years before Tilly died of cancer in New York, I was in London, where on my visits we always got together for lunch or dinner, or just to talk about the past and the present. One of the very last times was when she came to my Thanksgiving dinner—an American custom that I continued to observe at the house I had bought in Knightsbridge. She was then divorced from Porchy, who was now an Earl.

Later that evening, after I had accompanied her back to her flat in Eaton Square—she was always afraid to walk alone at night, even though London then was, and to some extent still is, one of the safer cities in the world—she showed me a photograph of the turreted Highclere Castle, one of the homes of the Carnarvons. "There were so many servants. I had my own maid; all she had to do was dress me and undress me." "How could you let all that go?" I asked somewhat enviously. "It was beautiful," she sighed, "but so dull!"

In her last years, Tilly had become suspicious of people, even those close to her. In her mind she had set herself up as some kind of aristocrat, although her beginnings had been fairly humble. All the rest of us were peasants. I was her pet peasant. I remember how annoyed she was when the maître d' at Le Bicyclette in Chelsea gave us a table in the back room. "It's because you are carrying a package," she stormed at me.

In her old age, Tilly also became miserly. She was always pleading poverty, and her friends, feeling sorry for the once great star, would treat her to lunches, dinners, and the theatre. She often sent her bills to Porchy, who usually paid them.

After her agonizing death in a New York hospital, the executors of her will discovered a $300,000 bank account in Switzerland, and other valuable properties. She had really been quite well off, with an apartment near Fifth Avenue on 68th Street in New York, where I was also living—how she worried over that lease, assuring me they were trying to cheat her—and the expensive flat in London. But I couldn't help loving her, and I wished I could have helped her more.

CHAPTER 26

Hollywood Today

IT WAS truly a different Hollywood that I came to in the eighties. Where orange groves had bloomed in the center of the city, there were skyscrapers, banks, savings and loan associations, and insurance companies. Wilshire Boulevard, north and south, resembled the New York skyline. The bridle path where the Strip becomes Beverly Hills now has a cement divider for the north and south side of Sunset Boulevard. In my time it was a meeting place for the horsey starlets and handsome young actors.

But one of the biggest changes for me was driving through what used to be the Twentieth Century–Fox studio—the hundred and seventy acres between Santa Monica and Pico Boulevards. Except for forty acres in the south-west corner there are towering condominiums, skyscraper office blocks, hotels, restaurants, stock exchanges, and clubs.

Marvin Davis would like to sell his forty acres for the building of more condominiums. But there has been a glut in that market. When and if he does, it is said that he will move his studio to the CBS lot in the Valley. Century City, the hundred and thirty acres which Mr. Davis does not own, is privately called Elizabeth Taylor City. The land was sold to prevent the bankruptcy of Twentieth Century–Fox after the financial disappointment of *Cleopatra*. Tom Mix, the long-ago silent Western star, owned the original acres. I hope he is not turning in his grave.

With so many studio back lots sold to the real estate agents, the producers who are still making movies for the theatres are forced

262

to use real locations. Tony Curtis, for instance, would be saying, "Yonda lies the castle of my fadda" (in pure Bronx) somewhere in Arabia, and not (as he did say it in 1952 in *The Son of Ali Baba*) on the back lot at Universal, where so much is now covered with tall hotels and office buildings.

To make *New Moon* today, MGM would not send Jeanette MacDonald and Nelson Eddy to lot 3. They would fly the whole company to the bayous of Louisiana. Lot 3 does not exist anymore. Neither does lot 2. They were sold to pay for owner Kirk Kerkorian's Grand Hotel in Las Vegas, and for the millions of dollars in interest on the $700 million that was owed by the studio.

But the glamorous stars of the old MGM are not entirely forgotten. Their names are carved in stone on the old buildings. In addition to a Clark Gable building, there is one apiece for Jean Harlow, Joan Crawford, John Barrymore, Norma Shearer, Leslie Howard, and William Powell.

At Warners, I was surprised to find that the Green Room is now the Blue Room; and instead of lunching near Errol Flynn, Bette Davis, Bogey and Baby, Jimmy Cagney, Alfred Hitchcock, or Ronald Reagan, I found the tables occupied by young faces I had seen only on my television screen. Hold on! One face belonged to Jane Wyman, who is playing the evil Angela Channing in "Falcon Crest" for the smaller screen, of course.

The wall that divided RKO from Paramount is no longer there. In fact RKO hasn't been there since Lucille Ball bought the studio for her Desilu television company. That name is still on the tall water tower in the section that used to be RKO, but Lucille's name has been painted out, much to her annoyance.

I had lunch in the new restaurant that serves both studios. It was hard to get a table because so many people were working there for television, mostly very young people. Before lunch, an elderly gentleman whom I was told to call Fritz took me around the combined lots in his small open paddy wagon. "That parking lot," he said, pointing to a huge tract crammed with the cars of the actors and set workers, "that used to be where all the Westerns were made." I thought sadly of Kirk Douglas facing Burt Lancaster, weapons at the draw, for a scene in *Gunfight at the O.K. Corral*. And of the remake of *The Virginian* in 1946, with Joel McRea.

Fritz dutifully took me to five sound stages given over to "sit-coms"—situation (so called) comedies for television. One of them, cancelled shortly after my visit, "Joannie Loves Chachi," made a millionaire of young Scott Baio. "Chachi" was being taped on the same sound stage where Marlene Dietrich had loved Cary Cooper in *Desire.* Scott—you will, I am sure, be delighted to know—is now playing a nineteen-year-old college student in the series "Charles in Charge."

For me, the best part of Paramount today was the wardrobe department. It's enormous. Most of the other studios have given up not only their wardrobes but also their hairdressing and make-up departments. Claire Trevor was amazed, she told me, when she had to fix her own hair and make-up for *Kiss Me Goodbye.* But at Paramount, every dress, suit, sword, boot, shoe, and period costume that was ever used in a film from 1913 on is preserved on shelves in glass cupboards—Rudolph Valentino's sequined matador vest from *Blood and Sand* (1922); Mae West's busty brocade gown from *Belle of the Nineties* (1934); Grace Kelly's flowing gold ballroom gown from *High Society* (1956); Elvis Presley's glittering silver jacket from *King Creole* (1958). And Ronald Reagan's knee-high riding boots from *The Last Outpost* (1951).

But alas, little of it was for present-day Paramount use. With the high cost of film-making, studios are now sometimes hard up for what they call "daily running money" and every device has been exploited to earn extra cash. Paramount is renting out its glorious memorabilia to other studios and independent producers. At MGM there is a "nostalgia" department, and there is a charge when you write for a photograph of an old favourite.

It was fascinating to visit the new Hollywood and remember the old. I would have thought that the Universal money men would be content with all the millions made from *E.T.* But they are still giving the studio tours that helped them in leaner days. Did you know that the Universal tour is the second biggest attraction in Southern California, second only to Disneyland? Every day, year in and out, between 20,000 and 25,000 people pour through the gates for a ninety-minute walking tour with a guide—$15.75 for adults, $9.75 for children over five and under eleven.

Twentieth Century–Fox, which is now aligned with CBS Video in the Valley, has twice-daily tours for visitors. While the success of the *Star Wars* trilogy made this studio rich, a little extra cash is always useful. Columbia has been riding the crest of prosperity since *Close Encounters of the Third Kind.* For many years now they have shared the Warner Brothers acreage under the name I still can't get used to, the Burbank Studios. I expect them to open the gates for the profitable studio tours, even though Warner Communications, which owns this whole area, is worth close to $3 billion.

In my day, the media was flown for premieres and visits to all parts of America and the rest of the world—Hawaii, Europe, the Middle East, and even Russia. Such junkets have been out for a long time. Today the burden of publicity is mostly carried by the stars of the film, that is, if they want to be co-operative.

Barbra Streisand usually prefers to have the film speak for itself. It was interesting that she went out of her way to publicize *Yentl* (in the U.S., London, Paris, and Israel). As star, director, producer, and co-scripter, she was determined to make it a success. The reviews, as you know, were mixed.

Robert Redford, who shies away from personal publicity, actually made a speech onstage to launch *Ordinary People,* which he directed. Of course, in the past, it was not expected that big stars like Garbo, Dietrich, and Hepburn would help to promote their own pictures—although Mae West, who had rarely put in an appearance for her films, was in New York for the premiere of her last (unsuccessful) movie.

But when I was in Hollywood to visit some of the people who are still around, I was invited by Twentieth Century–Fox to a junket. Not too far. To New York, where I have a home. It was for film critics from all over the United States and major cities abroad. There would be two hundred of us, and I was impressed. The film, *Kiss Me Goodbye,* was not in the blockbuster class. Neither were the stars: Sally Field (so good in *Norma Rae*), James Caan, and Jeff Bridges. For me the star of the film was Claire Trevor, who was listed in the supporting category.

I would guess that *Kiss Me Goodbye* had cost around $5 million. To promote it in New York, there was a dinner, a screening of the film, and, the next day, press, radio, and television interviews, en

masse and individually, and a luncheon. I was surprised when someone asked if I was attending a different screening entirely, of a film
from Columbia, that evening. I had not been invited. Then I learned
that the cost of the junket was being shared by Columbia and Twentieth Century–Fox. It made sense. These two studios have also been
sharing the cost of a $30 million movie in Europe. Again it makes
sense. But this could never have happened between rival studios
during my time in Hollywood.

Whenever I return to Hollywood I expect to find a museum, a
centre, a record, under one roof, of all the fabulous happenings
there since 1913, when it all started. They have been talking about
it for at least twenty years. The Academy has a fine library and shows
films every Sunday, but only for Academy members. Whereas the
British Film Institute runs films seven days a week for weeks on end,
changing the bill daily, and has all kinds of retrospectives, with the
stars and directors who worked on the films present to answer
questions.

There have been several attempts to start a Hollywood museum. I mean a true industry-supported institution—not a small-
scale tourist attraction like the one or two that have sprung up. Bart
Lytton—his Savings and Loan Bank covered the acres where the
Garden of Allah once stood—made a strong effort in the late fifties
to get something started, but politics, personalities, and mishan-
dling turned the project into a nasty snarl. Of course, a museum, a
film institute, would take a lot of money to start, and there seems
to be no one now in Hollywood who cares enough to do it. Or
perhaps it is that the people who have the money don't care enough.

Another new enterprise in Hollywood today is the big business
done in buying ready-made films from independent production
companies here and abroad, and sending them out with the name
and expertise of a major studio. Which, as I may have mentioned,
are run and controlled by big business—Gulf and Western for Paramount; Warner Communications for Warners; Las Vegas real estate
billionaire Kirk Kerkorian for MGM–United Artists; Texas oil man
Marvin Davis, who with his partner Marc Rich paid $725 million to
own all of what is left of Twentieth Century–Fox. At this studio
there are two vice presidents—male—who are in their twenties.

I was glad to see that while there aren't many star actresses today, there are, at most big studios, more women in executive positions, attractive young women at that. More like it was in the Hollywood teens and twenties—Lois Weber in 1913, Lillian Gish in 1920, Dorothy Arzner in 1927, Mrs. Wallace Reid in 1929. Miss Arzner was directing films until 1943, when she made some training documentaries for World War Two. In my time we were surprised when the actress Ida Lupino (who is descended from a long line of vaudevillians) was allowed to produce and direct some films. In more recent years, we've had Jane Fonda, in addition to her supporting role, producing *On Golden Pond* for her own company. Stephanie Powers has been a producer. And Sherry Lansing, in her thirties, was president of Twentieth Century–Fox until friction with Marvin Davis caused her to bow out. She is now president of her own company. One reason for the quarrel with Mr. Davis was her annoyance when he allowed the Ladd Company, which had produced the British-made *Chariots of Fire,* to take it with them when they moved to Warner Communications. The revenues, forty million dollars at last report, are still rolling in.

An interesting development in Hollywood is studio backing for plays on Broadway. This always used to happen, but in the past fifteen years movie money for the New York theatre has accelerated, with some successes and some failures. Columbia has long since received its investment back for *Dancin',* and Universal added to its profits with *The Best Little Whorehouse in Texas* onstage.

In 1980 Columbia had a flop in *Clothes for a Summer Hotel,* a Tennessee Williams play about the dead Scott and Zelda Fitzgerald renewing their quarrels in heaven. It closed on Broadway after five performances. But Columbia is still collecting dollars from *Sugar Babies,* an awful but hilarious musical starring Mickey Rooney and Ann Miller. It had a long Broadway run and then went on the road.

Warners lost money with *Mass Appeal* and *Piaf,* but made money with the long-running *Woman of the Year.* Debbie Reynolds' lack of box office appeal finally closed it on Broadway, but it then went on tour with Lauren Bacall, who had originated the stage role. And there is David Geffen, one of the most successful backers of plays in New York. Mr. Geffen, a producer of films and top-selling records, is not only very rich but also very lucky. He put his money into two of the top shows on Broadway—*Cats* and *Dreamgirls.*

Nowhere on the list do I see the name of Metro-Goldwyn-Mayer. This company was too busy getting out of the financial mess it was in, slowly working to bring down the high interest on that original $700 million loan, to risk the uncertainties of backing a play. It makes me sad, remembering how great and respected it was, the top studio when I first came to Hollywood, and for many years afterwards.

One of the differences in Hollywood today is the method of publicizing a picture or a personality. Press agents used to tumble over themselves for a mention of their clients in a column. It was worth thousands of dollars in free publicity. The syndicated Hollywood columns have diminished with the newspapers. Too frequently you read of another paper going under. And our role as Hollywood purveyors of juicy tidbits has been usurped by such weeklies as *People,* the *Star,* the *Globe;* and let's not forget the old *National Enquirer.*

"The function of the gossip columnist," said my favourite London psychiatrist, "is to remind the celebrities that they are human. They are larger than life. You bring them down to size. You remind them of reality." This was fine when we had the tycoons and the glamorous people in Hollywood. But how do you bring a robot down to size, or a star-ship from outer space? It reminds me of a recent cartoon in *The New Yorker.* Two teenagers are leaving a movie theatre specializing in films of yesterday. On the marquee: *Casablanca,* starring Humphrey Bogart and Ingrid Bergman. One youngster says to the other: "What a ripoff. No special effects."

The Hollywood gossip made our columns interesting. I always took on the giants, the Louis B. Mayers, the Sinatras, the Bette Davises, the Yul Brynners. There aren't the same sort of giants in Hollywood today, which is part of the reason why the Hollywood gossip columnist is becoming an endangered species. Today no one cares what the people there are doing in their private lives unless it's scandalous. Hard news, yes. Hollywood will always be fascinating reading for most of the world when a really juicy scandal breaks, but even that has to involve a famous name. In actual fact, the best gossip has always come from Washington, D.C. There are enough vulnerable giants there for the Jacks to kill.

But for the press agents in Hollywood there are still radio and

TV talk shows, reserved for the tops in their field. Sylvester Stallone was talking on a hundred ABC radio stations when his movie *First Blood* was released around the country. And NBC gave Lana Turner five mornings on the "Today" show for her book.

There are also personal appearances and charitable causes to keep old stars in the news. Danny Kaye, for instance, has not made a feature film since 1969, but he tours the world for UNICEF. And he has also given his time and amateur baton to raise six million dollars for the American Musicians' Pension Fund. Gene Kelly has not done much in the movies since his on-screen narration in 1974 for MGM's mammoth presentation of its great stars in *That's Entertainment,* but he appears now and then on television specials. His press agent, Warren Cowan, tells me Gene is developing a play for Ben Vereen (one of the stars of "Roots") titled *Satchmo,* about the late Louis Armstrong.

Would I want a Hollywood column today? No. I had a long run and it was interesting, but no, I would not want to try it again now. You might enjoy this put-down of me by a young taxi driver on my recent visit there. "I seem to remember your face," he said. He obviously had seen me on a talk show. He asked my name. "Sheilah Graham," I told him. He also quite obviously had never heard of me. I jogged his memory. "I was a columnist here for a long time." "Oh, you mean someone like Rona Barrett?" I was duly flattered.

The last time I was in Hollywood, I was amused to see a "Rent a Rolls Royce" sign in a parking lot on Santa Monica Boulevard. For thirty-nine dollars you could impress acquaintances and producers that you were in the money. But now, some of the people who are doing well patronize a place called "Rent-a-Wreck," because they don't want to seem pretentious. The car inside is in perfect condition. But outside the fenders are bent, and the doors are hanging by a thread. So those who don't have money are renting Rolls Royces, while those who do are driving wrecks. Isn't it a kind of reverse pretentiousness?

It parallels, for me, the rise of stars who look like Dustin Hoffman, Al Pacino, Robert De Niro, and Burt Reynolds. To me, brought up on the classic faces of Tyrone Power, Cary Grant, Gregory Peck, and Laurence Olivier, the contrast is remarkable and meaningful. (I am for talent, but I confess I am not anti-glamour.)

The handsome movie actor went out with the sixties. Today's primarily young audience, brought up on the harsh realities of Vietnam, want their stars to look more like themselves. And perhaps it's better this way. After all, what was glamour? False eyelashes, paint and powder, an enormous publicity machine. Perhaps today's thriving Hollywood is more honest.

So, as you see, I do not maintain that Hollywood is dead. As I've said before, Hollywood is not dead; it's different. Agreed, Burt Reynolds is not Errol Flynn. But, all things considered, is that so bad?

Index

273